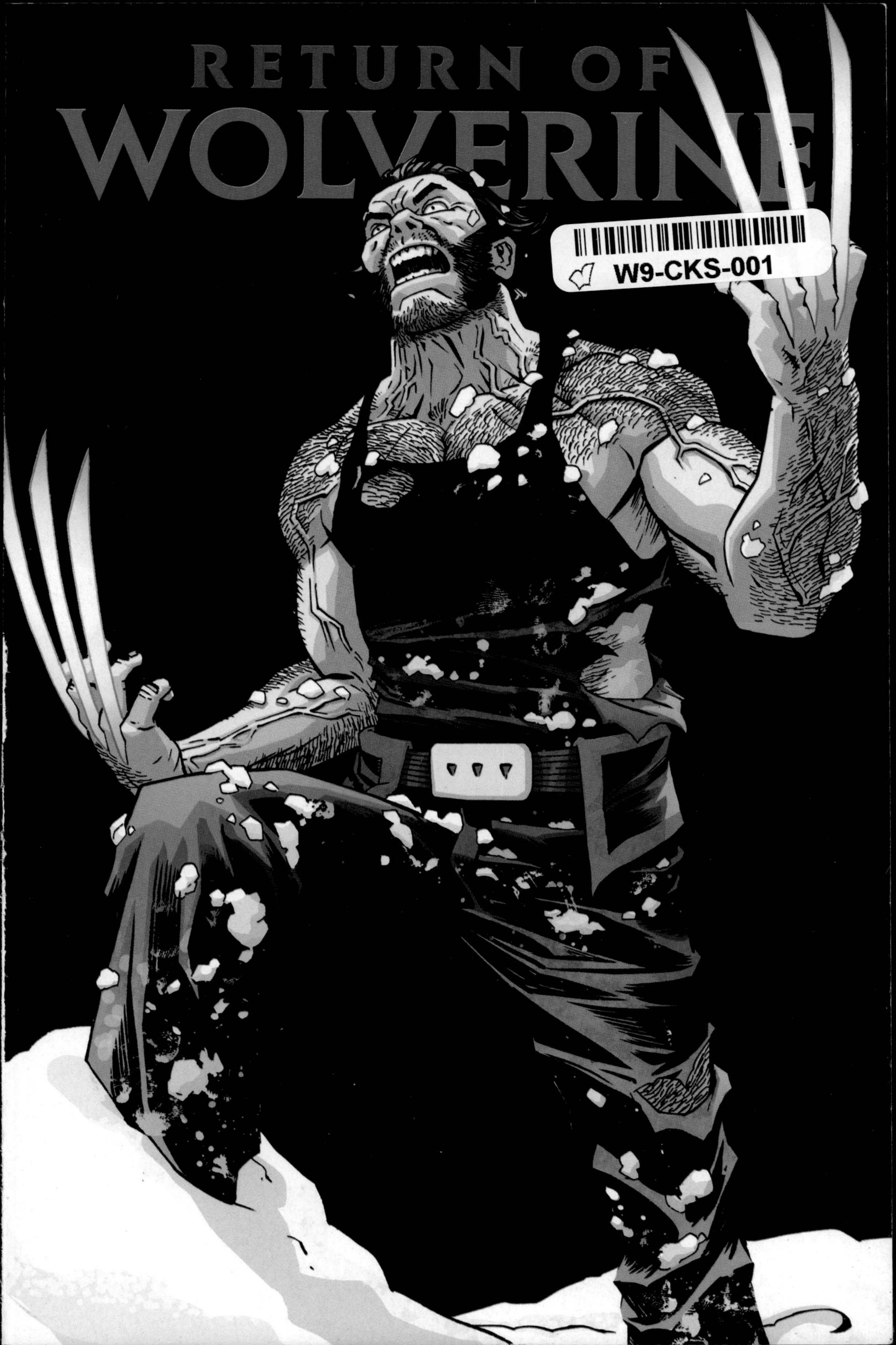
RETURN OF
WOLVERINE

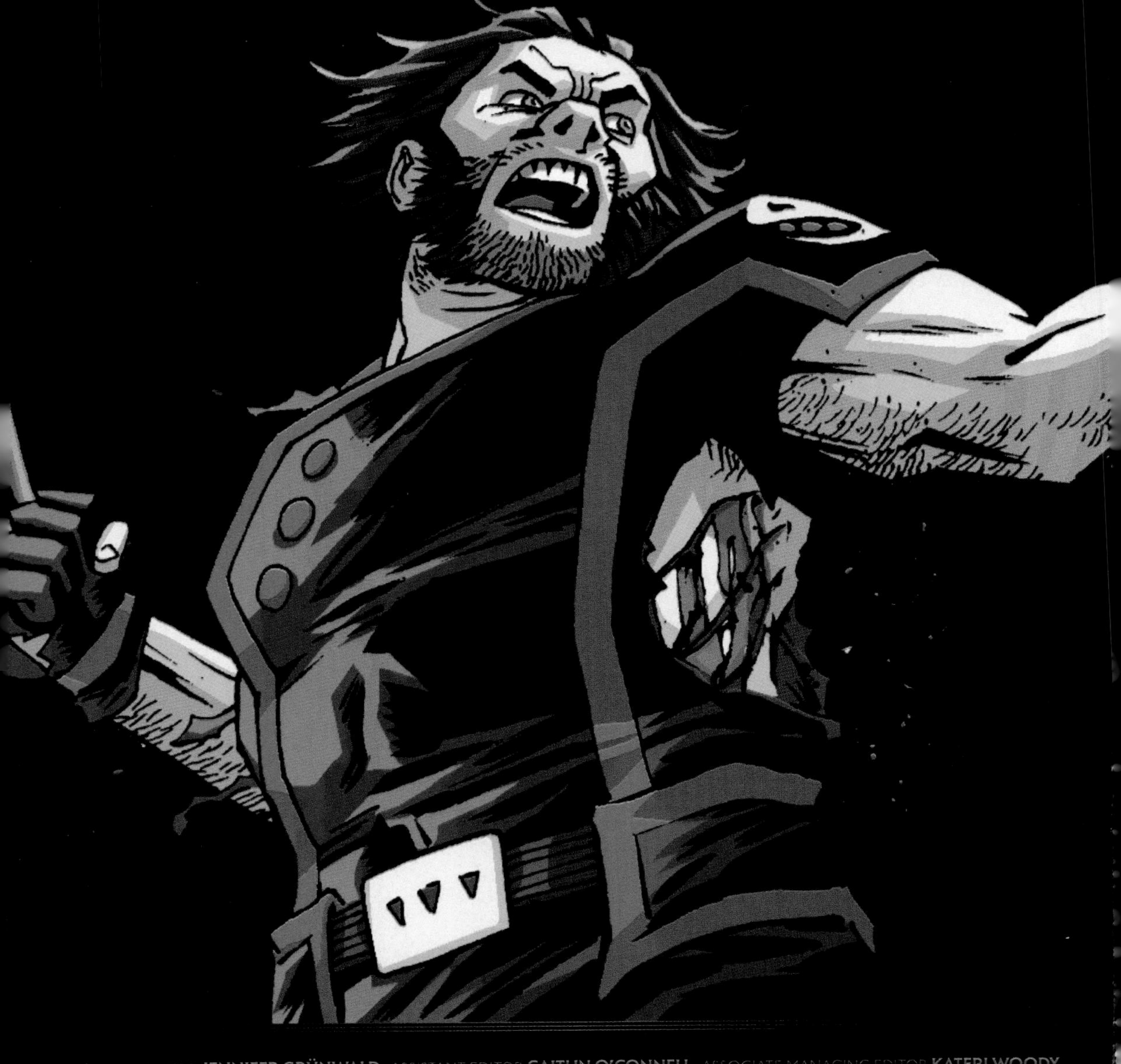

COLLECTION EDITOR **JENNIFER GRÜNWALD** ASSISTANT EDITOR **CAITLIN O'CONNELL** ASSOCIATE MANAGING EDITOR **KATERI WOODY**
EDITOR, SPECIAL PROJECTS **MARK D. BEAZLEY** VP PRODUCTION & SPECIAL PROJECTS **JEFF YOUNGQUIST**
SVP PRINT, SALES & MARKETING **DAVID GABRIEL** BOOK DESIGNER **JAY BOWEN**

EDITOR IN CHIEF **C.B. CEBULSKI** CHIEF CREATIVE OFFICER **JOE QUESADA**
PRESIDENT **DAN BUCKLEY** EXECUTIVE PRODUCER **ALAN FINE**

RETURN OF WOLVERINE. Contains material originally published in magazine form as RETURN OF WOLVERINE #1-5. First printing 2019. ISBN 978-1-302-91198-0. Published by MARVEL WORLDWIDE, INC., a subsidiary of MARVEL ENTERTAINMENT, LLC. OFFICE OF PUBLICATION: 135 West 50th Street, New York, NY 10020. **Printed in the U.S.A.** DAN BUCKLEY, President, Marvel Entertainment; JOHN NEE, Publisher; JOE QUESADA, Chief Creative Officer; TOM BREVOORT, SVP of Publishing; DAVID BOGART, SVP of Business Affairs & Operations, Publishing & Partnership; DAVID GABRIEL, SVP of Sales & Marketing, Publishing; JEFF YOUNGQUIST, VP of Production & Special Projects; DAN CARR, Executive Director of Publishing Technology; ALEX MORALES, Director of Publishing Operations; DAN EDINGTON, Managing Editor; SUSAN CRESPI, Production Manager; STAN LEE, Chairman Emeritus. For information regarding advertising in Marvel Comics or on Marvel.com, please contact Vit DeBellis, Custom Solutions & Integrated Advertising Manager, at vdebellis@marvel.com. For Marvel subscription inquiries, please call 888-511-5480. **Manufactured between 1/25/2019 and 2/26/2019 by LSC COMMUNICATIONS INC., KENDALLVILLE, IN, USA.**

10 9 8 7 6 5 4 3 2 1

RETURN OF WOLVERINE

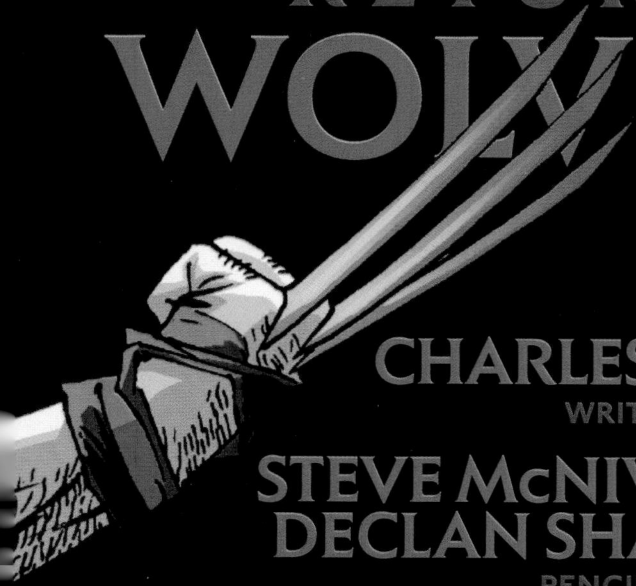

CHARLES SOULE
WRITER

STEVE McNIVEN (#1, #5) &
DECLAN SHALVEY (#2-4)
PENCILERS

JAY LEISTEN (#1, #5) &
DECLAN SHALVEY (#2-4)
INKERS

LAURA MARTIN
COLOR ARTIST

VC's JOE SABINO
LETTERER

STEVE McNIVEN WITH
LAURA MARTIN (#1-2)
& **SUNNY GHO** (#3-5)
COVER ART

ANNALISE BISSA
ASSISTANT EDITOR

MARK PANICCIA &
JORDAN D. WHITE
EDITORS

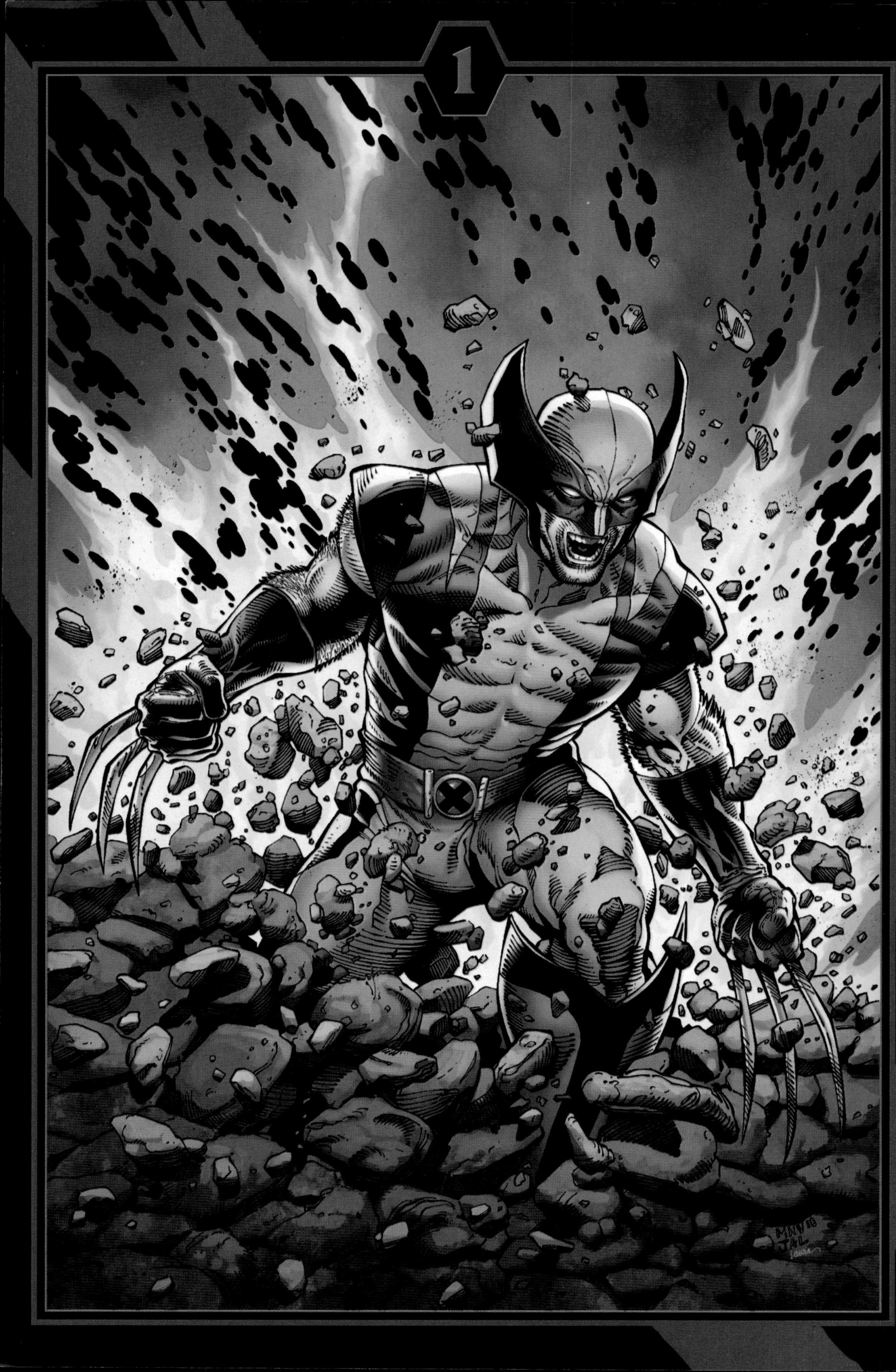
1

WOLVERINE.

A GREAT HERO.

SELFLESS, STRONG, BRAVE.

AN X-MAN. AN AVENGER.

A STEADFAST FRIEND.

AN IMPLACABLE ENEMY.

HE WAS DEAD.

NOW...

...HE'S NOT.

CHAPTER ONE
HELL

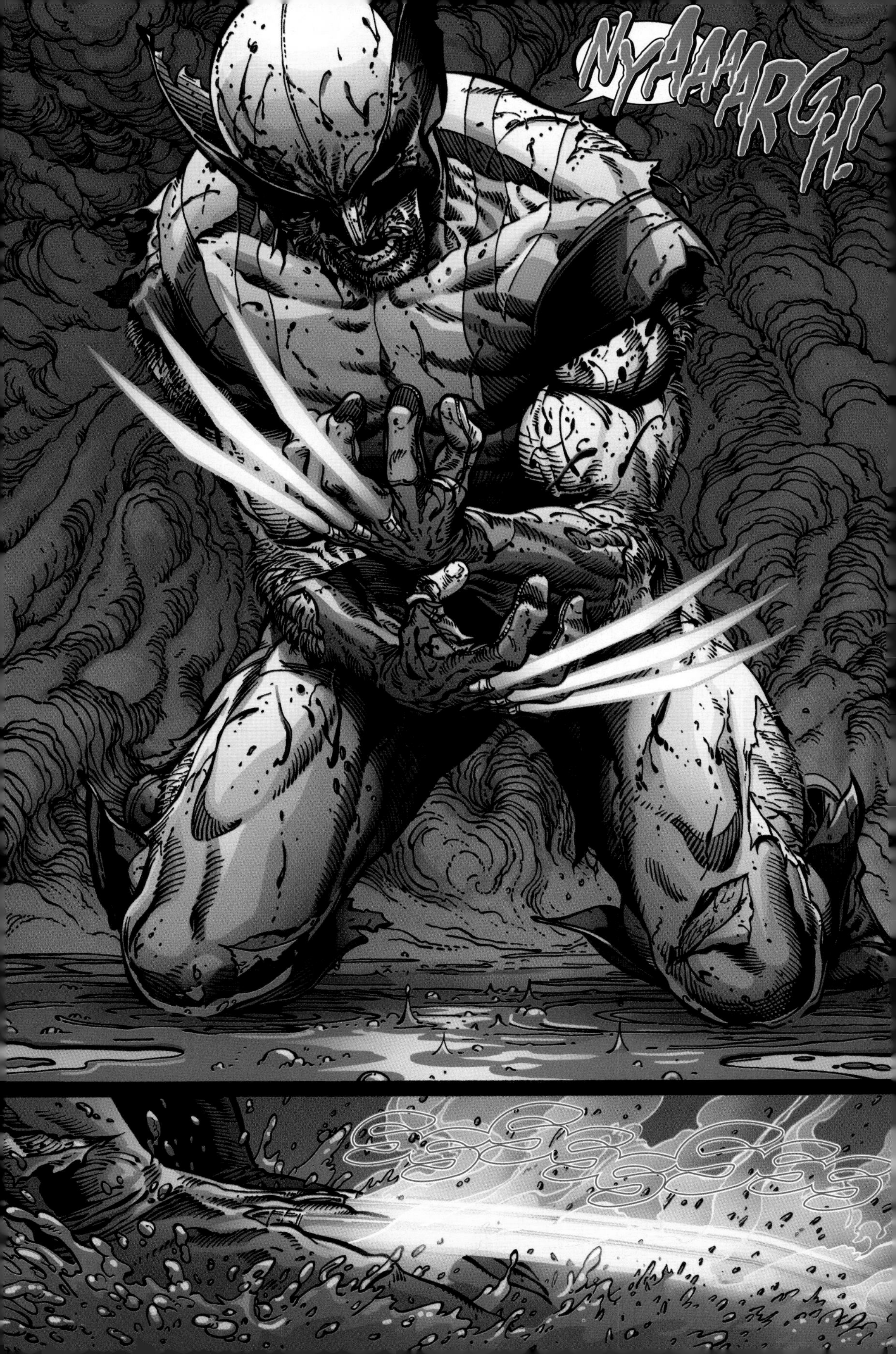
NYAAAARGH!

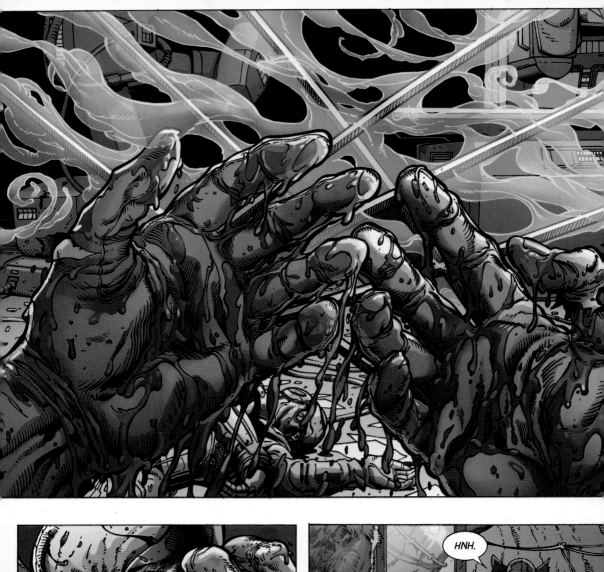

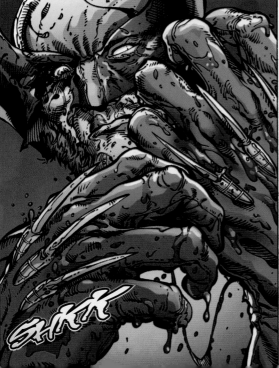

SHKK

HNH.

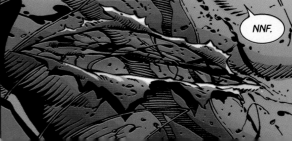

NNF.

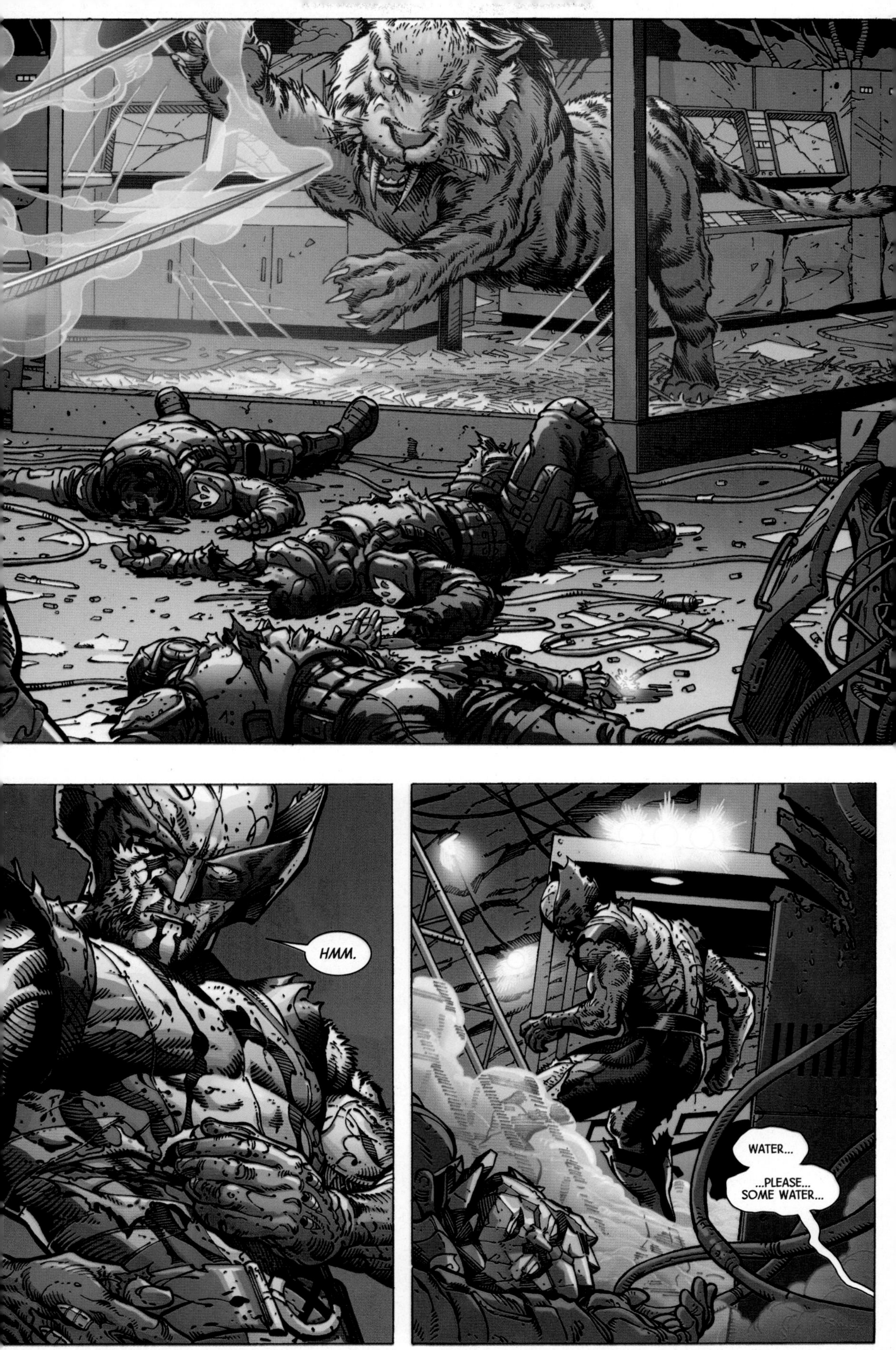
HMM.
WATER...
...PLEASE... SOME WATER...

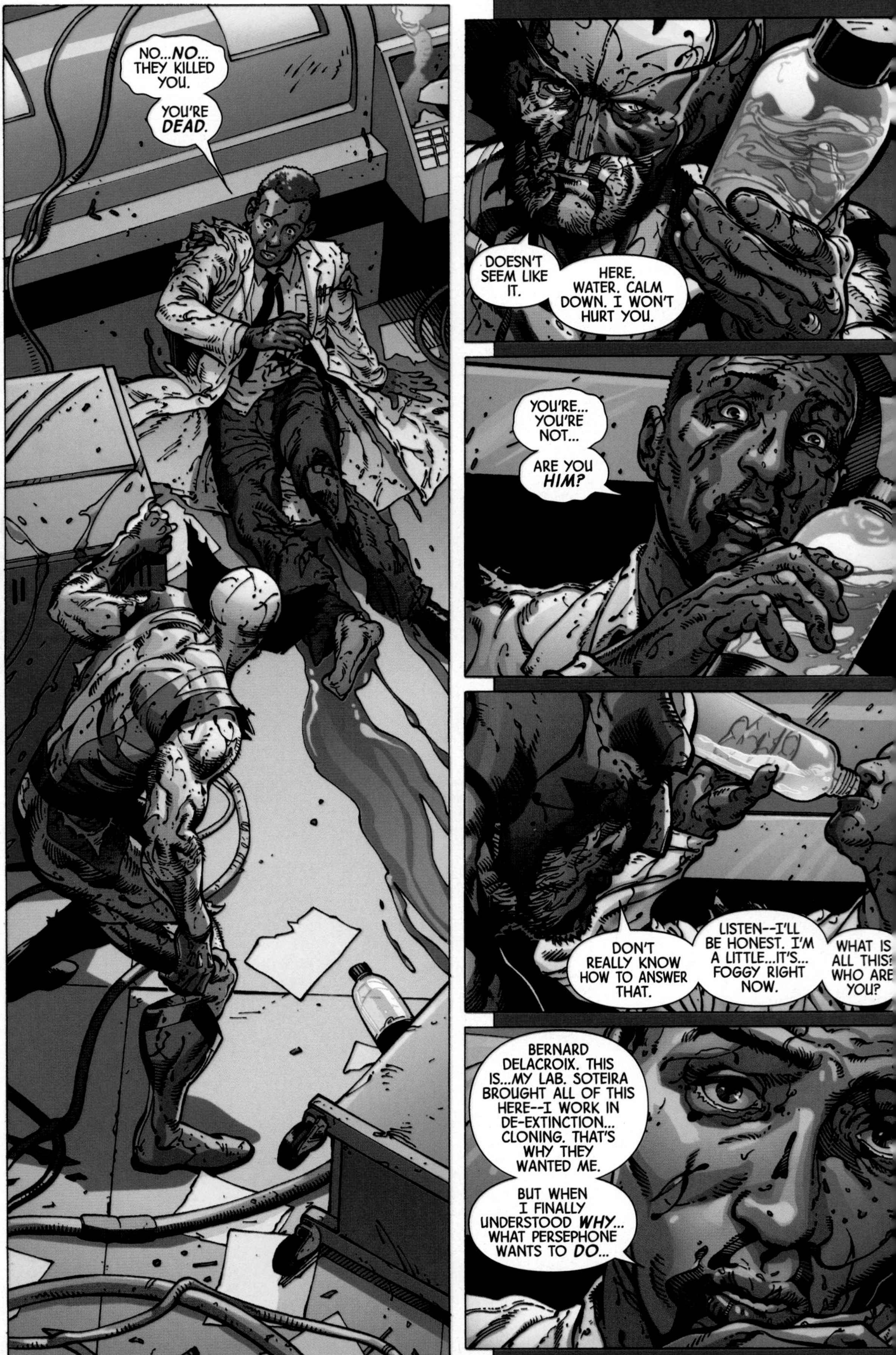
NO...NO... THEY KILLED YOU.
YOU'RE DEAD.
DOESN'T SEEM LIKE IT.
HERE. WATER. CALM DOWN. I WON'T HURT YOU.
YOU'RE... YOU'RE NOT...
ARE YOU HIM?
DON'T REALLY KNOW HOW TO ANSWER THAT.
LISTEN--I'LL BE HONEST. I'M A LITTLE...IT'S... FOGGY RIGHT NOW.
WHAT IS ALL THIS? WHO ARE YOU?
BERNARD DELACROIX. THIS IS...MY LAB. SOTEIRA BROUGHT ALL OF THIS HERE--I WORK IN DE-EXTINCTION... CLONING. THAT'S WHY THEY WANTED ME.
BUT WHEN I FINALLY UNDERSTOOD WHY... WHAT PERSEPHONE WANTS TO DO...

I JUST SAID NO. DO YOU UNDERSTAND? THAT'S ALL I DID.

ALL OF THIS...JUST BECAUSE I TOLD THEM *NO.*

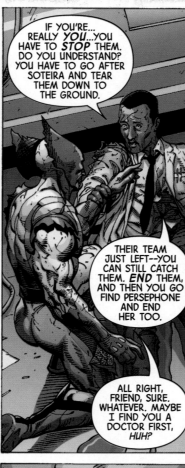

IF YOU'RE... REALLY *YOU*...YOU HAVE TO *STOP* THEM. DO YOU UNDERSTAND? YOU HAVE TO GO AFTER SOTEIRA AND TEAR THEM DOWN TO THE GROUND.

THEIR TEAM JUST LEFT--YOU CAN STILL CATCH THEM. *END* THEM, AND THEN YOU GO FIND PERSEPHONE AND END HER TOO.

ALL RIGHT, FRIEND, SURE. WHATEVER. MAYBE I FIND YOU A DOCTOR FIRST, *HUH?*

NO! TRY TO REMEMBER. YOU WERE A *GREAT MAN,* UNTIL SOTEIRA STOLE THAT FROM YOU.

PERSEPHONE WANTS TO DO THAT TO *EVERYONE ON EARTH.* SHE WANTS TO TAKE OUR...OUR *GREATNESS.*

BRING HER DOWN...IF NOT FOR THE WORLD, FOR WHAT SHE DID TO *YOU.*

LOOK. I MIGHT BE FUZZY ON THE DETAILS, BUT I CAN STILL *COUNT.* I'M JUST ONE MAN.

I'M SUPPOSED TO SAVE THE WHOLE DAMN *PLANET?*

YOU'VE DONE IT BEFORE.

...WHAT?

I DON'T HAVE TIME TO EXPLAIN. YOU NEED TO GO, NOW. CATCH UP TO THE SOTEIRA TEAM, MAKE THEM BRING YOU TO PERSEPHONE. SAVE US, AND SAVE YOURSELF.

BUT BEFORE THAT...

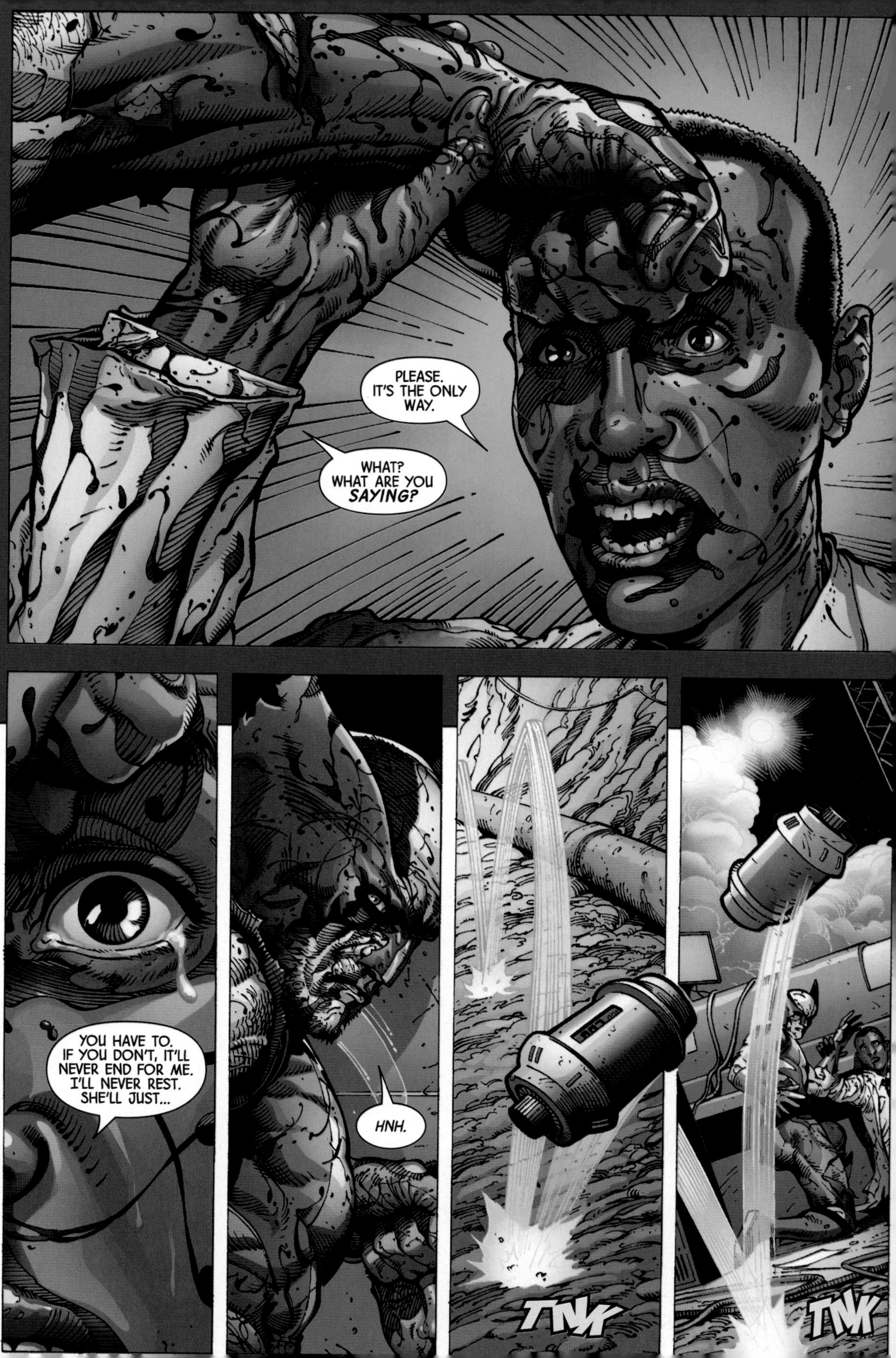
PLEASE. IT'S THE ONLY WAY.
WHAT? WHAT ARE YOU *SAYING?*
YOU HAVE TO. IF YOU DON'T, IT'LL NEVER END FOR ME. I'LL NEVER REST. SHE'LL JUST...
HNH.
TNK
TNK

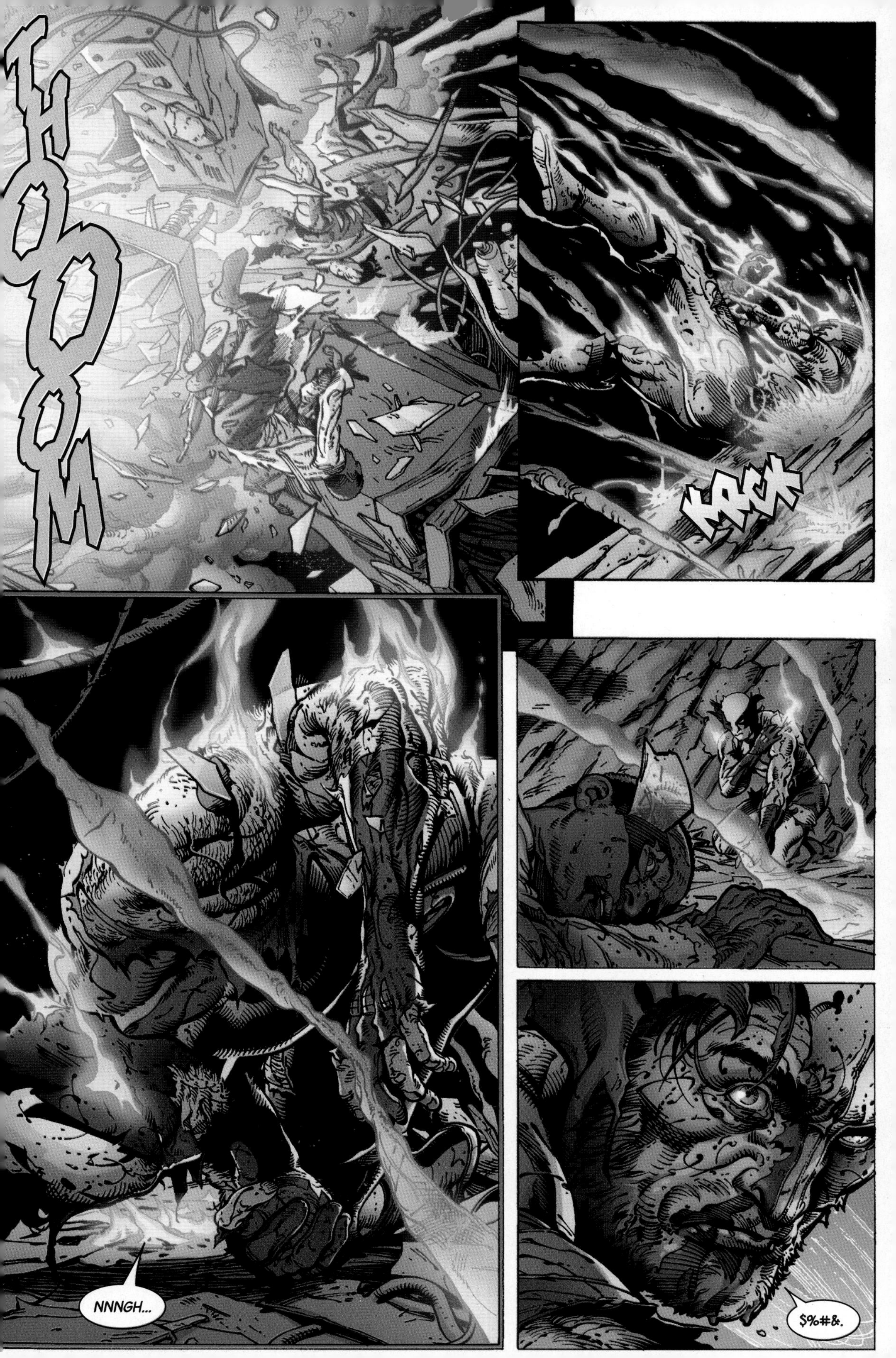
THOOOM
KRCK
NNNGH...
$%#&.

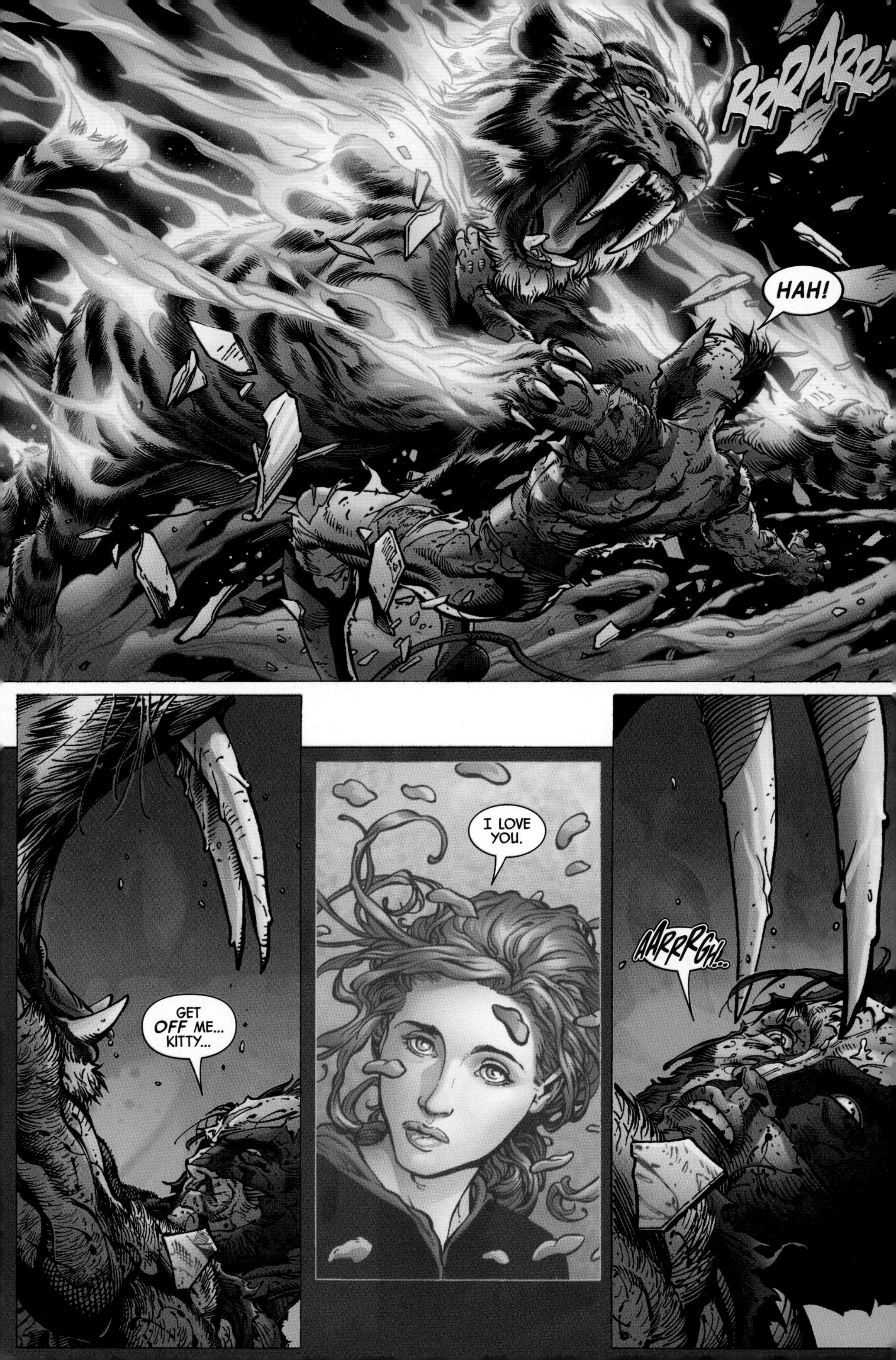
RRRARR!
HAH!
GET OFF ME... KITTY...
I LOVE YOU.
AARRRGH...

THWM

KRCK

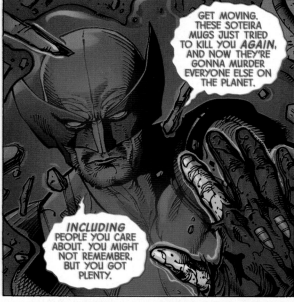

RATATTATT

GET MOVING. THESE SOTEIRA MUGS JUST TRIED TO KILL YOU *AGAIN*, AND NOW THEY'RE GONNA MURDER EVERYONE ELSE ON THE PLANET.

INCLUDING PEOPLE YOU CARE ABOUT. YOU MIGHT NOT REMEMBER, BUT YOU GOT PLENTY.

GO STOP THESE BASTARDS. YOU'RE A *HERO*.

WHAT DOES THAT EVEN *MEAN*?

BUB... IT AIN'T THAT COMPLICATED.

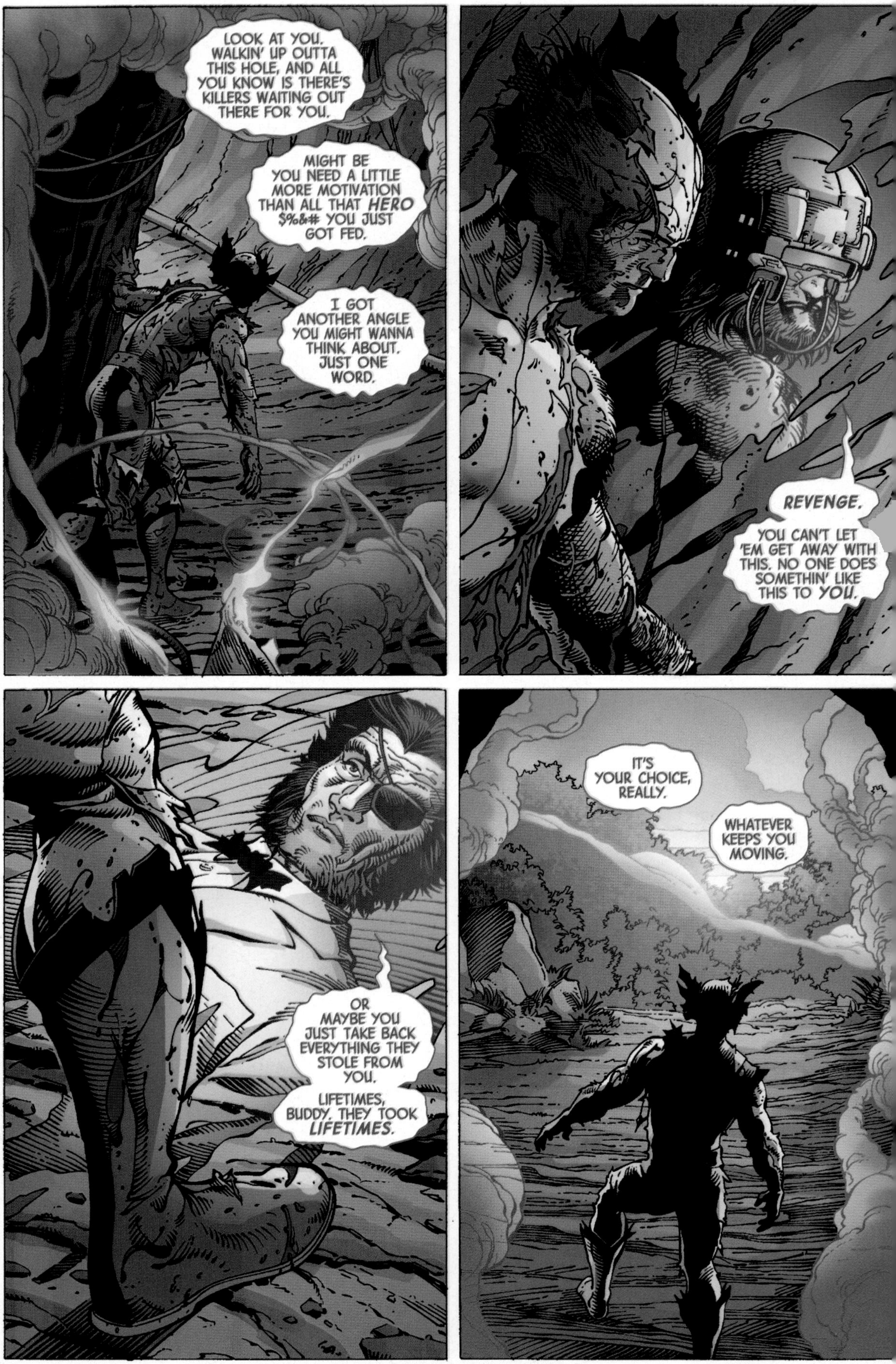
LOOK AT YOU. WALKIN' UP OUTTA THIS HOLE, AND ALL YOU KNOW IS THERE'S KILLERS WAITING OUT THERE FOR YOU.
MIGHT BE YOU NEED A LITTLE MORE MOTIVATION THAN ALL THAT HERO $%&# YOU JUST GOT FED.
I GOT ANOTHER ANGLE YOU MIGHT WANNA THINK ABOUT. JUST ONE WORD.
REVENGE.
YOU CAN'T LET 'EM GET AWAY WITH THIS. NO ONE DOES SOMETHIN' LIKE THIS TO YOU.
OR MAYBE YOU JUST TAKE BACK EVERYTHING THEY STOLE FROM YOU.
LIFETIMES, BUDDY. THEY TOOK LIFETIMES.
IT'S YOUR CHOICE, REALLY.
WHATEVER KEEPS YOU MOVING.

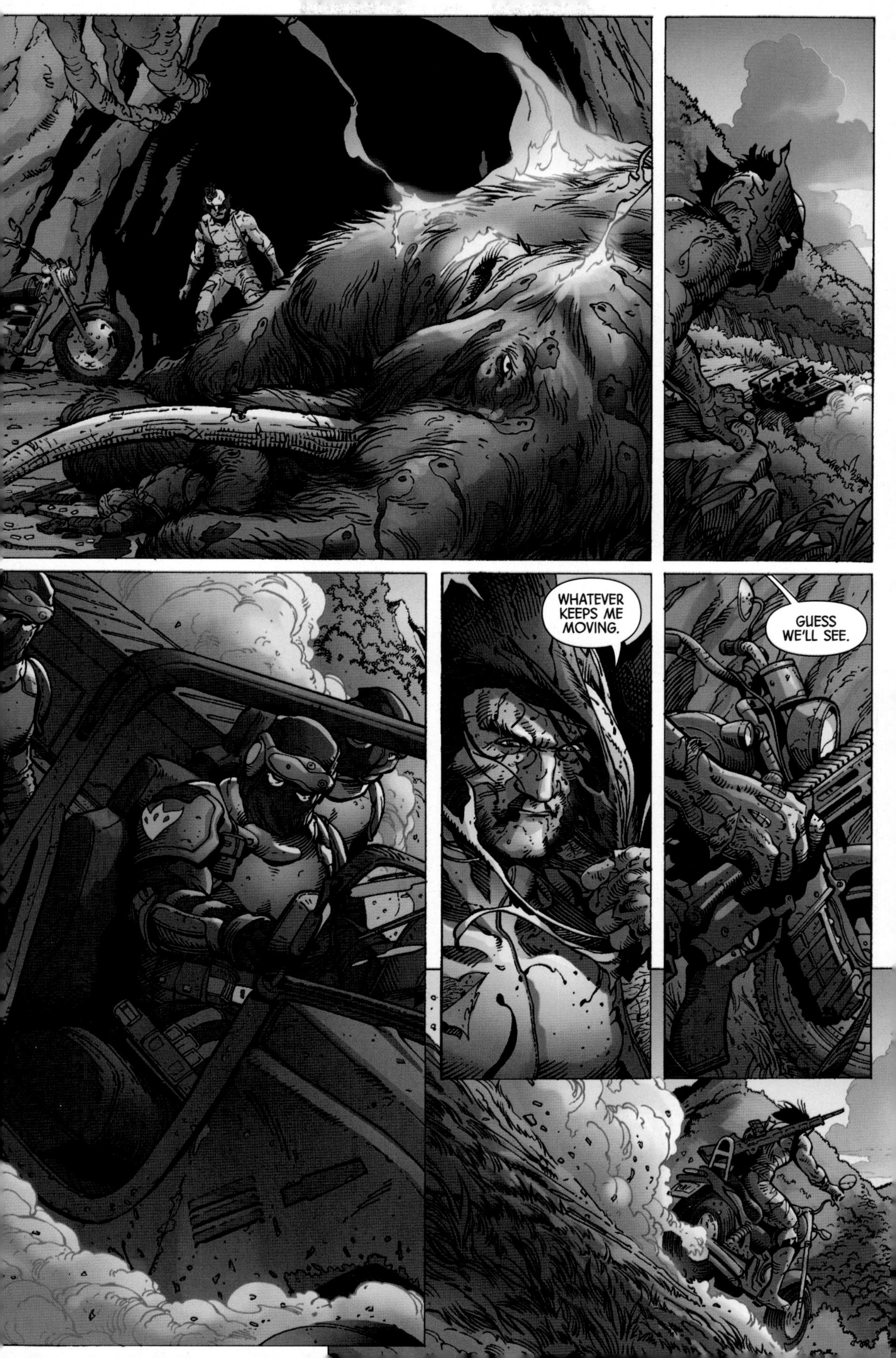
WHATEVER KEEPS ME MOVING.
GUESS WE'LL SEE.

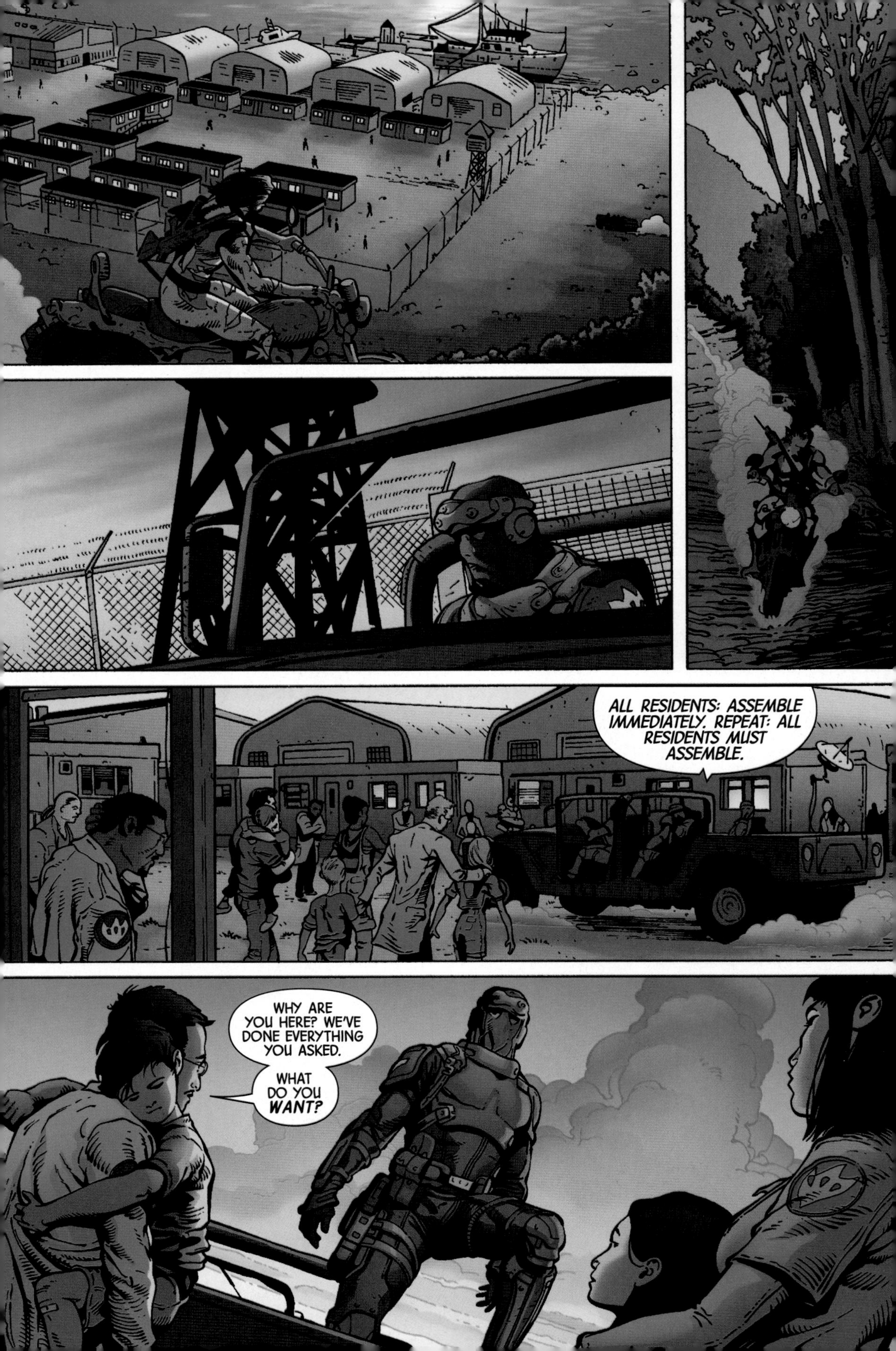
ALL RESIDENTS: ASSEMBLE IMMEDIATELY. REPEAT: ALL RESIDENTS MUST ASSEMBLE.
WHY ARE YOU HERE? WE'VE DONE EVERYTHING YOU ASKED.
WHAT DO YOU *WANT*?

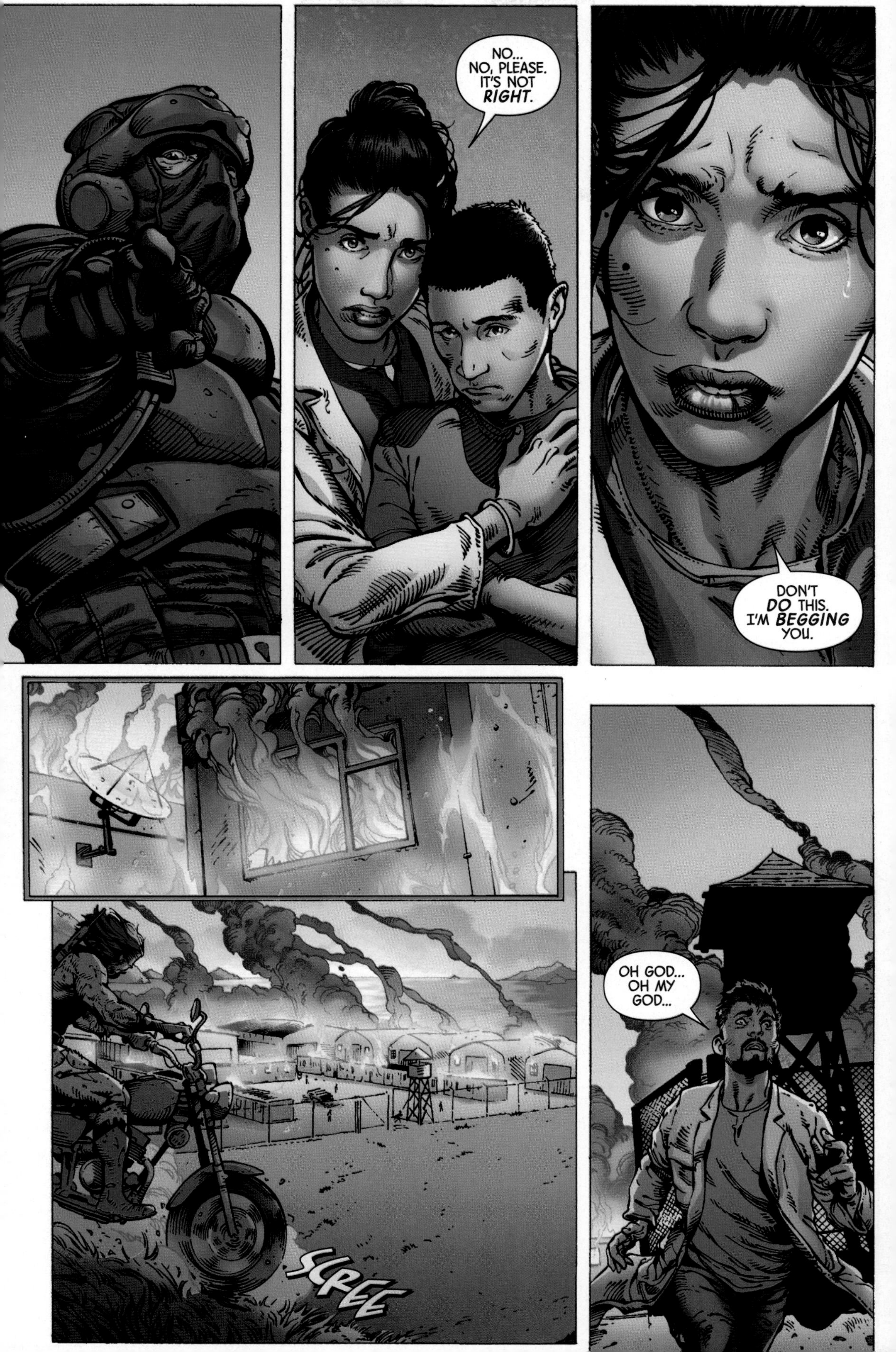
NO... NO, PLEASE. IT'S NOT RIGHT.
DON'T DO THIS. I'M BEGGING YOU.
SCREE
OH GOD... OH MY GOD...

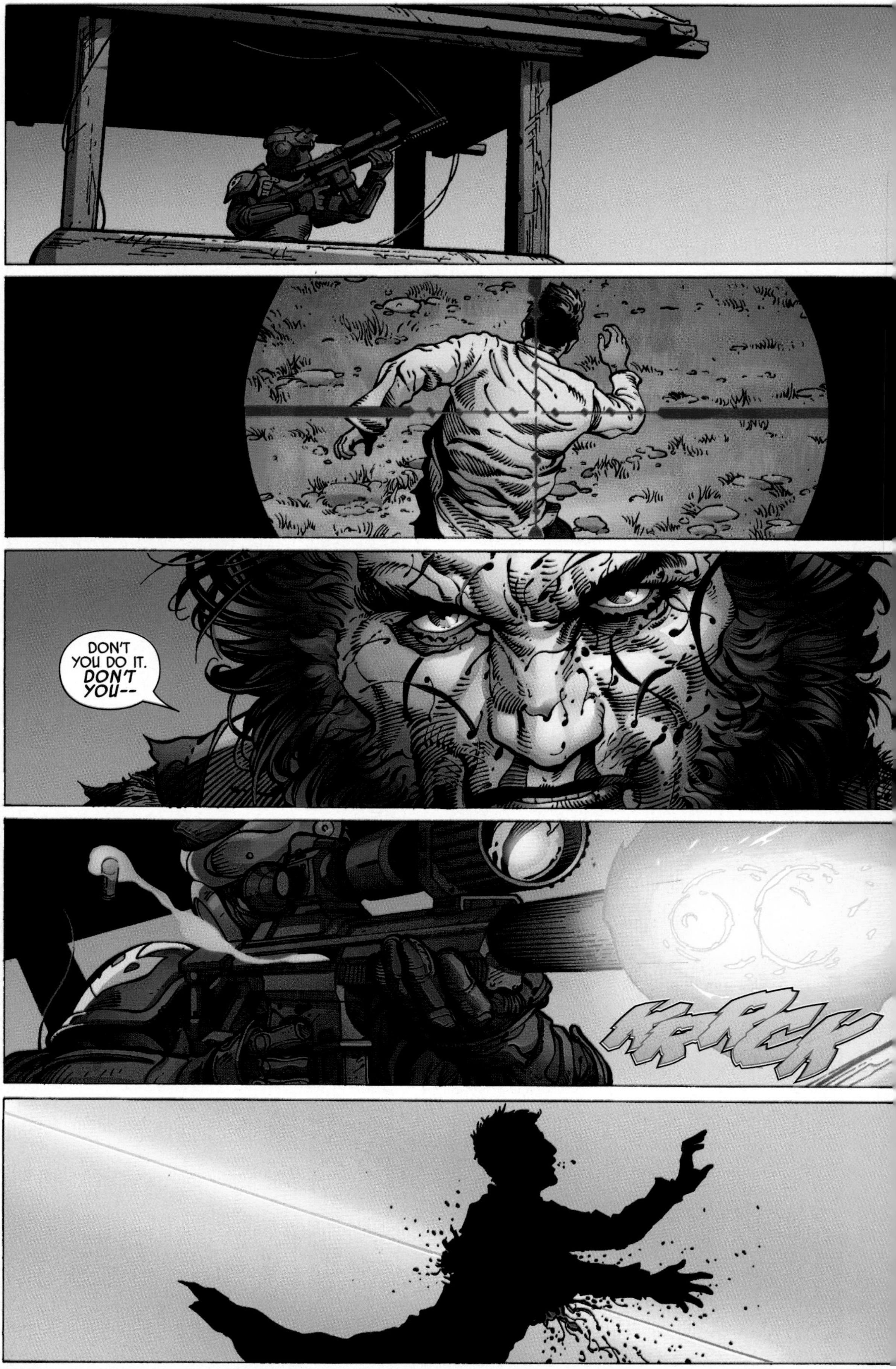
DON'T YOU DO IT. DON'T YOU--
KRRCK

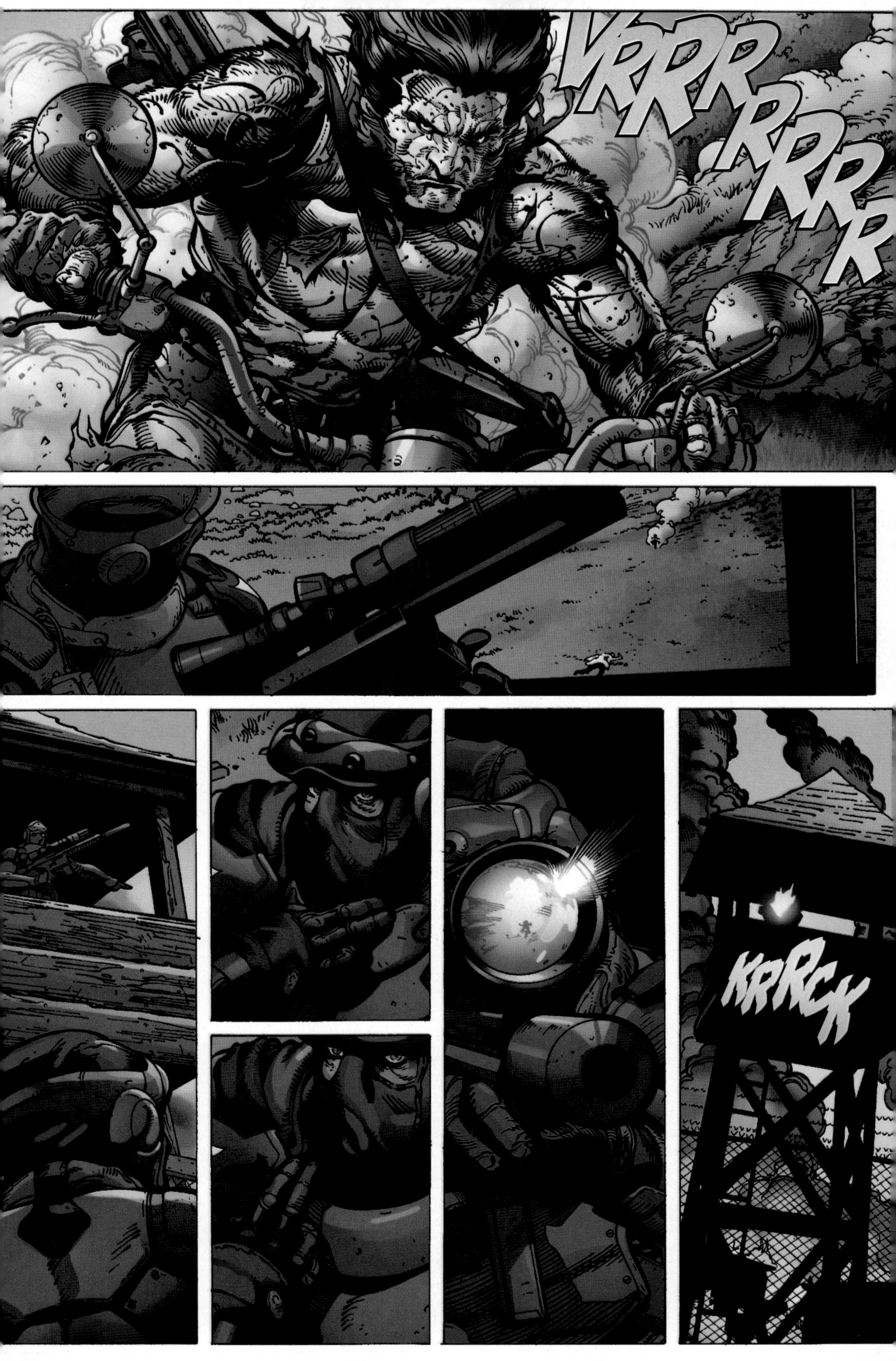
VRRRRRRRRR
KRRCK

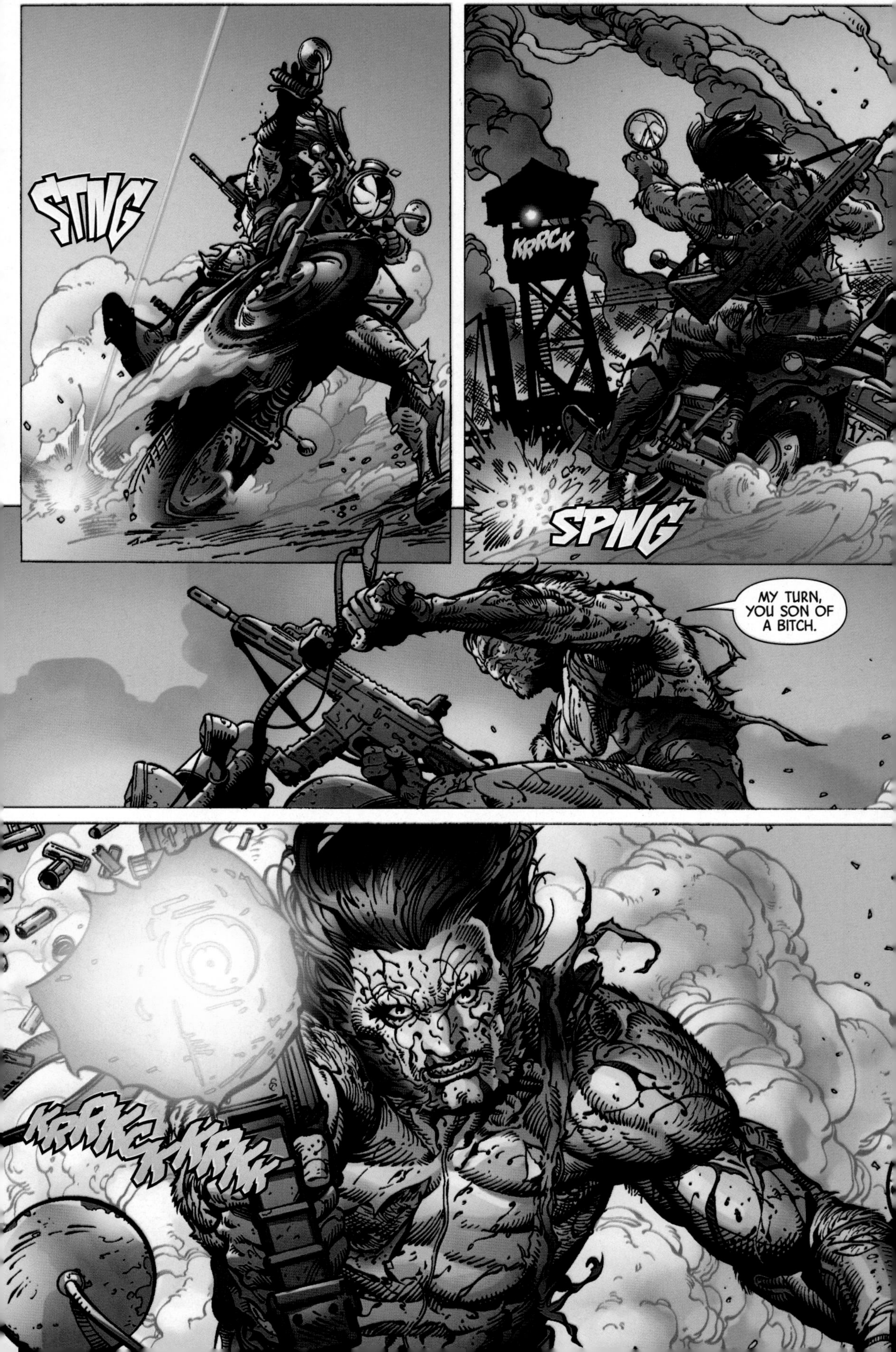
STNG
KRRCK
SPNG
MY TURN, YOU SON OF A BITCH.
KRRCK-KRRK

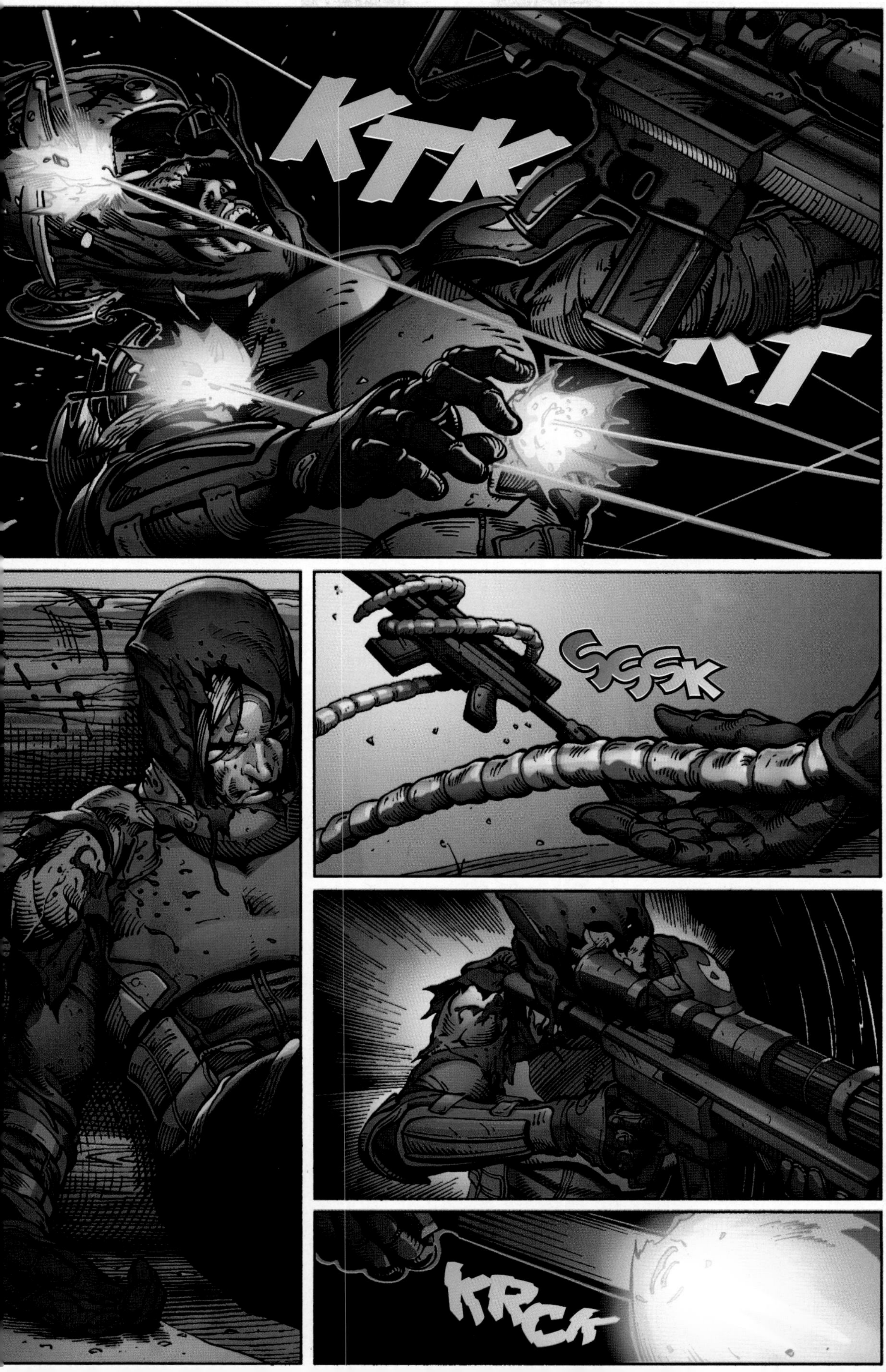
KTK
KT
SSSK
KRCK

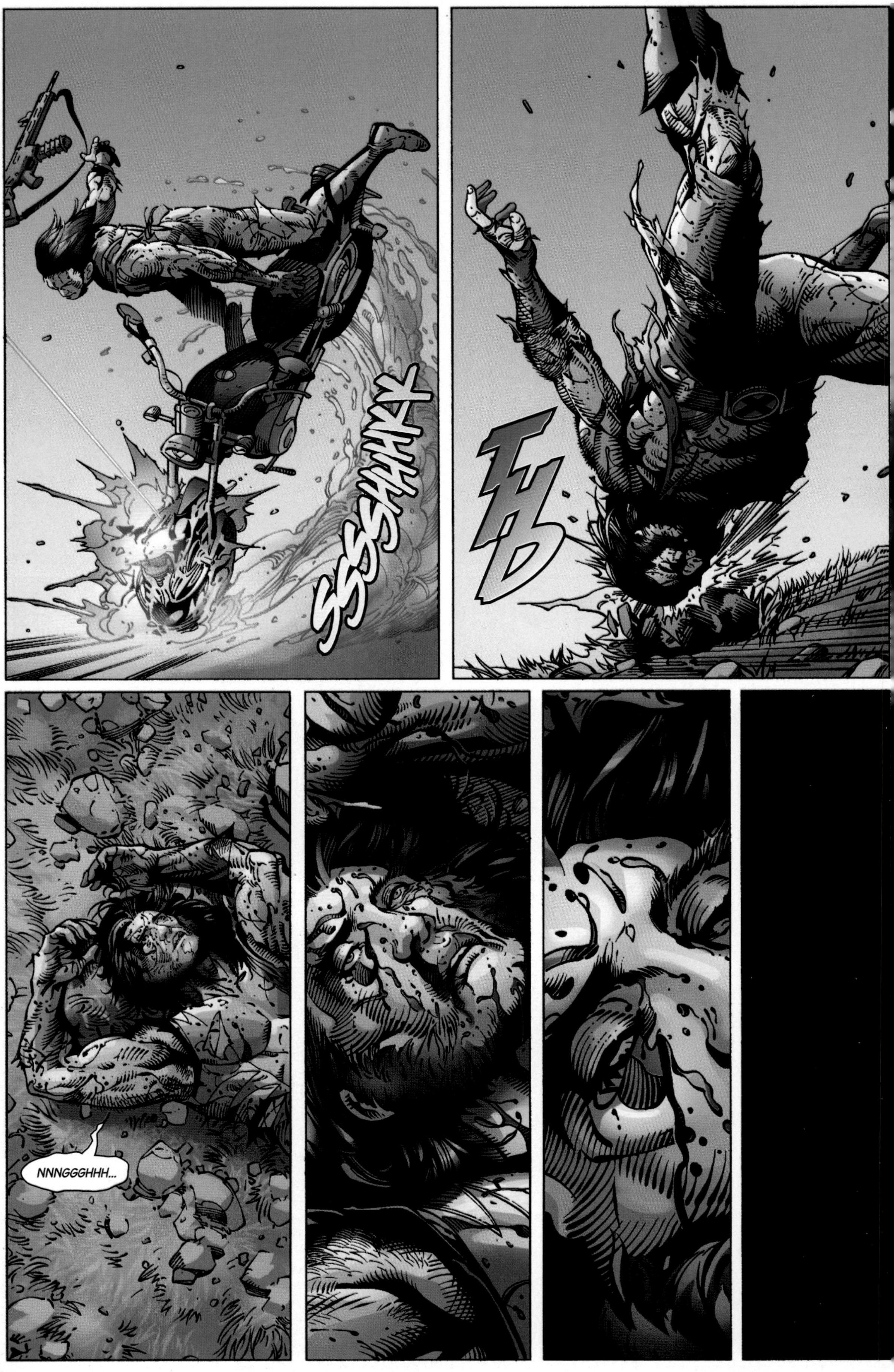
SSSSHHKK
TH
NNNGGGHHH...

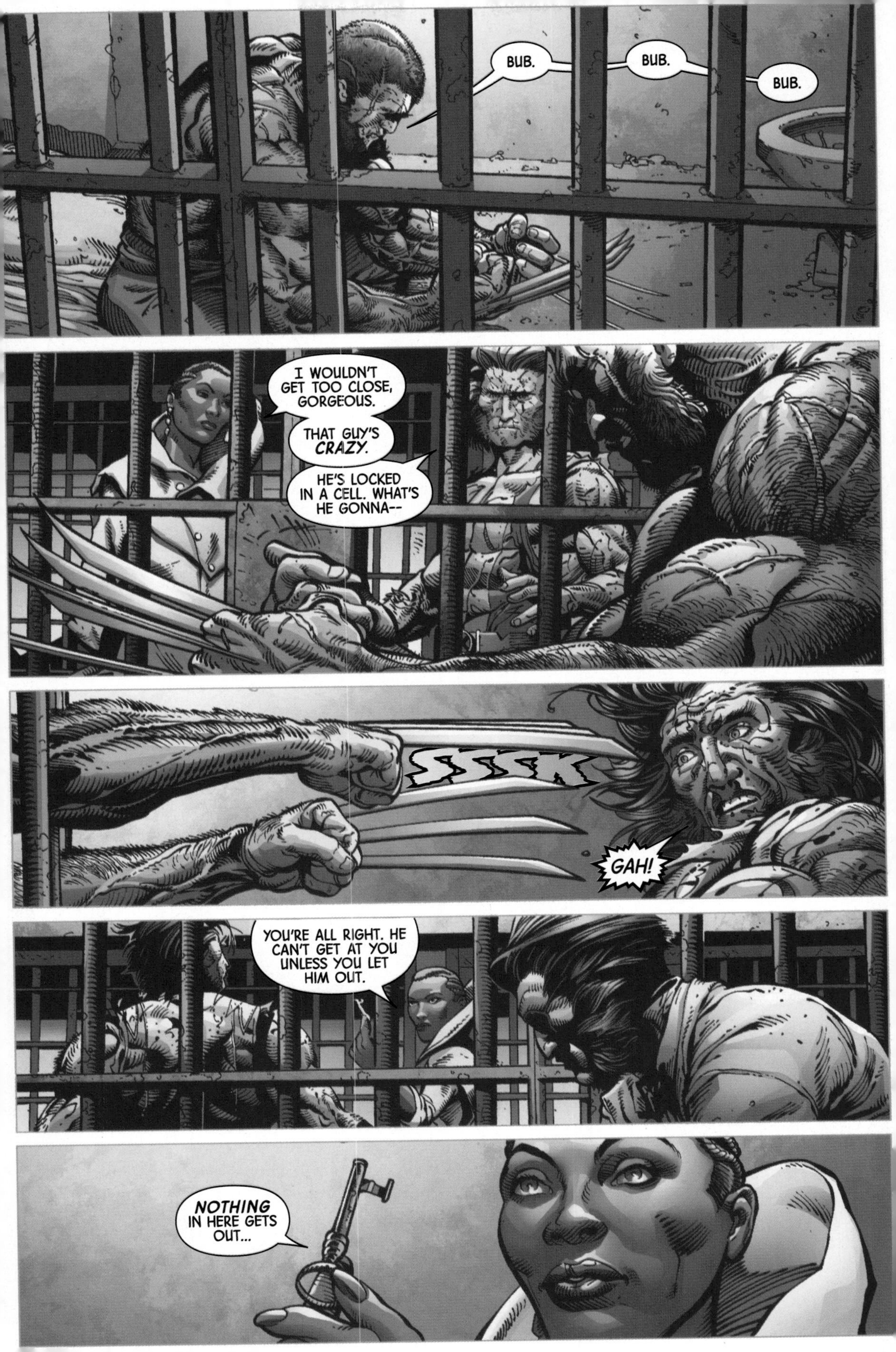
BUB.
BUB.
BUB.
I WOULDN'T GET TOO CLOSE, GORGEOUS.
THAT GUY'S CRAZY.
HE'S LOCKED IN A CELL. WHAT'S HE GONNA--
SSTIKT
GAH!
YOU'RE ALL RIGHT. HE CAN'T GET AT YOU UNLESS YOU LET HIM OUT.
NOTHING IN HERE GETS OUT...

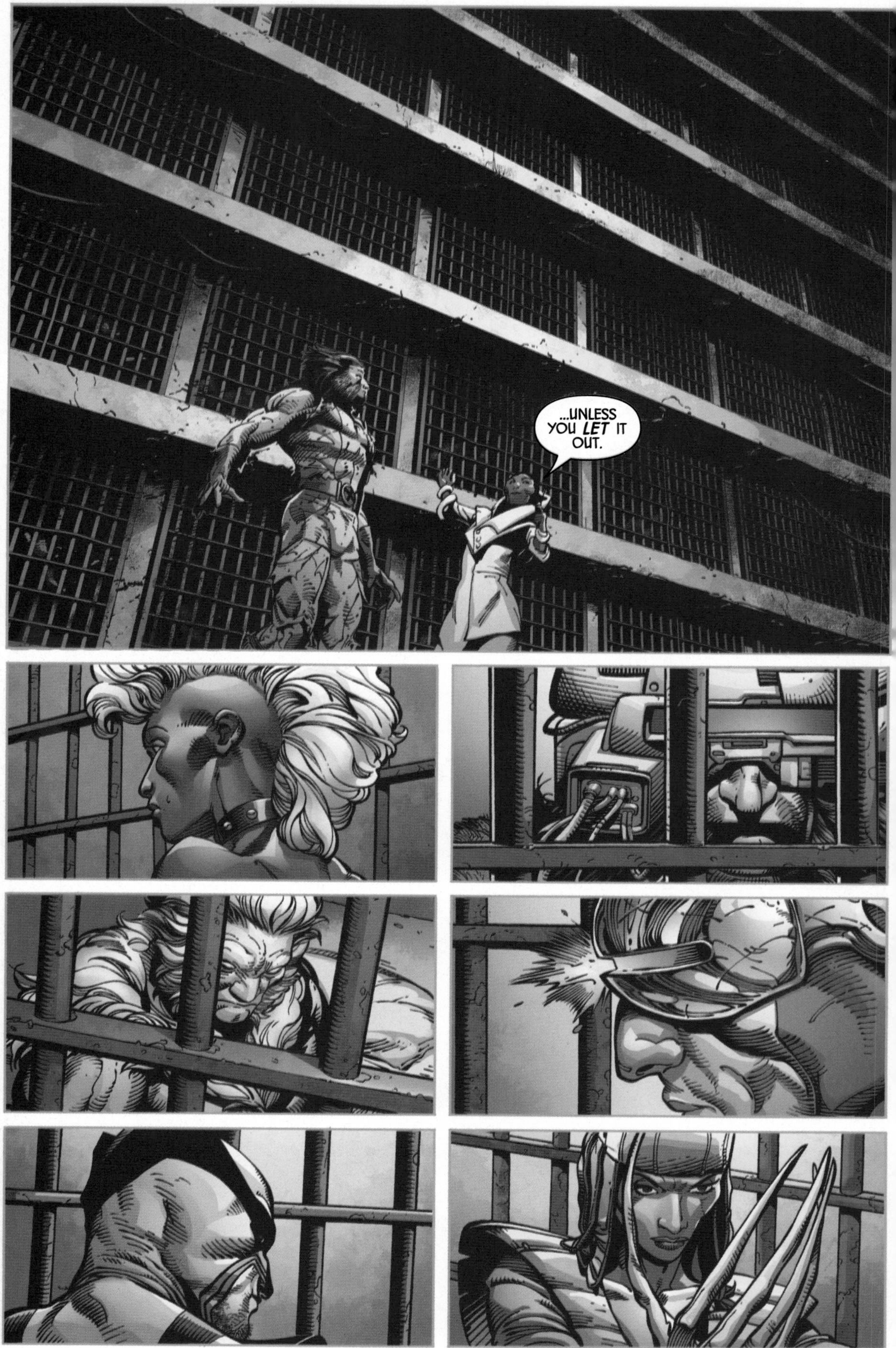
...UNLESS YOU LET IT OUT.

WHY DON'T YOU TAKE A LOOK AROUND? LOTS OF INTERESTING THINGS TO SEE. OPEN ANY DOOR YOU WANT.

HOW ABOUT *THAT*?

THAT'S NOT A DOOR. THAT'S A WALL, AND IT'S THERE FOR A REASON.

YOU DON'T WANT TO LOOK IN THERE, LOGAN. YOU'D BE... VERY UPSET. TRUST ME.

ANY DOOR?

WHO *ARE* YOU?

ME? MY NAME IS PERSEPHONE. WE'RE VERY GOOD FRIENDS.

PERSEPHONE, *HUH*? A DEAD MAN TOLD ME YOU'RE GOING TO DO SOMETHING TERRIBLE. SAID I SHOULD DO EVERYTHING I CAN TO STOP YOU.

THEN YOU WERE MISINFORMED.

BABY, I BROUGHT YOU BACK TO LIFE.

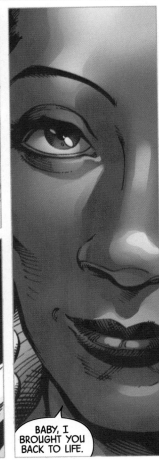

WOLVERINE!

WAKE UP!

PLEASE! YOU HAVE TO WAKE UP!

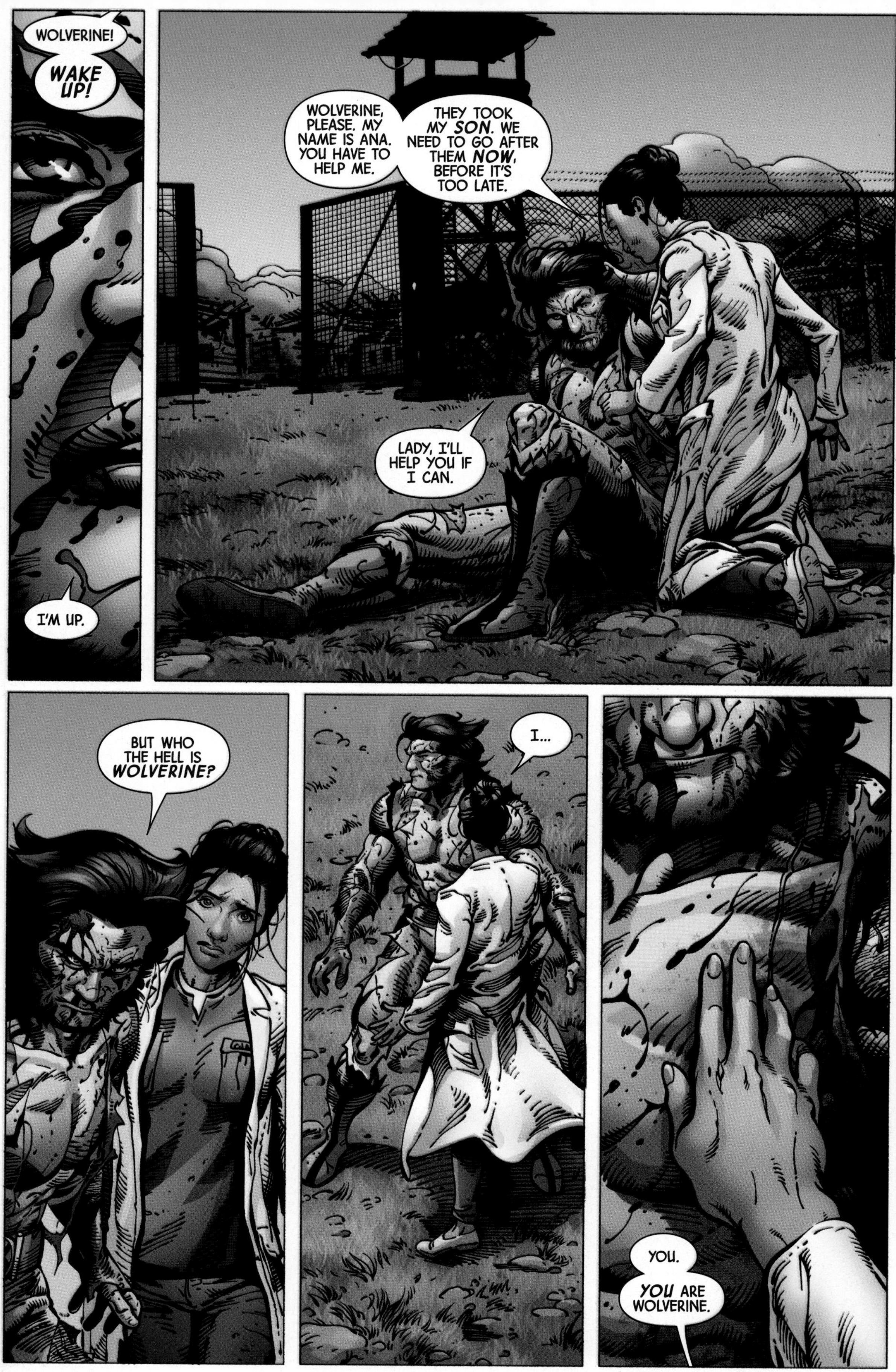
WOLVERINE!
WAKE UP!
I'M UP.
WOLVERINE, PLEASE. MY NAME IS ANA. YOU HAVE TO HELP ME.
THEY TOOK MY SON. WE NEED TO GO AFTER THEM NOW, BEFORE IT'S TOO LATE.
LADY, I'LL HELP YOU IF I CAN.
BUT WHO THE HELL IS WOLVERINE?
I...
YOU.
YOU ARE WOLVERINE.

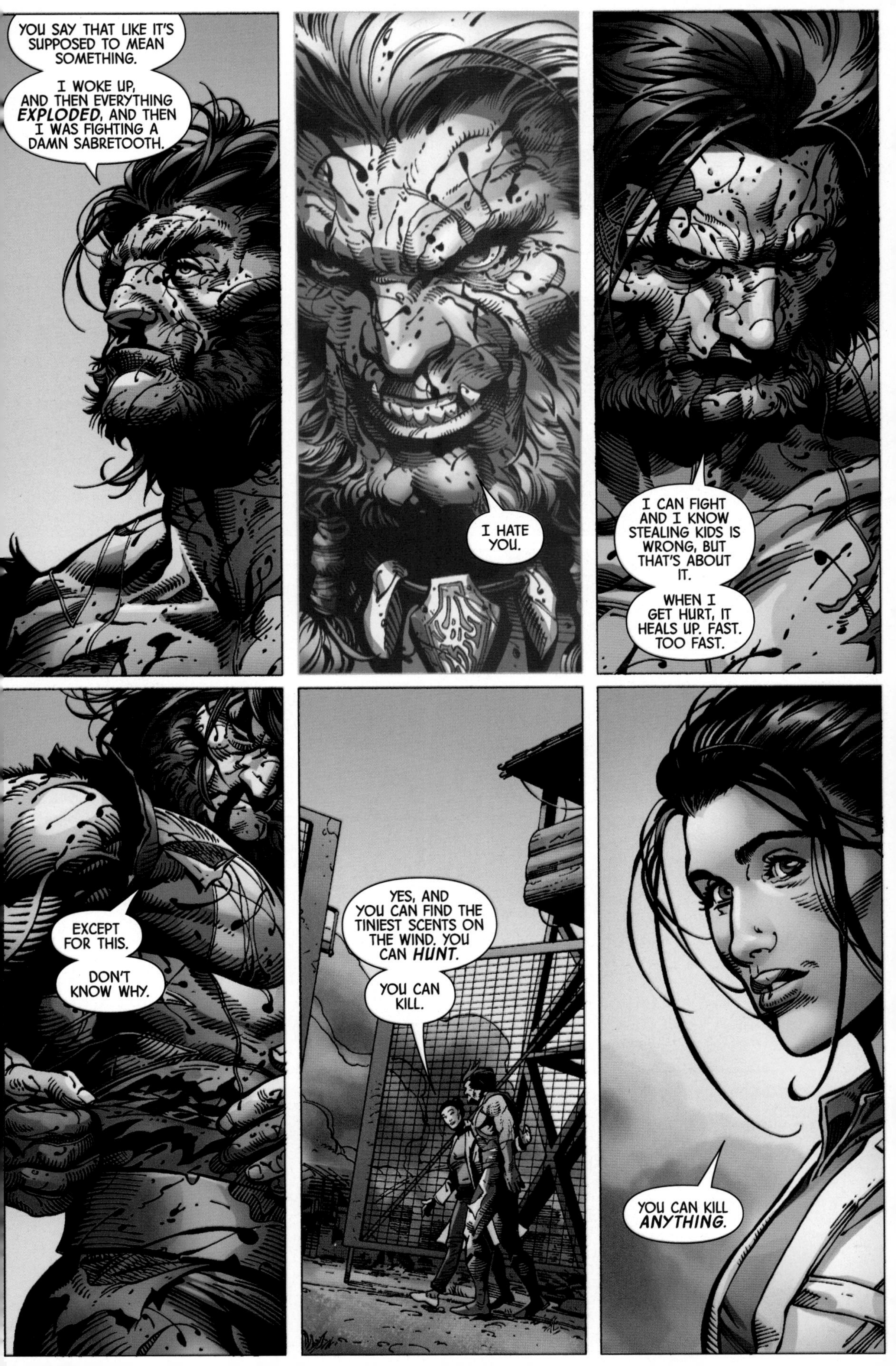
YOU SAY THAT LIKE IT'S SUPPOSED TO MEAN SOMETHING.
I WOKE UP, AND THEN EVERYTHING *EXPLODED*, AND THEN I WAS FIGHTING A DAMN SABRETOOTH.
I HATE YOU.
I CAN FIGHT AND I KNOW STEALING KIDS IS WRONG, BUT THAT'S ABOUT IT.
WHEN I GET HURT, IT HEALS UP. FAST. TOO FAST.
EXCEPT FOR THIS.
DON'T KNOW WHY.
YES, AND YOU CAN FIND THE TINIEST SCENTS ON THE WIND. YOU CAN *HUNT*.
YOU CAN KILL.
YOU CAN KILL *ANYTHING*.

ANYTHING, *HUH?*

YES. AND NOW I NEED YOU TO KILL THE PEOPLE WHO KILLED MY FRIENDS AND TOOK MY SON.

THOSE MONSTERS FROM *SOTEIRA.*

SOTEIRA. BEEN HEARING THAT NAME A LOT.

THIS WAS THEIR PLACE. A RESEARCH FACILITY. THEY WERE BRINGING *SCIENTISTS* HERE, COLLECTING THEM, ALL DIFFERENT KINDS, HELPING THEM WITH THEIR WORK.

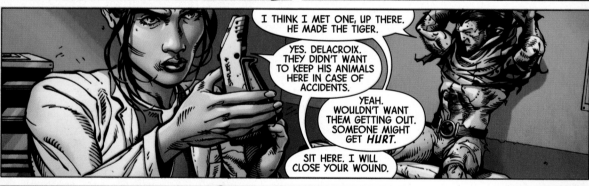

I THINK I MET ONE, UP THERE. HE MADE THE TIGER.

YES. DELACROIX. THEY DIDN'T WANT TO KEEP HIS ANIMALS HERE IN CASE OF ACCIDENTS.

YEAH. WOULDN'T WANT THEM GETTING OUT. SOMEONE MIGHT GET *HURT.*

SIT HERE. I WILL CLOSE YOUR WOUND.

HOW DO YOU KNOW ALL THIS? WHY'D THEY TAKE YOUR SON? HE A SCIENTIST TOO?

KCHK

NO...I WORKED HERE. IN THE CANTEEN. PEOPLE TALK WHEN THEY EAT, THEY DON'T EVEN REALIZE WHO'S LISTENING. YOU CAN LEARN A LOT.

MY SON... PERREN. HE'S 15. WHEN THE SOTEIRA TEAM CAME TO DESTROY THE FACILITY, THEY INJECTED HIM WITH SOMETHING FROM THE LABS.

WANTED TO MAKE HIM A LIVING INCUBATOR, MAYBE.

STICK HIM WITH SOMETHING, LET IT GROW INSIDE HIM, THEN HARVEST IT WHEN THEY GET WHERE THEY'RE GOING.

W-WHAT? *HARVEST* HIM? HOW DO YOU *KNOW* THAT?

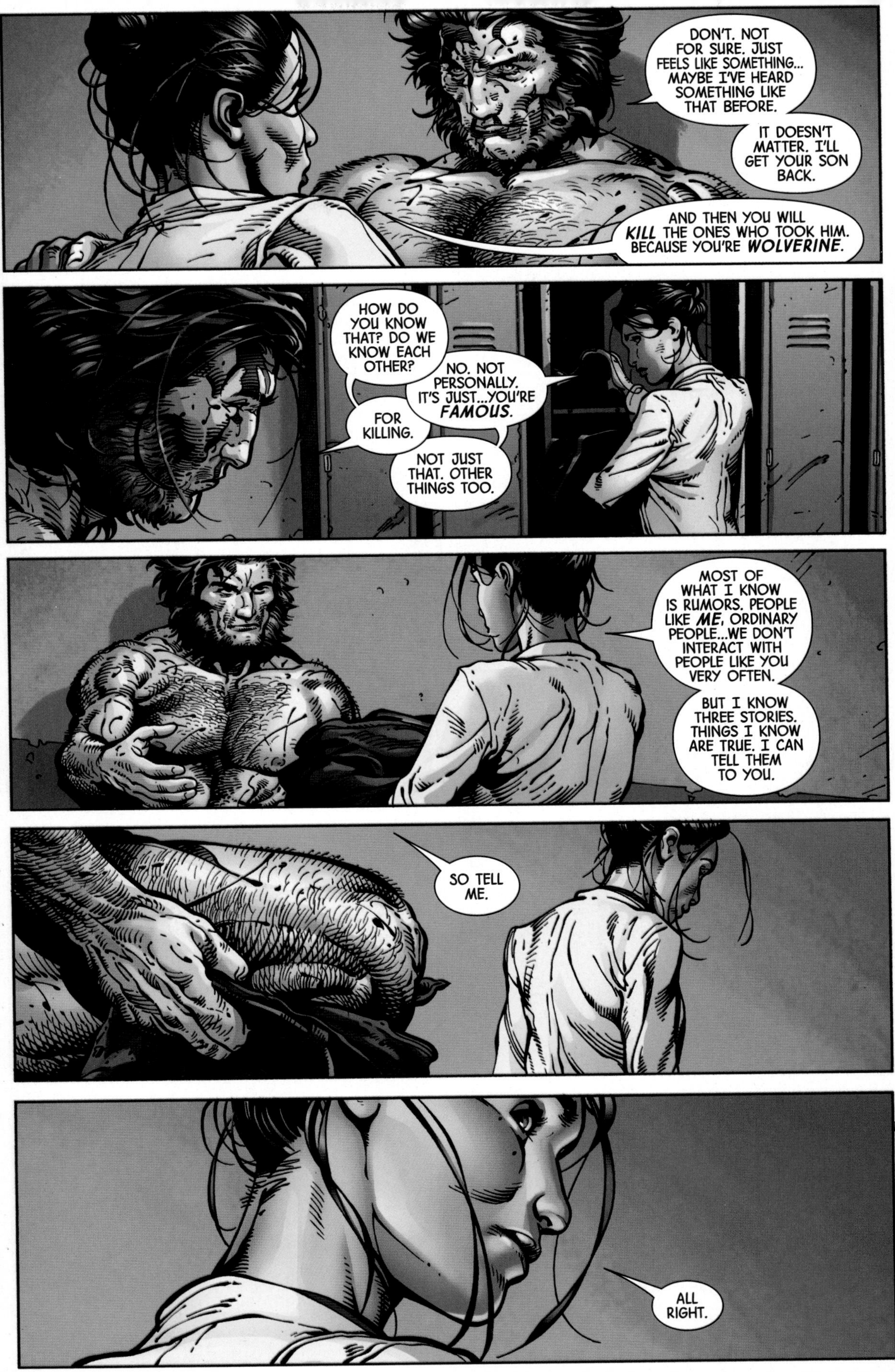

DON'T. NOT FOR SURE. JUST FEELS LIKE SOMETHING... MAYBE I'VE HEARD SOMETHING LIKE THAT BEFORE.
IT DOESN'T MATTER. I'LL GET YOUR SON BACK.
AND THEN YOU WILL **KILL** THE ONES WHO TOOK HIM. BECAUSE YOU'RE ***WOLVERINE***.
HOW DO YOU KNOW THAT? DO WE KNOW EACH OTHER?
NO. NOT PERSONALLY. IT'S JUST...YOU'RE ***FAMOUS***.
FOR KILLING.
NOT JUST THAT. OTHER THINGS TOO.
MOST OF WHAT I KNOW IS RUMORS. PEOPLE LIKE ***ME***, ORDINARY PEOPLE...WE DON'T INTERACT WITH PEOPLE LIKE YOU VERY OFTEN.
BUT I KNOW THREE STORIES. THINGS I KNOW ARE TRUE. I CAN TELL THEM TO YOU.
SO TELL ME.
ALL RIGHT.

"THIS IS THE FIRST STORY. I KNOW IT IS TRUE BECAUSE I SAW IT HAPPEN. I WAS THERE.

"IT IS THE STORY OF WHY YOU WEAR YELLOW AND BLUE.

"A MAN LOST TO ANGER CAME TO THE CITY ONE DAY.

"HE HAD BUILT A MACHINE, PUT WEAPONS ON IT AND PUT HIMSELF INSIDE IT.

"AND THEN HE USED THE WEAPONS.

"I DO NOT KNOW WHY, OR WHAT HE WANTED. MAYBE JUST TO HURT PEOPLE.

"MOST COULD RUN, AND DID, BUT THEN HE CAME TO A PLACE WHERE THE PEOPLE COULD *NOT* RUN. A HOSPITAL.

"IT SEEMED LIKE THIS WAS WHAT HE WANTED ALL ALONG.

"THE ANGRY MAN WAS ABOUT TO FIRE HIS WEAPONS, TO KILL ALL THOSE DEFENSELESS PEOPLE...

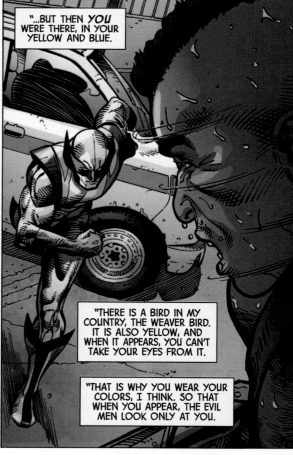

"...BUT THEN *YOU* WERE THERE, IN YOUR YELLOW AND BLUE.

"THERE IS A BIRD IN MY COUNTRY, THE WEAVER BIRD. IT IS ALSO YELLOW, AND WHEN IT APPEARS, YOU CAN'T TAKE YOUR EYES FROM IT.

"THAT IS WHY YOU WEAR YOUR COLORS, I THINK. SO THAT WHEN YOU APPEAR, THE EVIL MEN LOOK ONLY AT YOU.

"THE MAN FIRED HIS WEAPONS AT *YOU*, INSTEAD OF THE HOSPITAL. I THINK YOU KNEW HE WOULD.

"I BELIEVED YOU WERE DEAD. WE ALL DID. WHO COULD SURVIVE SUCH A THING?

"BUT YOU WERE ALIVE. YOU STOOD UP.

"AND THEN YOU DID THE OTHER THING THEY SAY WOLVERINE CAN DO.

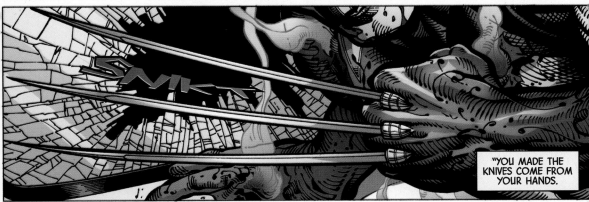

SNIK

"YOU MADE THE KNIVES COME FROM YOUR HANDS.

"YOU ARE A HERO."

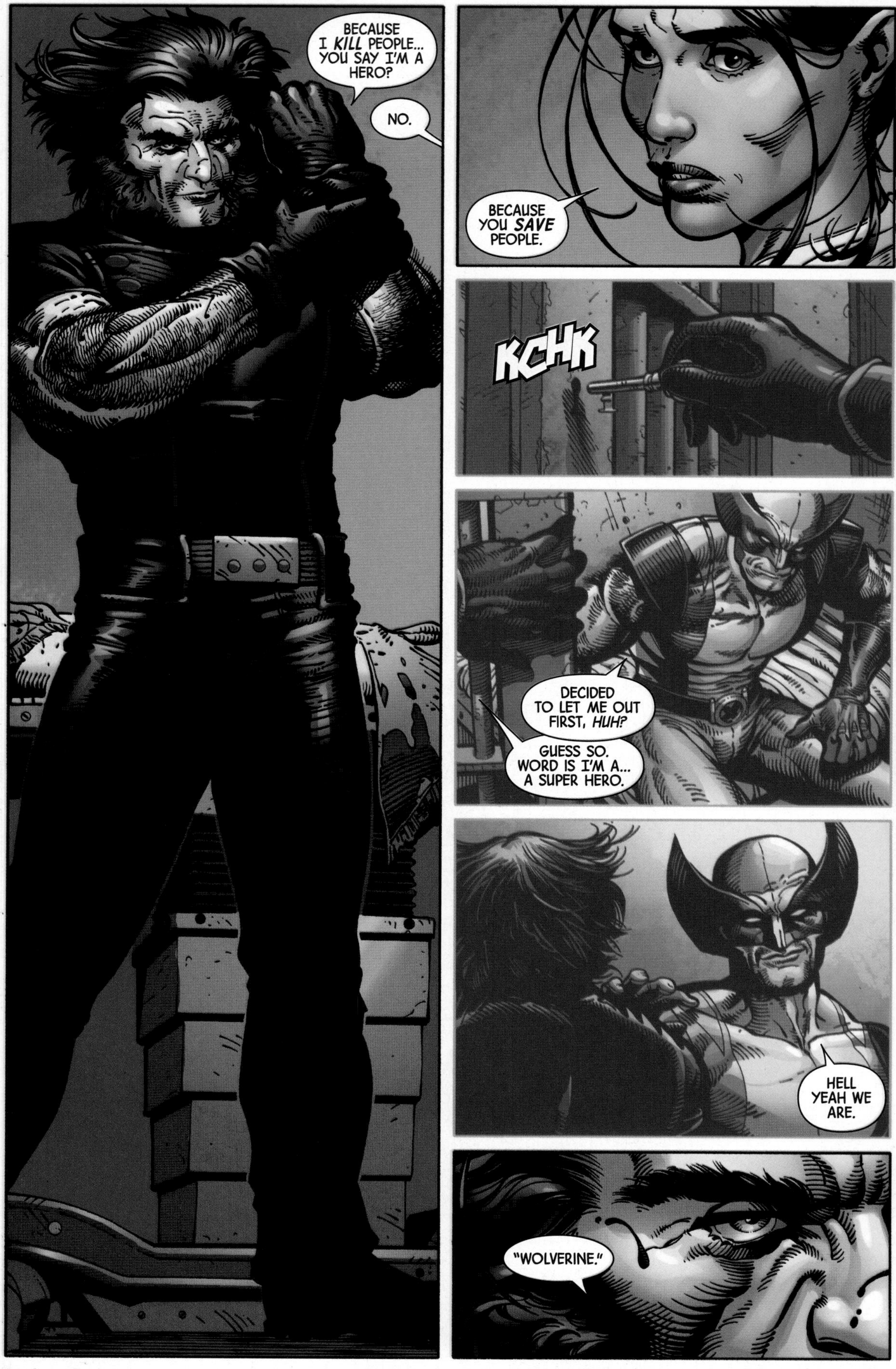
BECAUSE I *KILL* PEOPLE... YOU SAY I'M A HERO?
NO.
BECAUSE YOU *SAVE* PEOPLE.
KCHK
DECIDED TO LET ME OUT FIRST, *HUH?*
GUESS SO. WORD IS I'M A... A SUPER HERO.
HELL YEAH WE ARE.
"WOLVERINE."

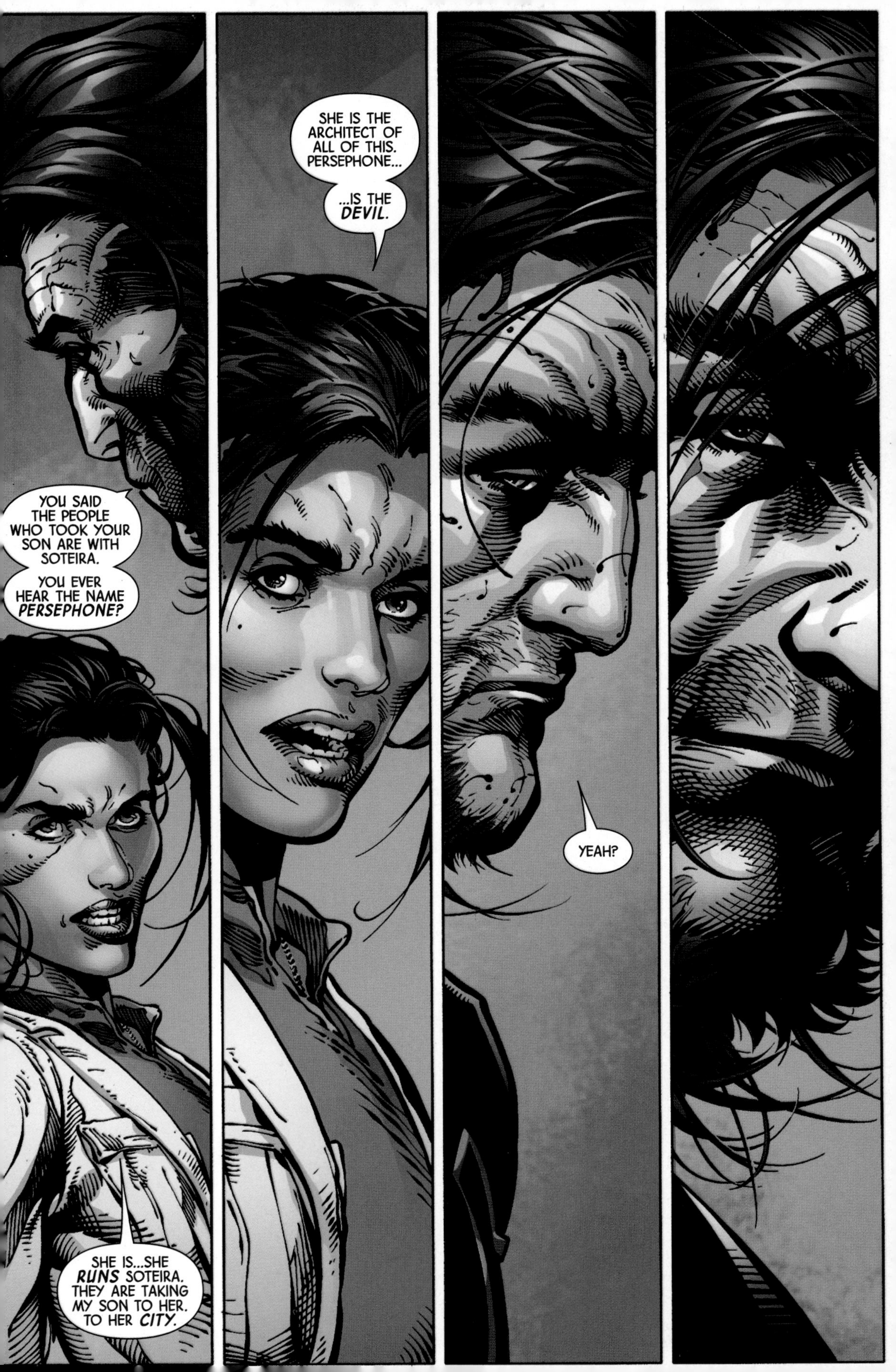
YOU SAID THE PEOPLE WHO TOOK YOUR SON ARE WITH SOTEIRA.
YOU EVER HEAR THE NAME *PERSEPHONE?*
SHE IS...SHE *RUNS* SOTEIRA. THEY ARE TAKING MY SON TO HER. TO HER *CITY*.
SHE IS THE ARCHITECT OF ALL OF THIS. PERSEPHONE...
...IS THE *DEVIL*.
YEAH?

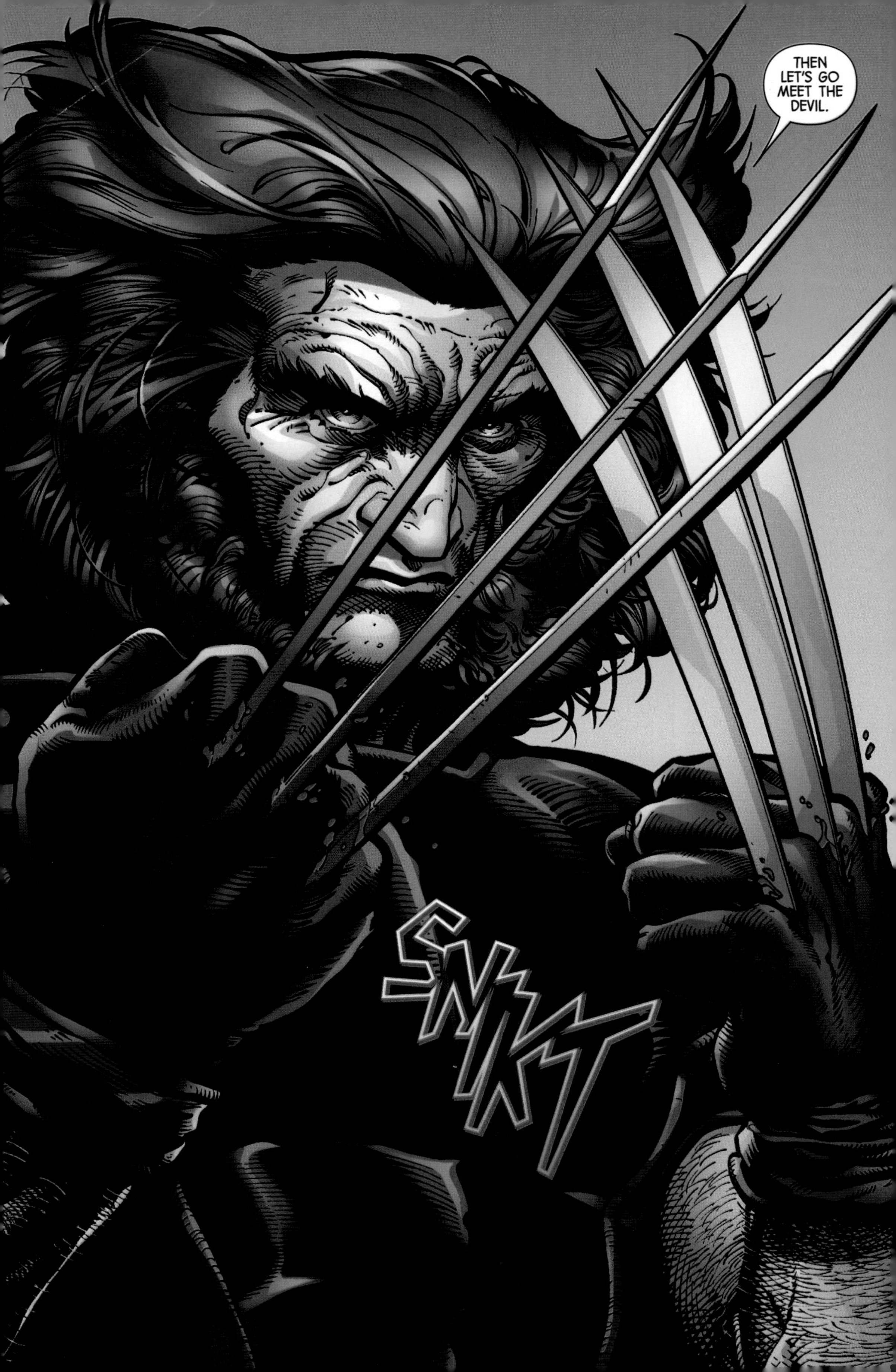
THEN LET'S GO MEET THE DEVIL.
SNIKT

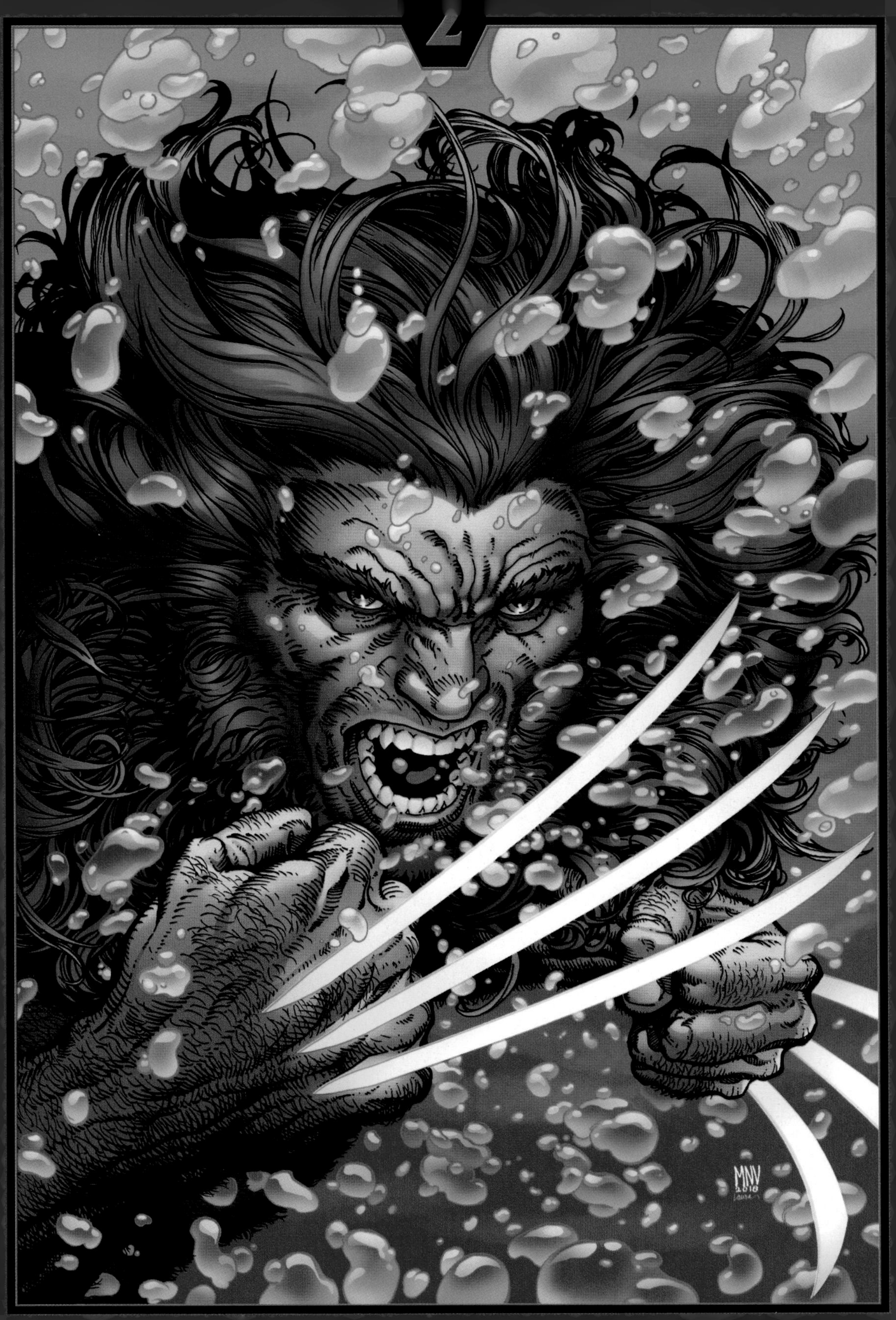
2

CHAPTER TWO
LIMBO

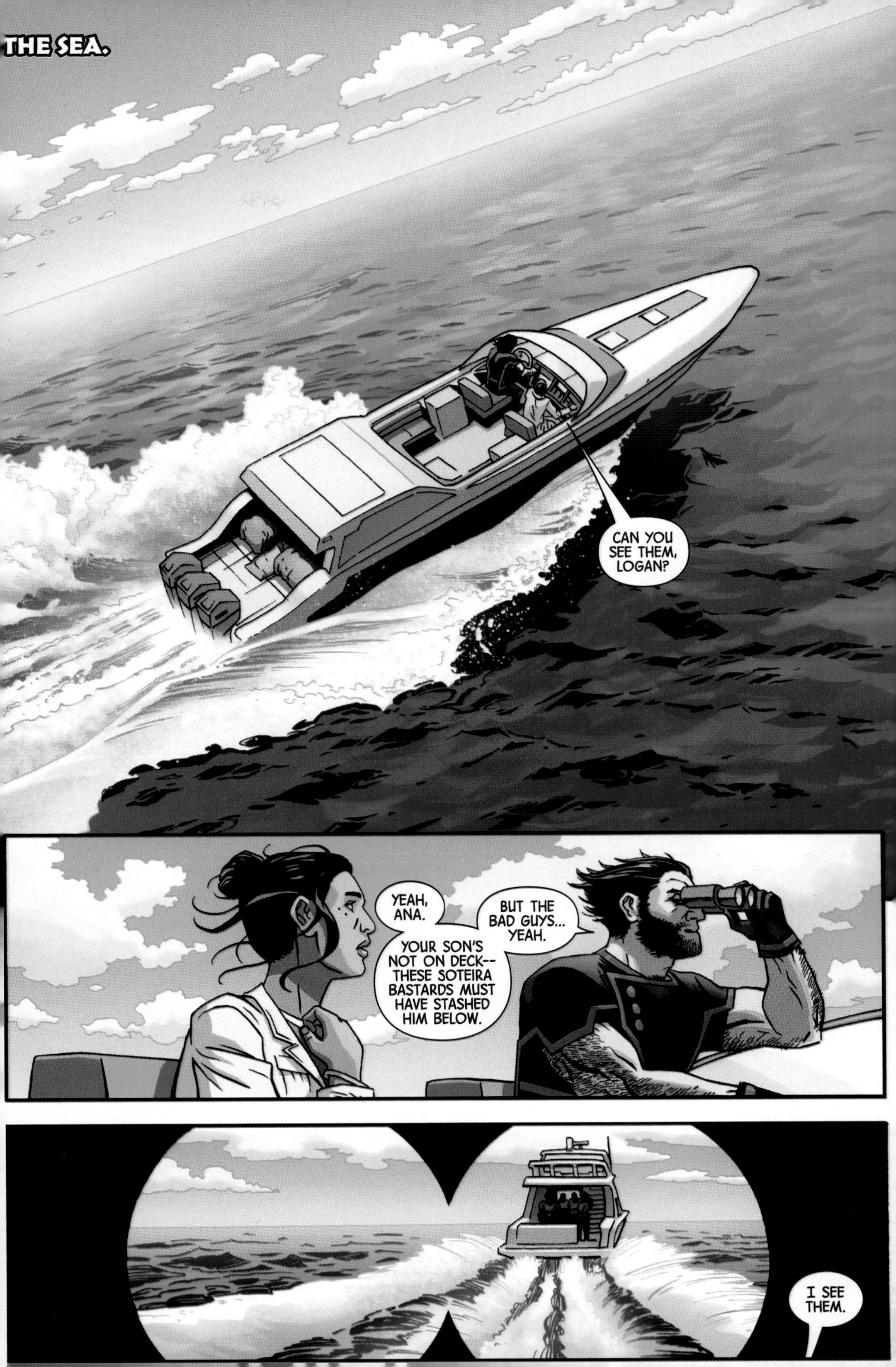
THE SEA.
CAN YOU SEE THEM, LOGAN?
YEAH, ANA.
BUT THE BAD GUYS... YEAH.
YOUR SON'S NOT ON DECK-- THESE SOTEIRA BASTARDS MUST HAVE STASHED HIM BELOW.
I SEE THEM.

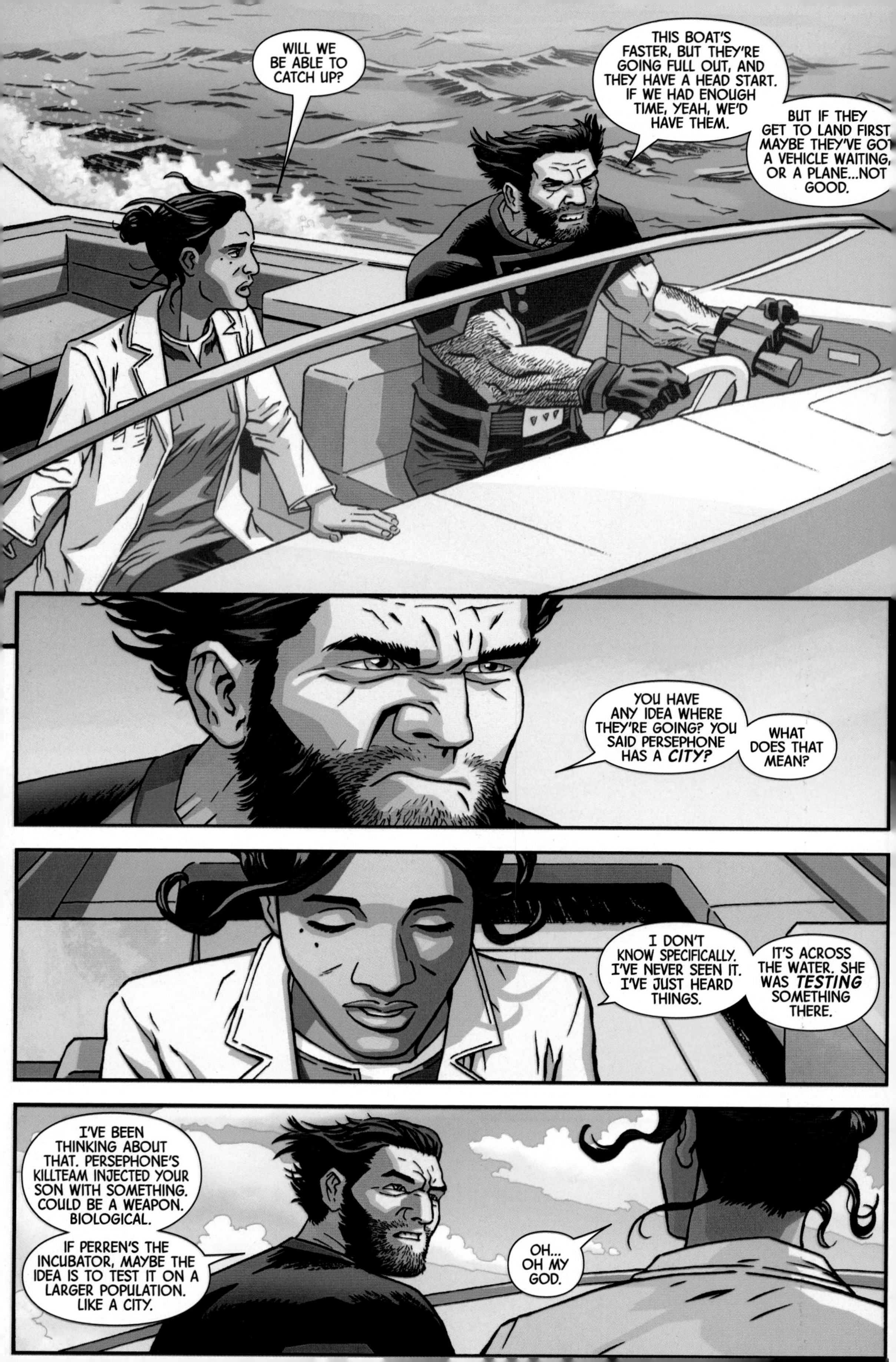
WILL WE BE ABLE TO CATCH UP?
THIS BOAT'S FASTER, BUT THEY'RE GOING FULL OUT, AND THEY HAVE A HEAD START. IF WE HAD ENOUGH TIME, YEAH, WE'D HAVE THEM.
BUT IF THEY GET TO LAND FIRST MAYBE THEY'VE GOT A VEHICLE WAITING, OR A PLANE...NOT GOOD.
YOU HAVE ANY IDEA WHERE THEY'RE GOING? YOU SAID PERSEPHONE HAS A *CITY?*
WHAT DOES THAT MEAN?
I DON'T KNOW SPECIFICALLY. I'VE NEVER SEEN IT. I'VE JUST HEARD THINGS.
IT'S ACROSS THE WATER. SHE WAS *TESTING* SOMETHING THERE.
I'VE BEEN THINKING ABOUT THAT. PERSEPHONE'S KILLTEAM INJECTED YOUR SON WITH SOMETHING. COULD BE A WEAPON. BIOLOGICAL.
IF PERREN'S THE INCUBATOR, MAYBE THE IDEA IS TO TEST IT ON A LARGER POPULATION. LIKE A CITY.
OH... OH MY GOD.

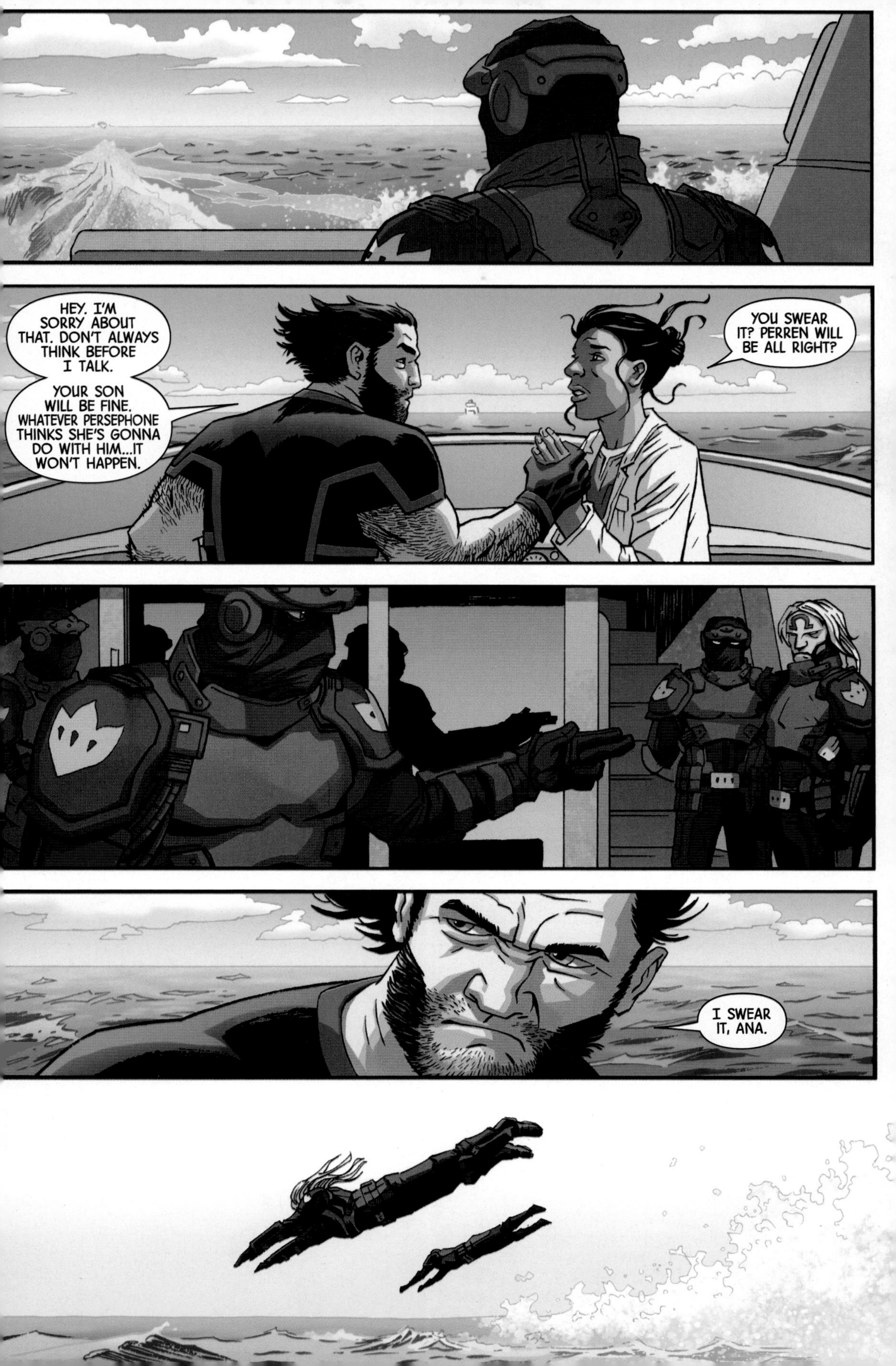
HEY. I'M SORRY ABOUT THAT. DON'T ALWAYS THINK BEFORE I TALK.
YOUR SON WILL BE FINE. WHATEVER PERSEPHONE THINKS SHE'S GONNA DO WITH HIM...IT WON'T HAPPEN.
YOU SWEAR IT? PERREN WILL BE ALL RIGHT?
I SWEAR IT, ANA.

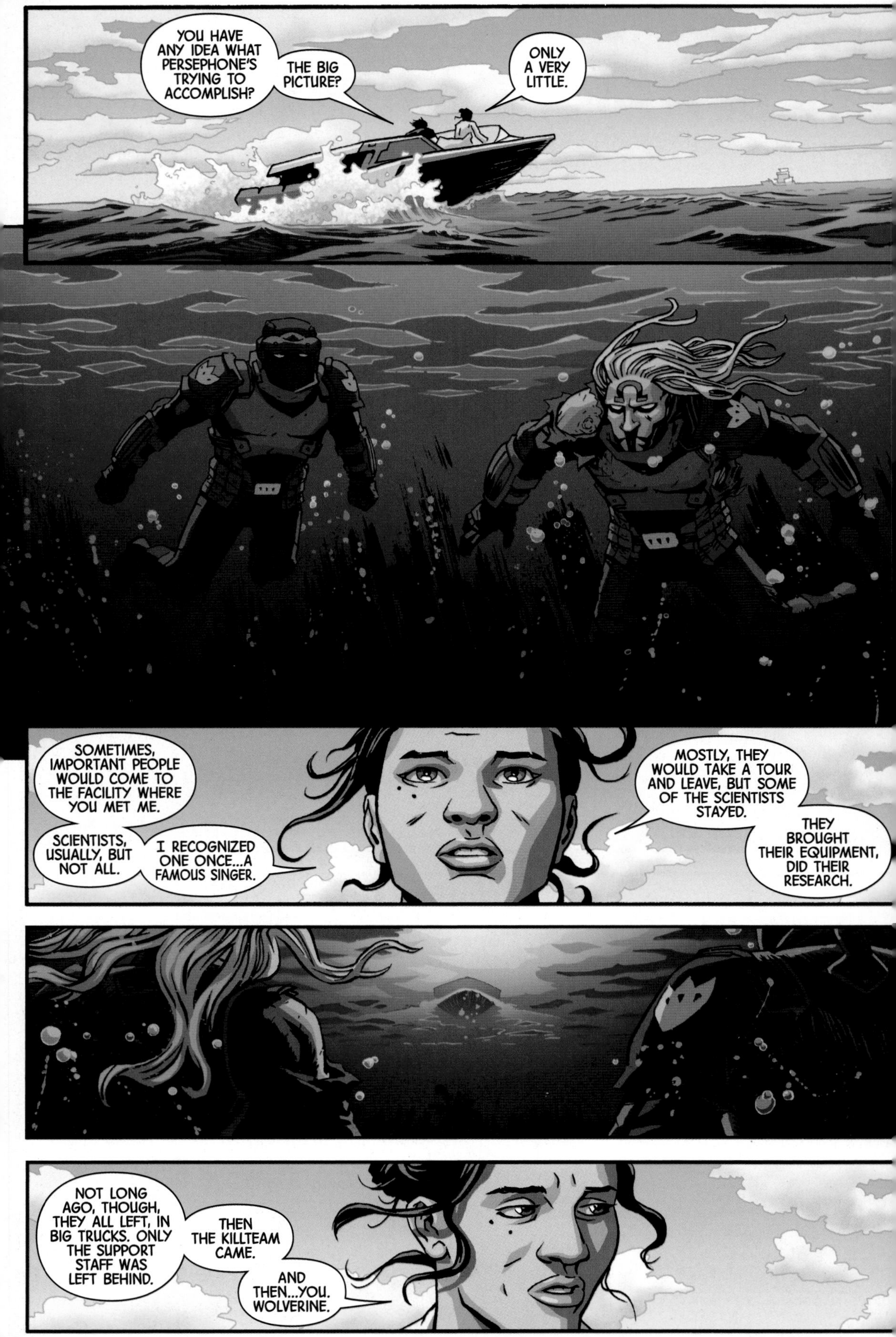
YOU HAVE ANY IDEA WHAT PERSEPHONE'S TRYING TO ACCOMPLISH?
THE BIG PICTURE?
ONLY A VERY LITTLE.
SOMETIMES, IMPORTANT PEOPLE WOULD COME TO THE FACILITY WHERE YOU MET ME.
SCIENTISTS, USUALLY, BUT NOT ALL.
I RECOGNIZED ONE ONCE...A FAMOUS SINGER.
MOSTLY, THEY WOULD TAKE A TOUR AND LEAVE, BUT SOME OF THE SCIENTISTS STAYED.
THEY BROUGHT THEIR EQUIPMENT, DID THEIR RESEARCH.
NOT LONG AGO, THOUGH, THEY ALL LEFT, IN BIG TRUCKS. ONLY THE SUPPORT STAFF WAS LEFT BEHIND.
THEN THE KILLTEAM CAME.
AND THEN...YOU. WOLVERINE.

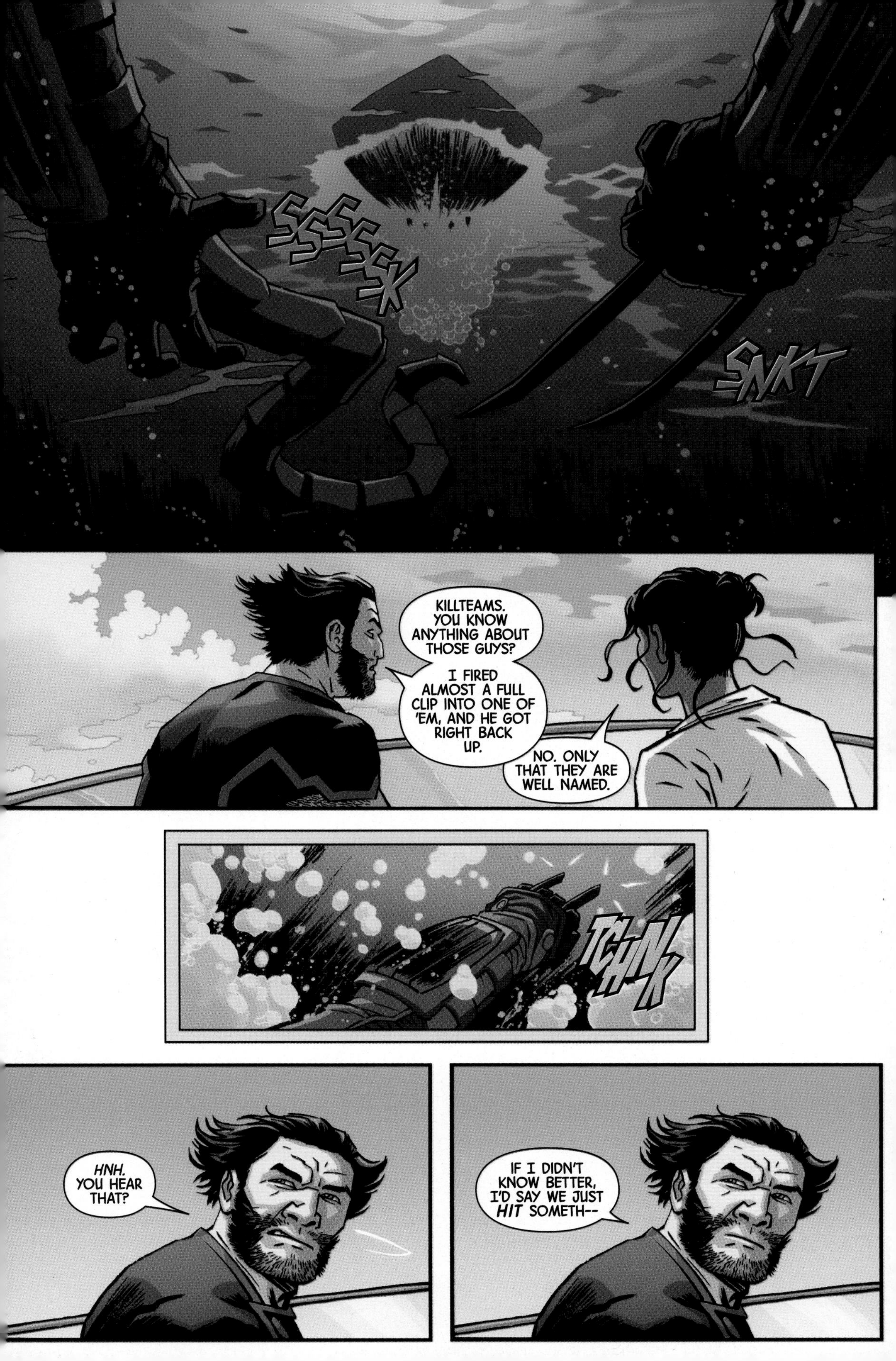
SSSSCCK
SNKT
KILLTEAMS. YOU KNOW ANYTHING ABOUT THOSE GUYS?
I FIRED ALMOST A FULL CLIP INTO ONE OF 'EM, AND HE GOT RIGHT BACK UP.
NO. ONLY THAT THEY ARE WELL NAMED.
TCHNK
HNH. YOU HEAR THAT?
IF I DIDN'T KNOW BETTER, I'D SAY WE JUST HIT SOMETH--

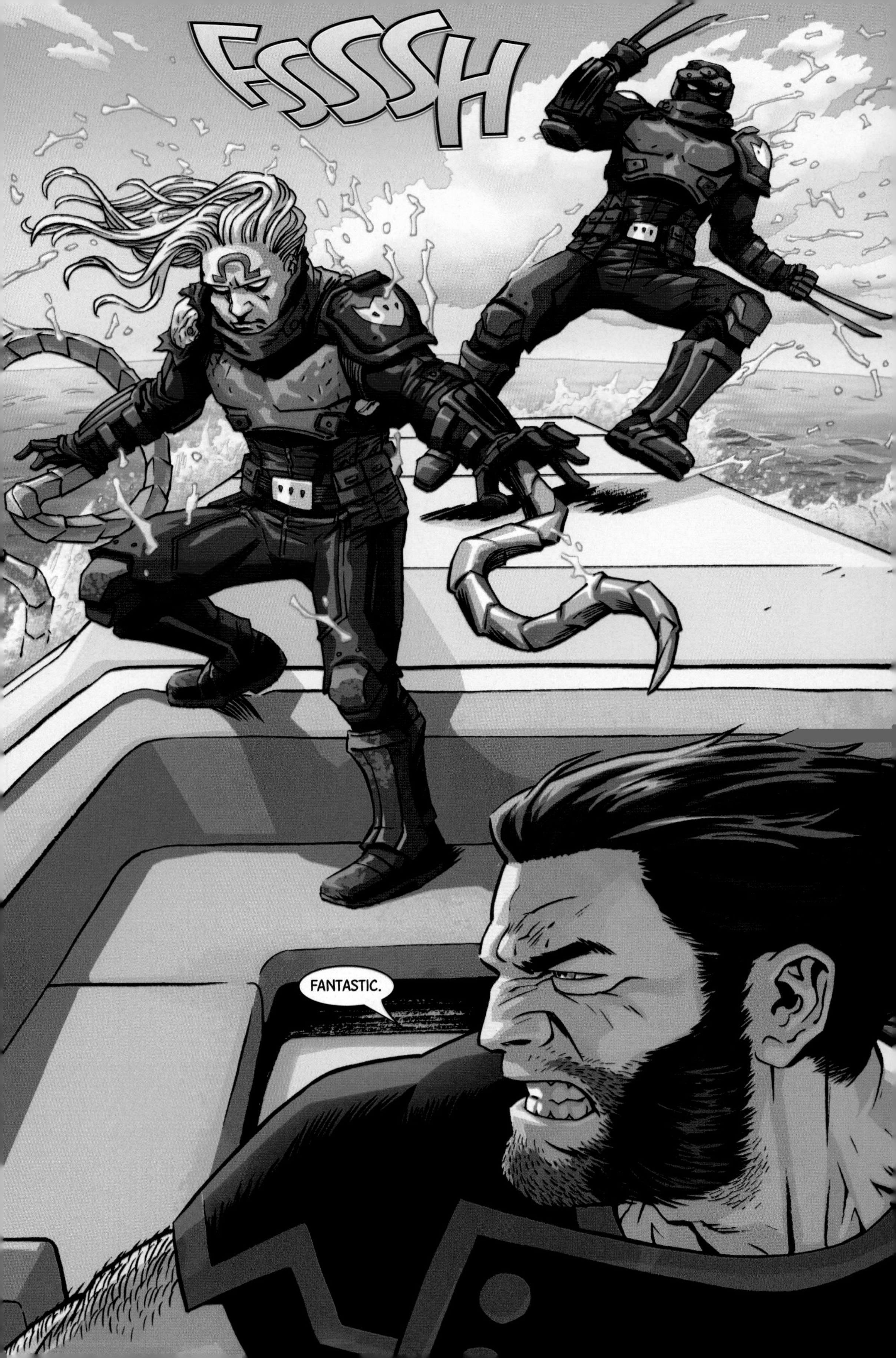
FSSSH
FANTASTIC.

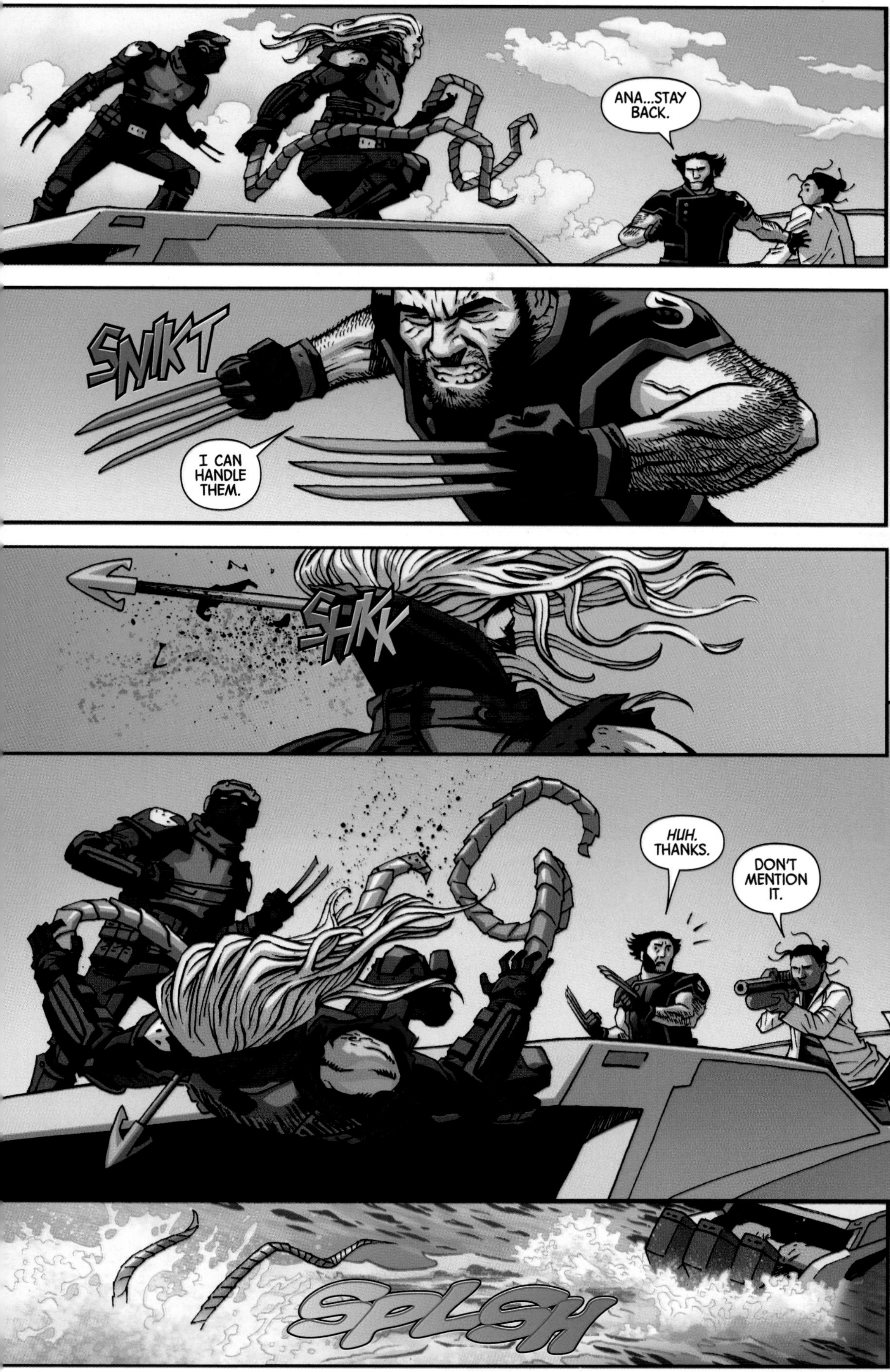
ANA...STAY BACK.
SNIKT
I CAN HANDLE THEM.
SHKK
HUH. THANKS.
DON'T MENTION IT.
SPLSH

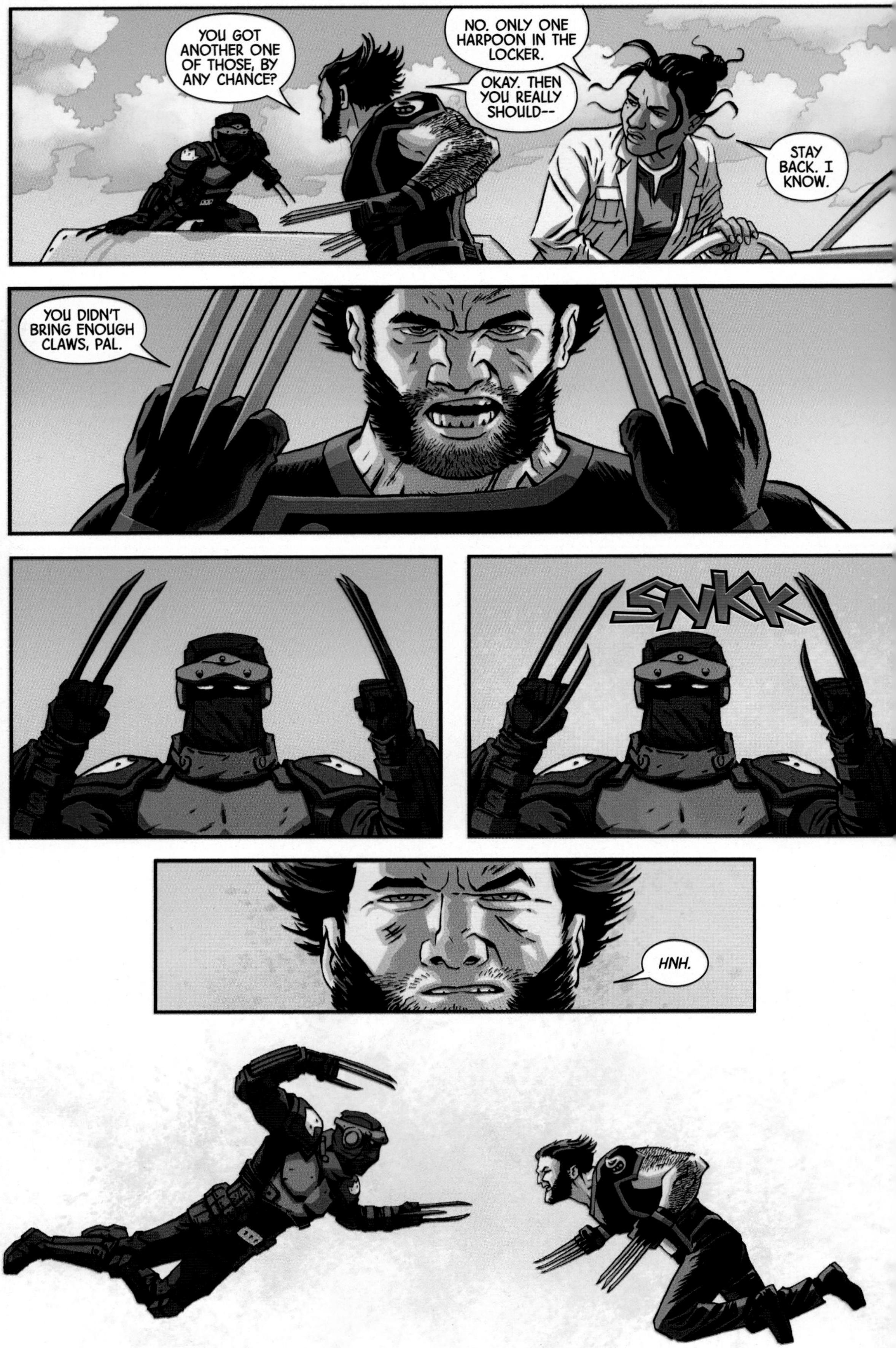
YOU GOT ANOTHER ONE OF THOSE, BY ANY CHANCE?
NO. ONLY ONE HARPOON IN THE LOCKER.
OKAY. THEN YOU REALLY SHOULD--
STAY BACK. I KNOW.
YOU DIDN'T BRING ENOUGH CLAWS, PAL.
SNKK
HNH.

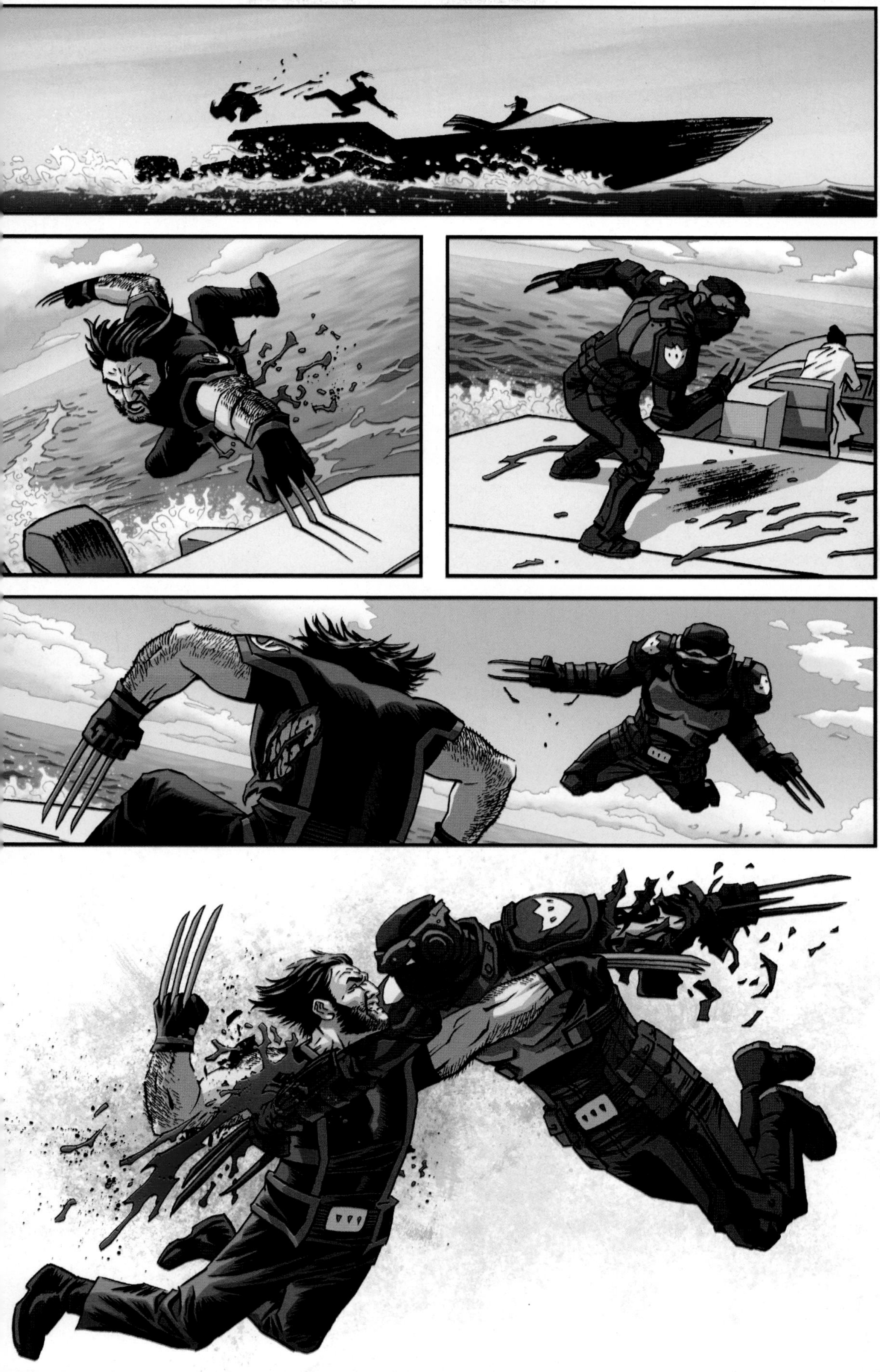

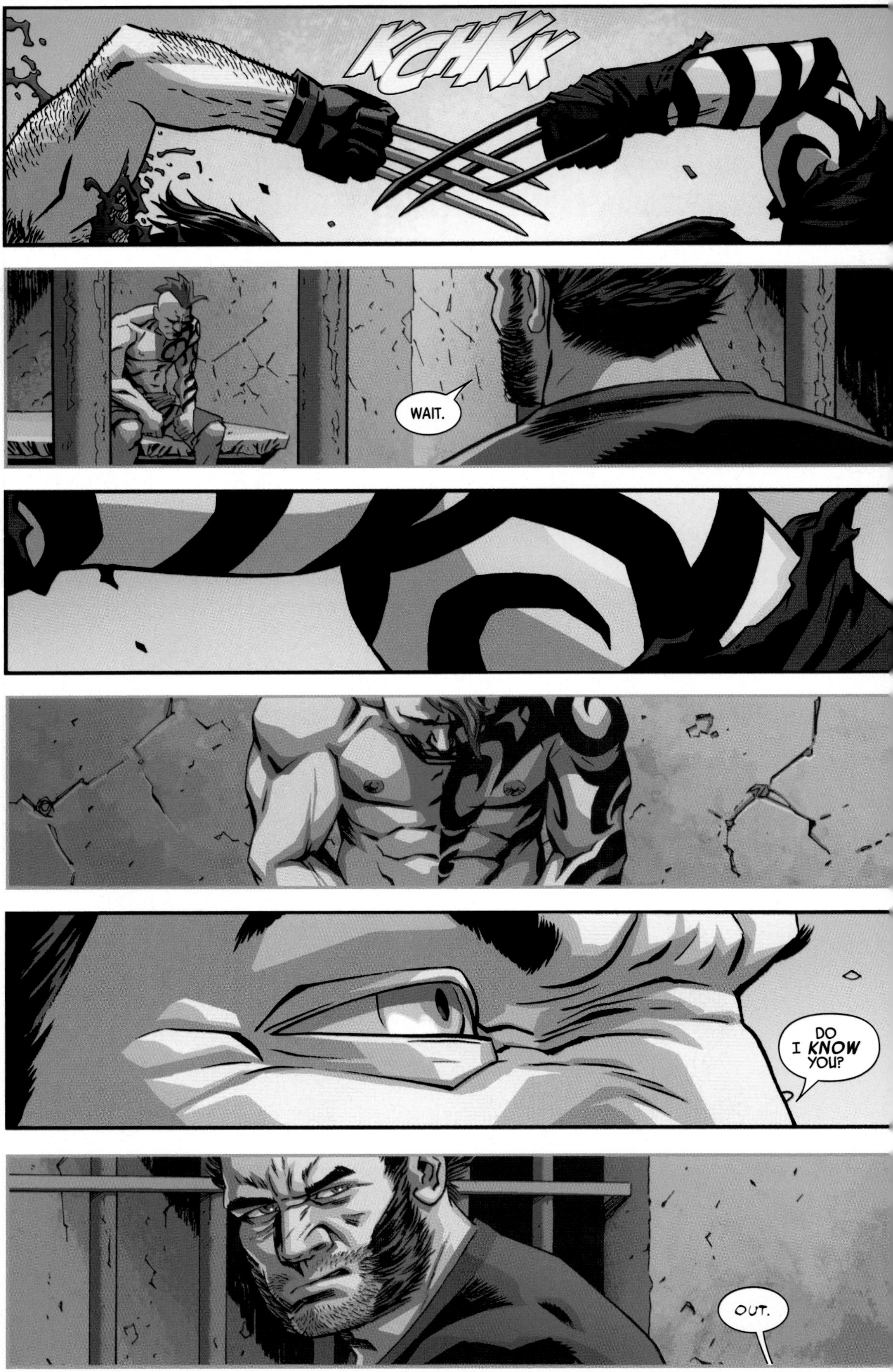
KCHKK
WAIT.
DO I KNOW YOU?
OUT.

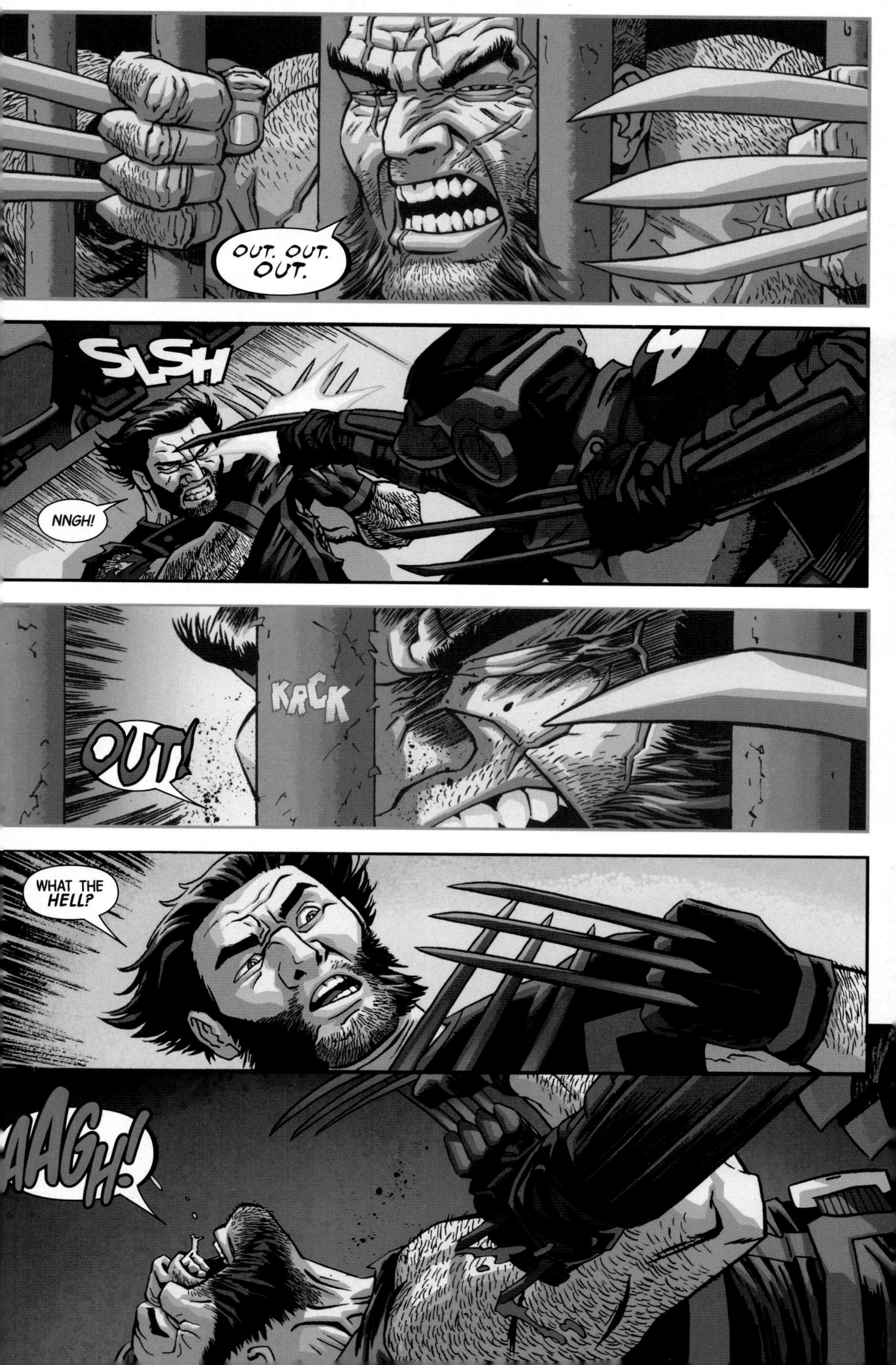
OUT. OUT. OUT.
SLSH
NNGH!
KRCK
OUT!
WHAT THE HELL?
AAGH!

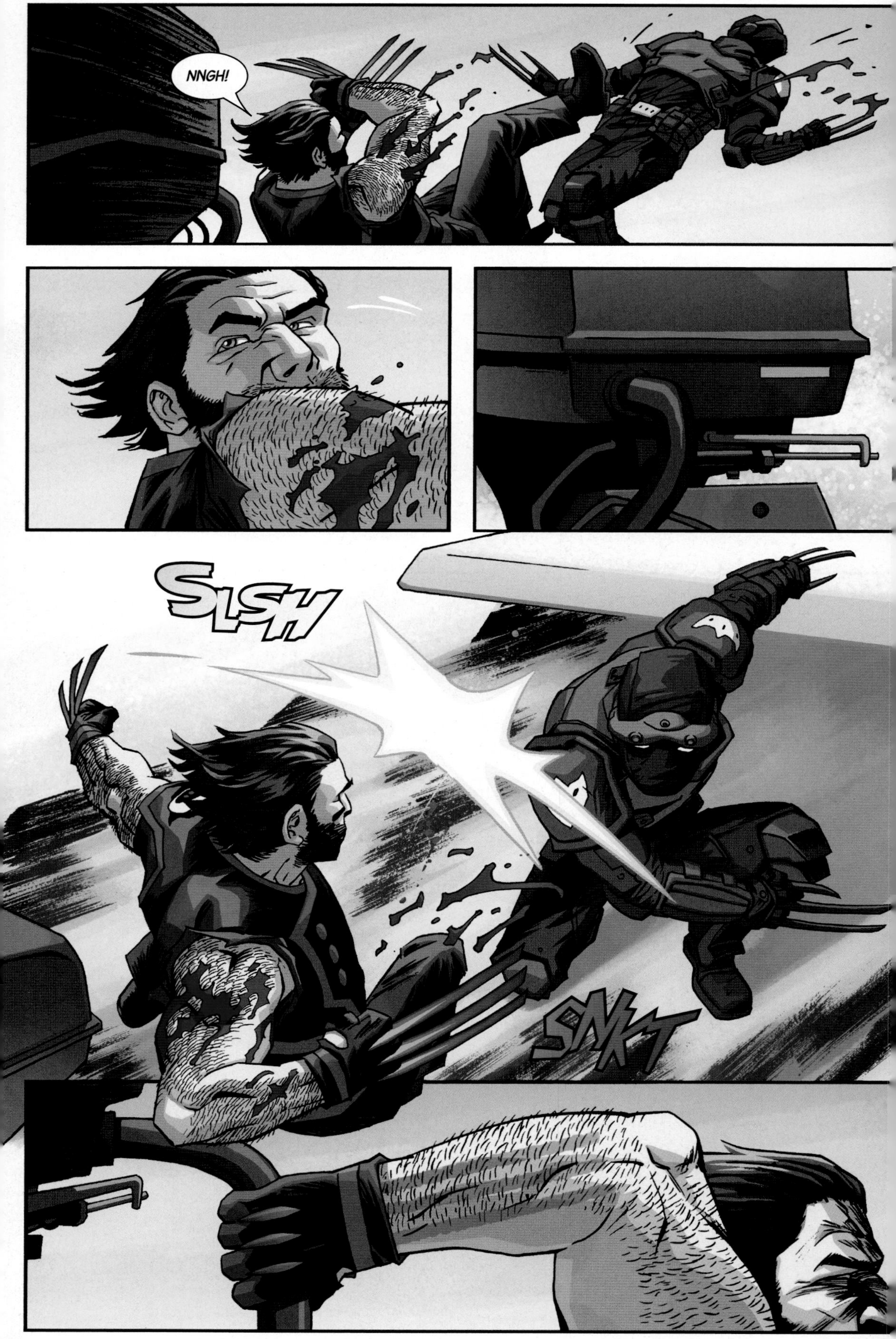
NNGH!
SLSH
SNKT

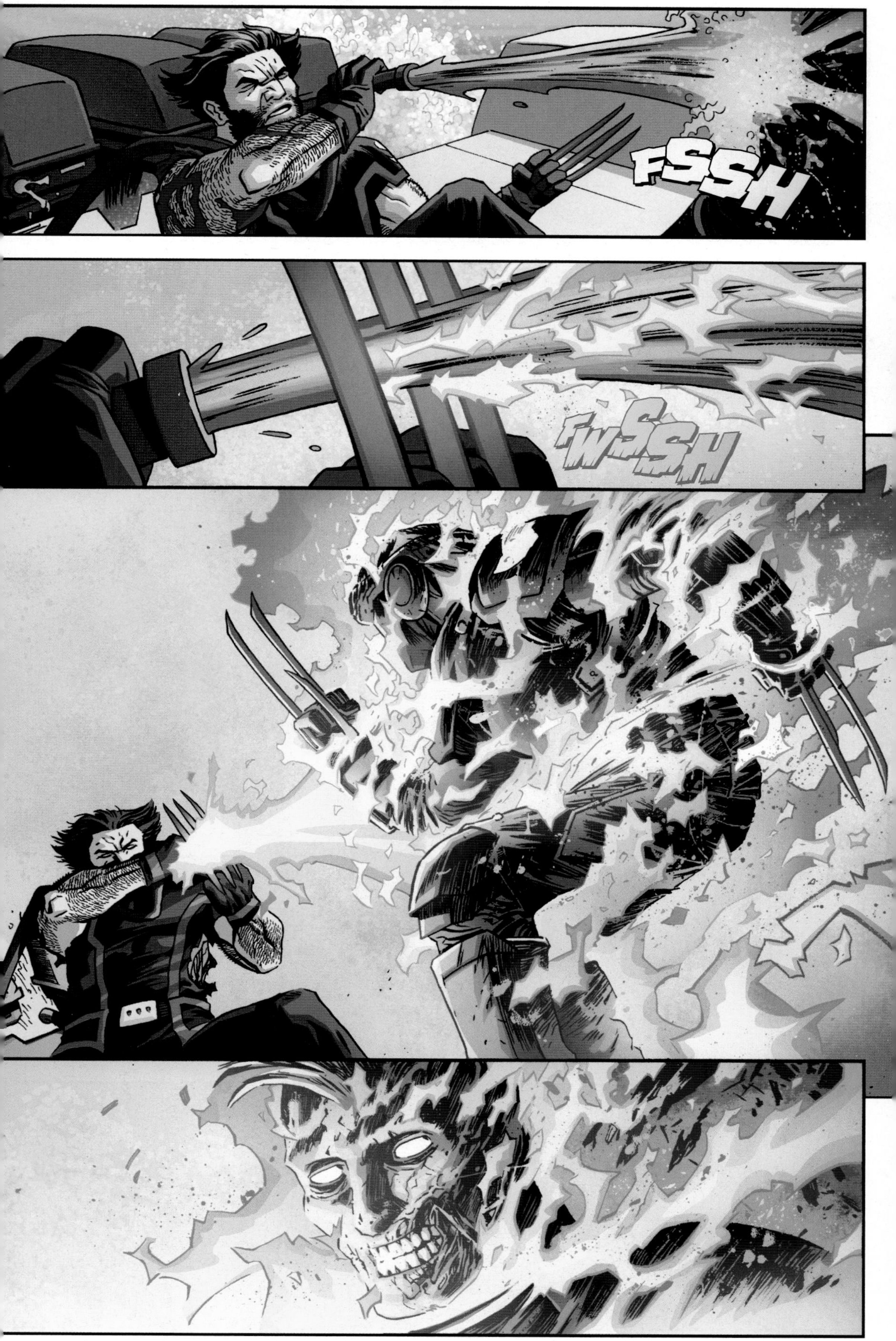
FSSH
FWSSH

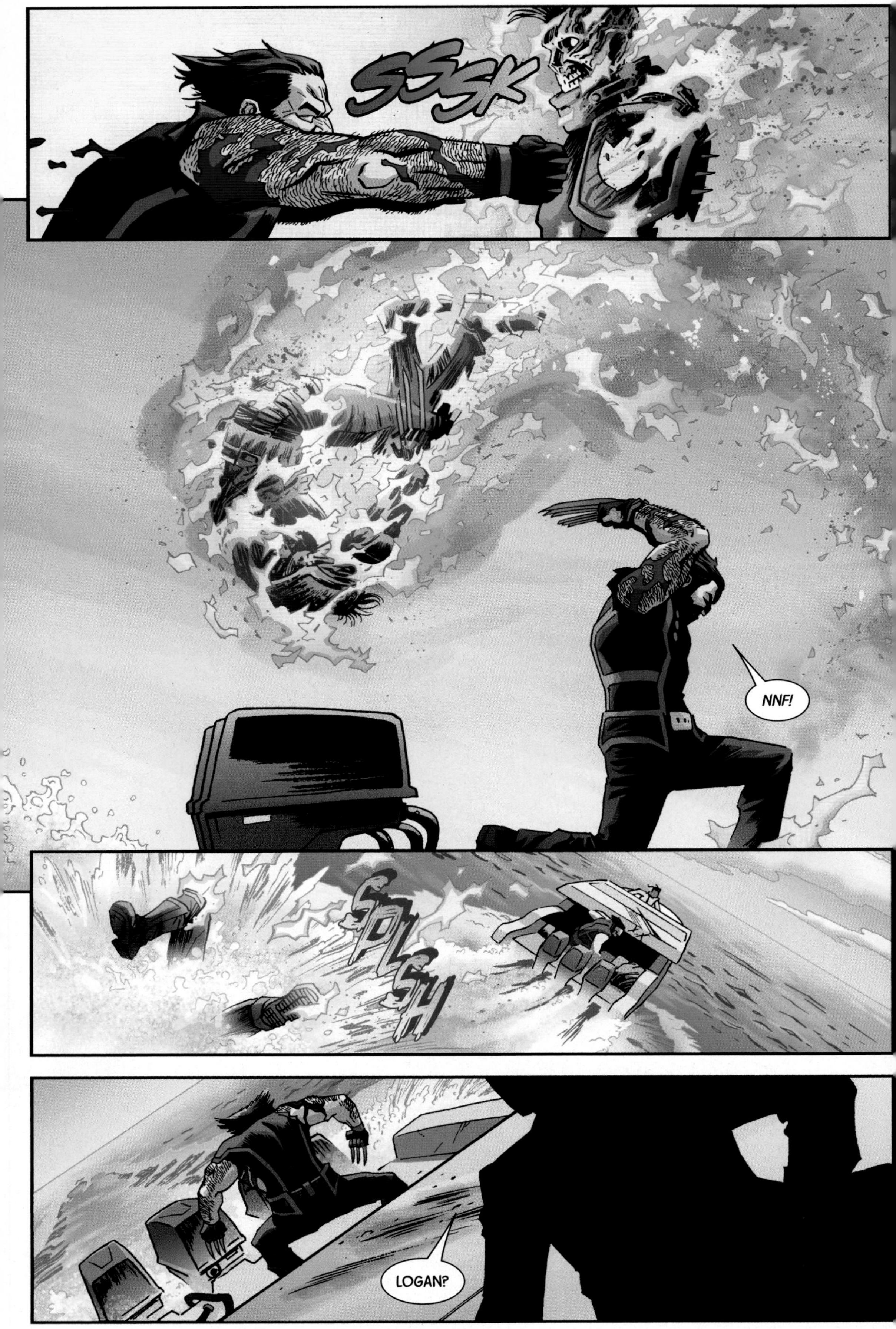
SSSK
NNF!
SPLSH
LOGAN?

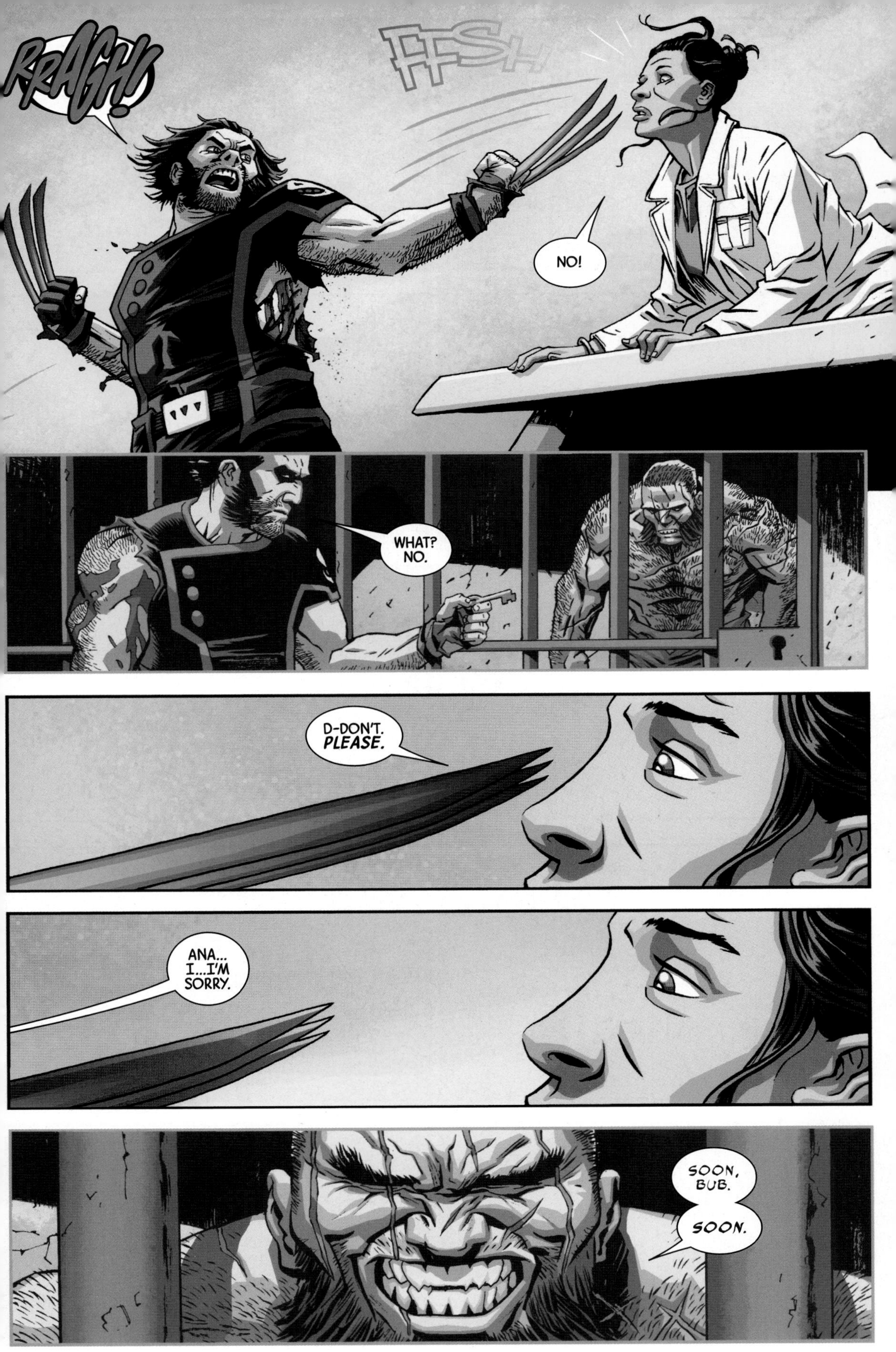
RRAGH!
FFSH
NO!
WHAT? NO.
D-DON'T. PLEASE.
ANA... I...I'M SORRY.
SOON, BUB.
SOON.

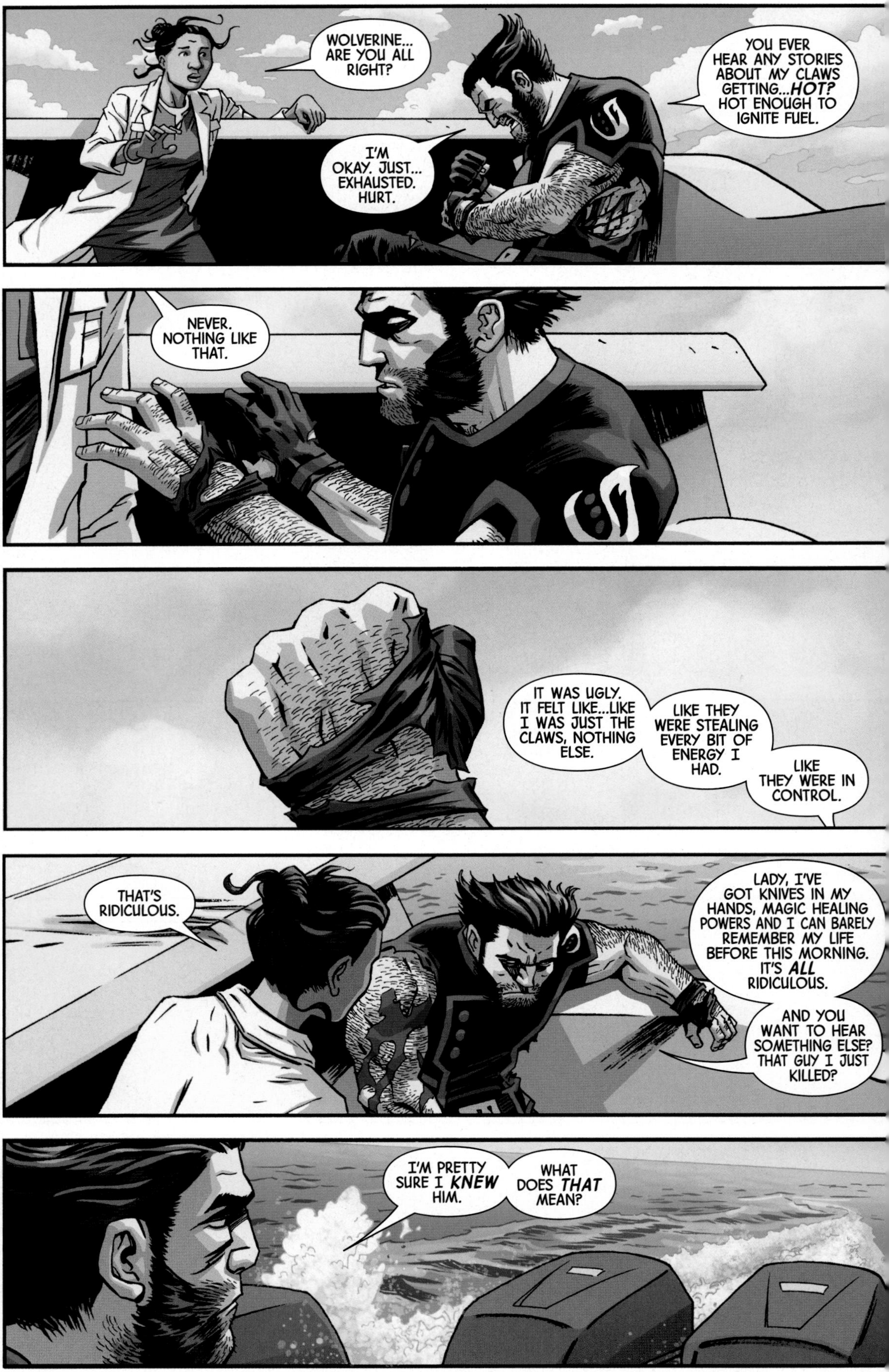
WOLVERINE... ARE YOU ALL RIGHT?
I'M OKAY. JUST... EXHAUSTED. HURT.
YOU EVER HEAR ANY STORIES ABOUT MY CLAWS GETTING...HOT? HOT ENOUGH TO IGNITE FUEL.
NEVER. NOTHING LIKE THAT.
IT WAS UGLY. IT FELT LIKE...LIKE I WAS JUST THE CLAWS, NOTHING ELSE.
LIKE THEY WERE STEALING EVERY BIT OF ENERGY I HAD.
LIKE THEY WERE IN CONTROL.
THAT'S RIDICULOUS.
LADY, I'VE GOT KNIVES IN MY HANDS, MAGIC HEALING POWERS AND I CAN BARELY REMEMBER MY LIFE BEFORE THIS MORNING. IT'S ALL RIDICULOUS.
AND YOU WANT TO HEAR SOMETHING ELSE? THAT GUY I JUST KILLED?
I'M PRETTY SURE I KNEW HIM.
WHAT DOES THAT MEAN?

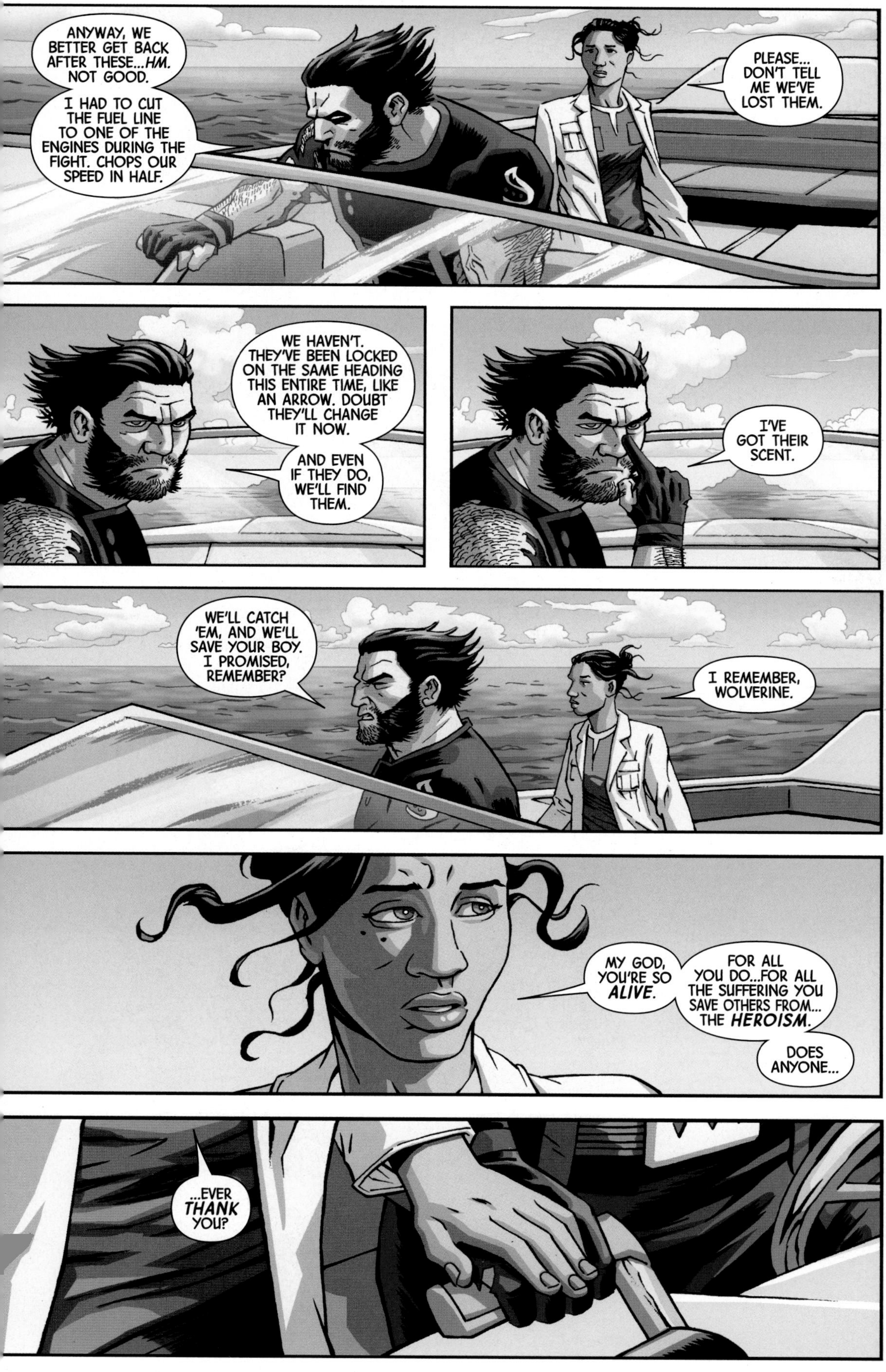
ANYWAY, WE BETTER GET BACK AFTER THESE...HM. NOT GOOD.
I HAD TO CUT THE FUEL LINE TO ONE OF THE ENGINES DURING THE FIGHT. CHOPS OUR SPEED IN HALF.
PLEASE... DON'T TELL ME WE'VE LOST THEM.
WE HAVEN'T. THEY'VE BEEN LOCKED ON THE SAME HEADING THIS ENTIRE TIME, LIKE AN ARROW. DOUBT THEY'LL CHANGE IT NOW.
AND EVEN IF THEY DO, WE'LL FIND THEM.
I'VE GOT THEIR SCENT.
WE'LL CATCH 'EM, AND WE'LL SAVE YOUR BOY. I PROMISED, REMEMBER?
I REMEMBER, WOLVERINE.
MY GOD, YOU'RE SO ALIVE.
FOR ALL YOU DO...FOR ALL THE SUFFERING YOU SAVE OTHERS FROM... THE HEROISM.
DOES ANYONE...
...EVER THANK YOU?

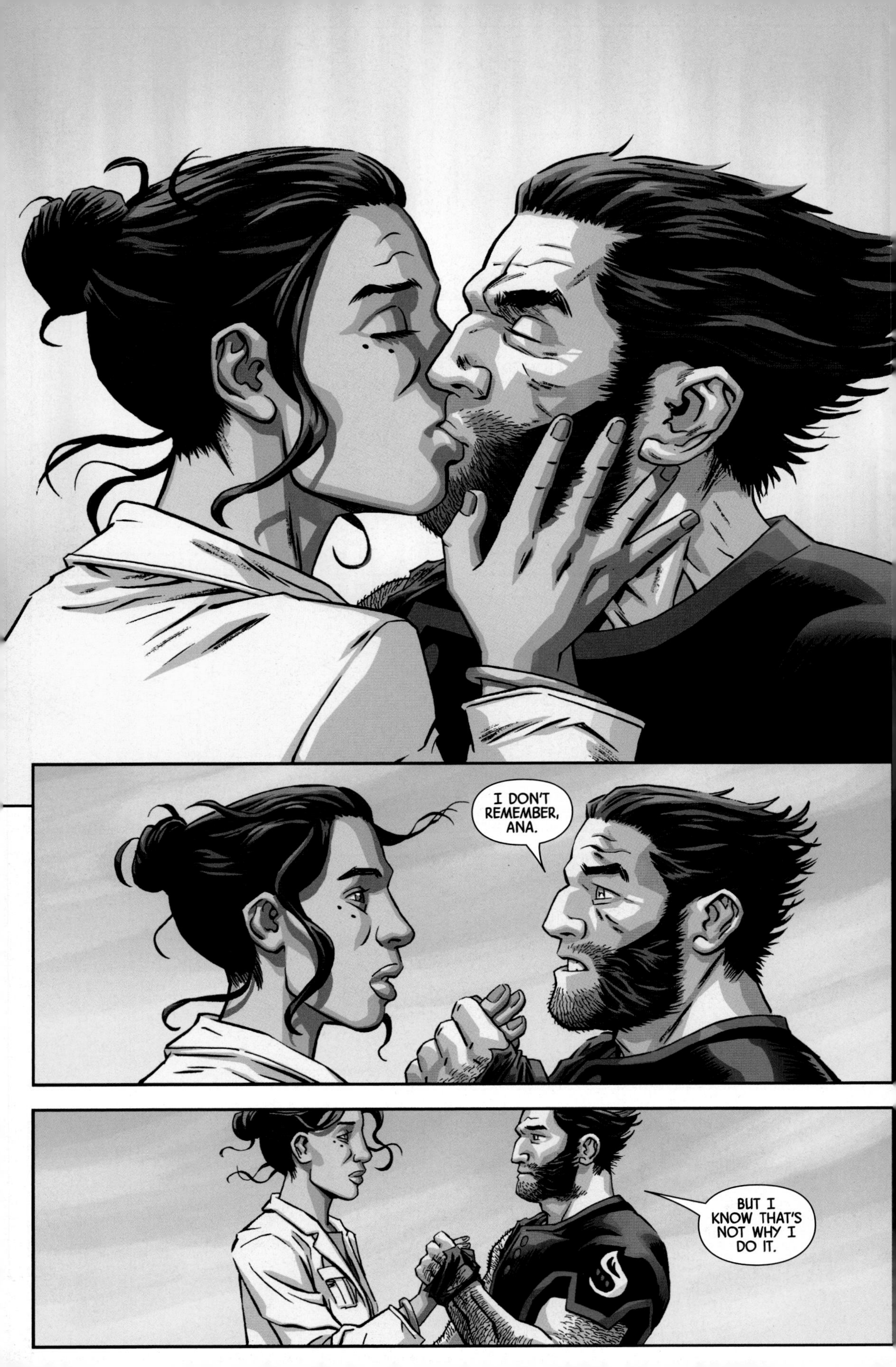
I DON'T REMEMBER, ANA.
BUT I KNOW THAT'S NOT WHY I DO IT.

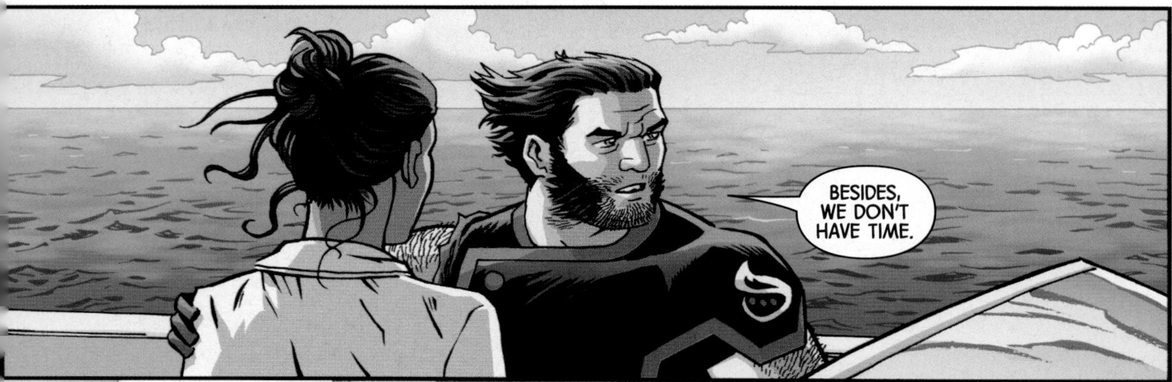
BESIDES, WE DON'T HAVE TIME.

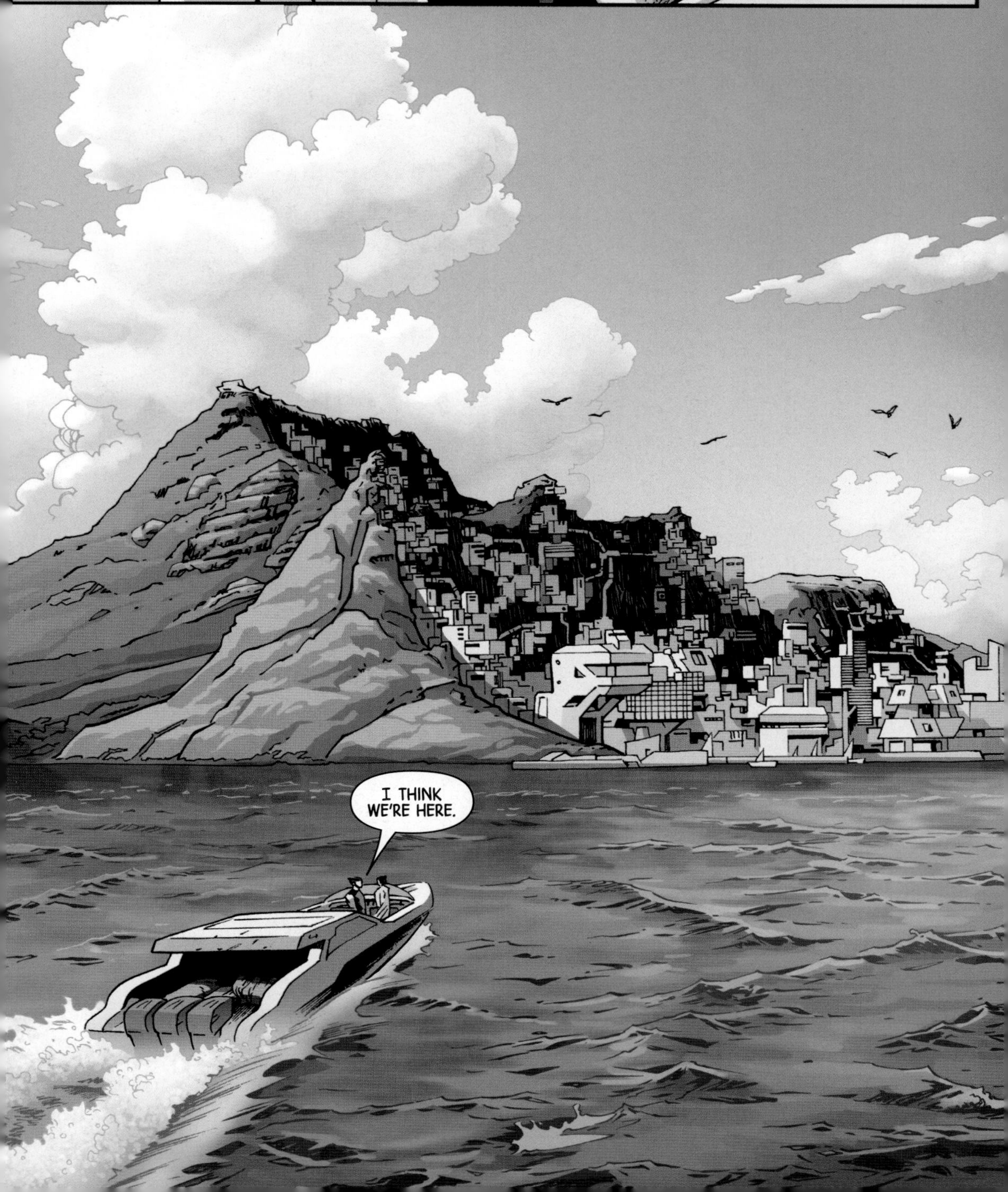
I THINK WE'RE HERE.

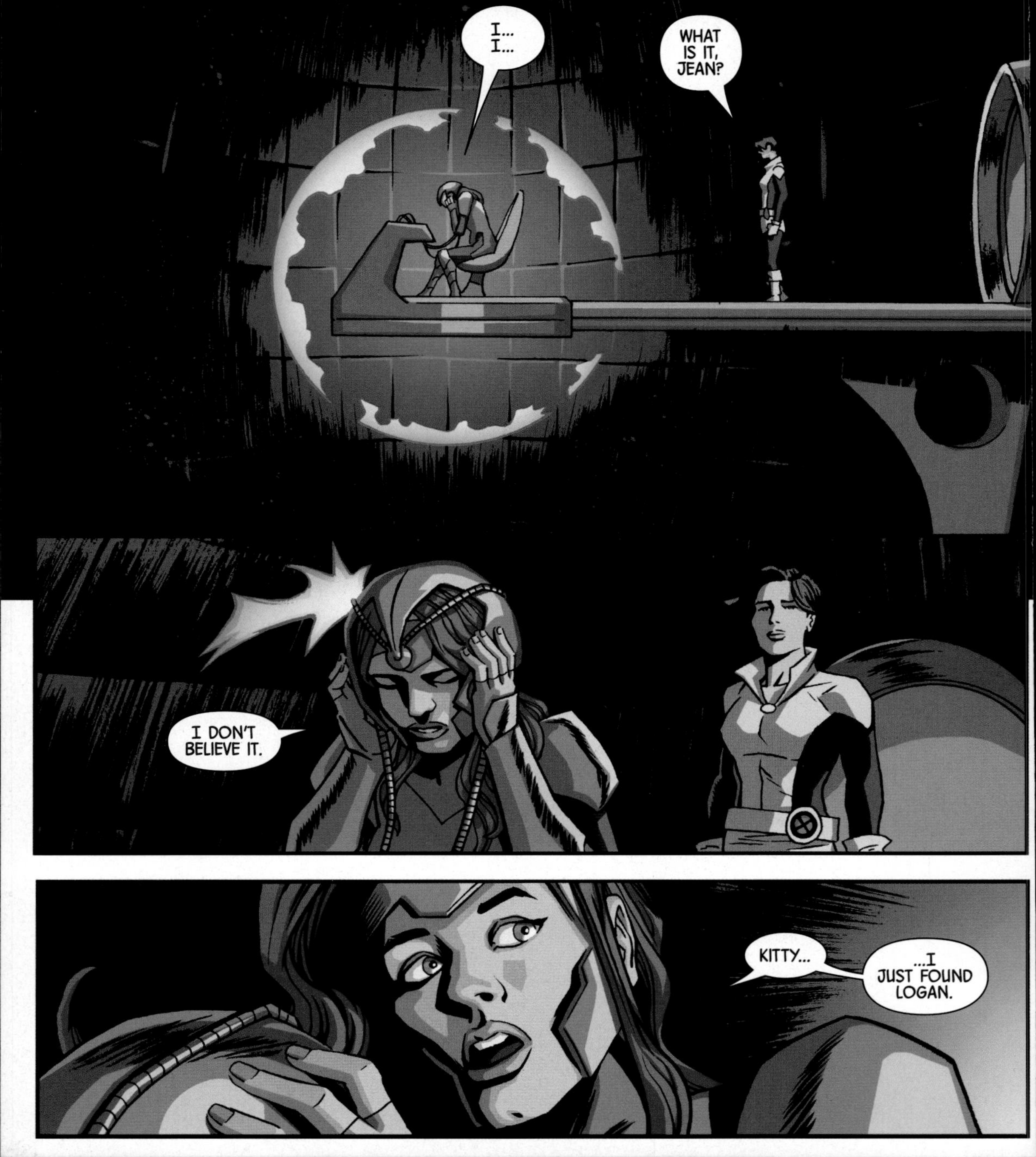
I...
I...
WHAT IS IT, JEAN?
I DON'T BELIEVE IT.
KITTY...
...I JUST FOUND LOGAN.

3

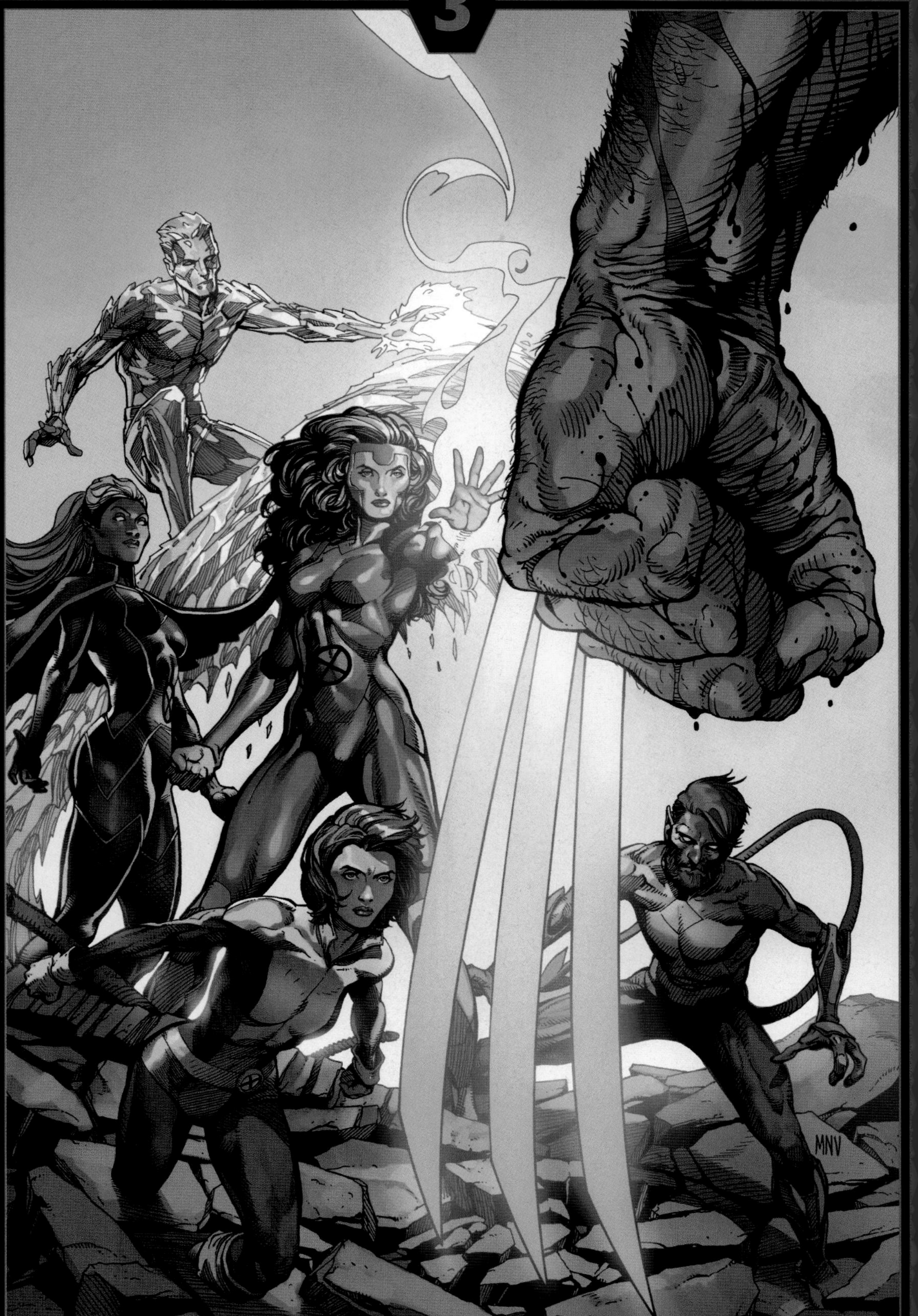
MNV

CHAPTER THREE
PURGATORY

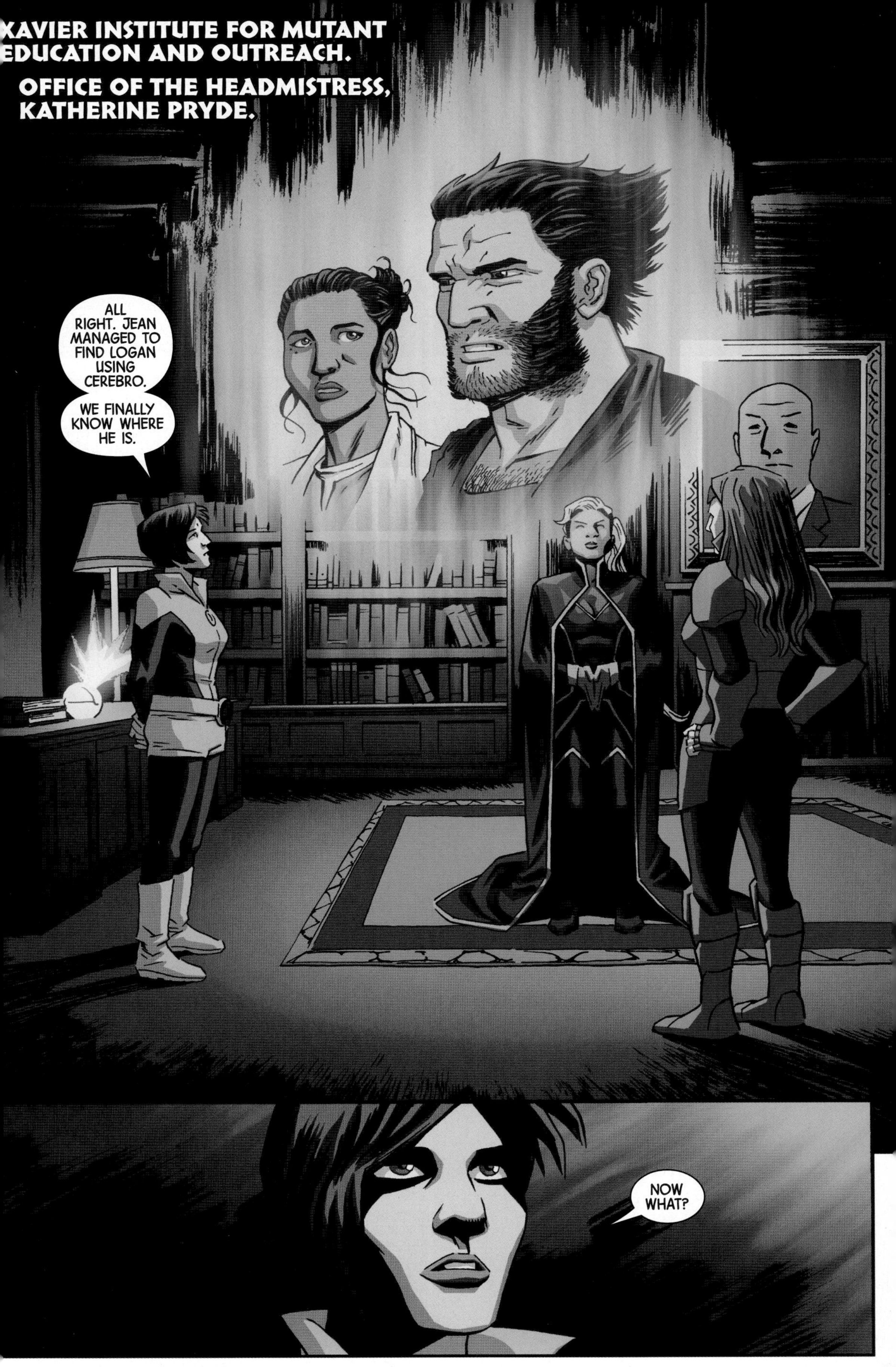
XAVIER INSTITUTE FOR MUTANT EDUCATION AND OUTREACH.
OFFICE OF THE HEADMISTRESS, KATHERINE PRYDE.
ALL RIGHT. JEAN MANAGED TO FIND LOGAN USING CEREBRO.
WE FINALLY KNOW WHERE HE IS.
NOW WHAT?

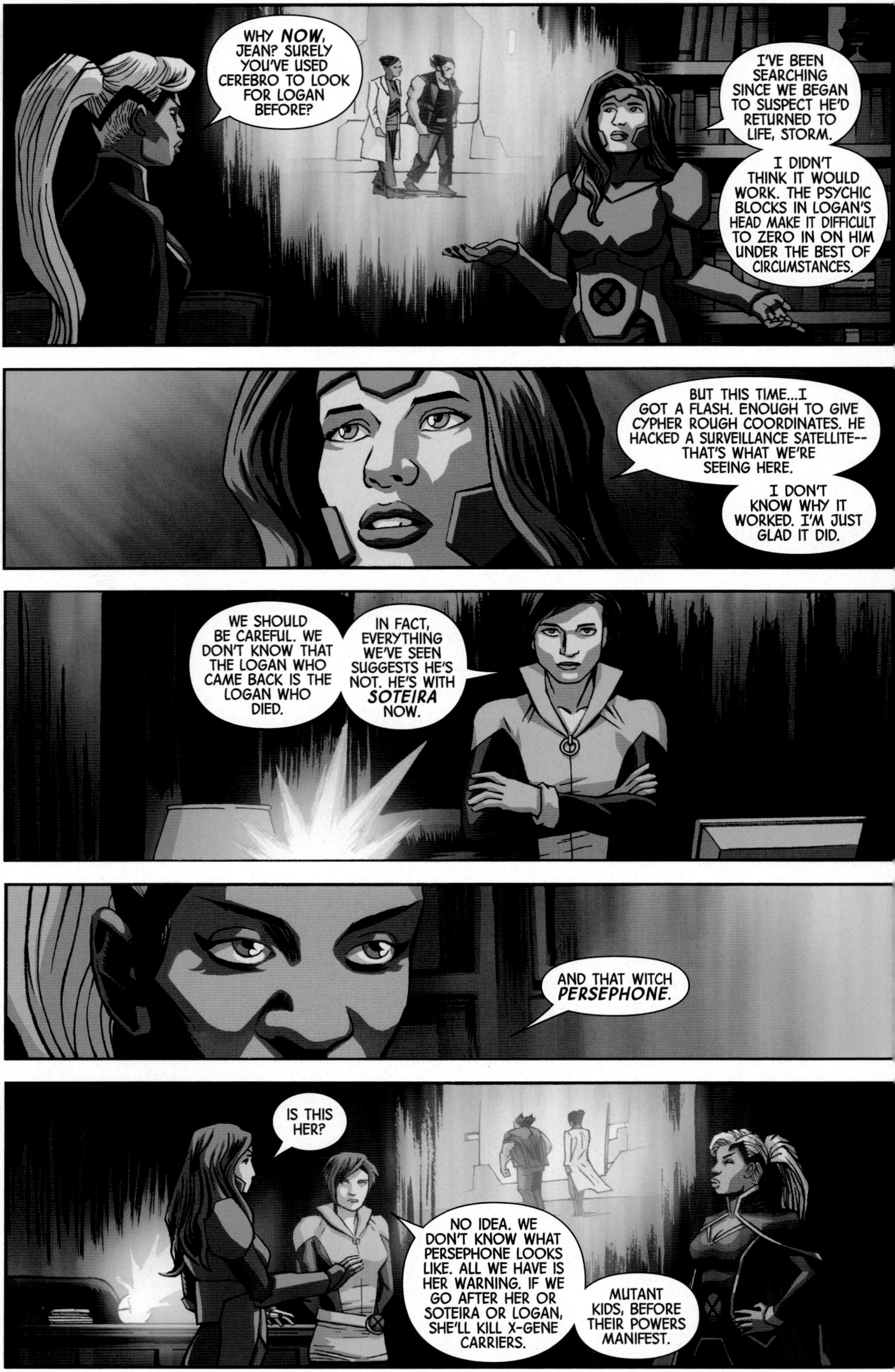
WHY NOW, JEAN? SURELY YOU'VE USED CEREBRO TO LOOK FOR LOGAN BEFORE?
I'VE BEEN SEARCHING SINCE WE BEGAN TO SUSPECT HE'D RETURNED TO LIFE, STORM.
I DIDN'T THINK IT WOULD WORK. THE PSYCHIC BLOCKS IN LOGAN'S HEAD MAKE IT DIFFICULT TO ZERO IN ON HIM UNDER THE BEST OF CIRCUMSTANCES.
BUT THIS TIME...I GOT A FLASH. ENOUGH TO GIVE CYPHER ROUGH COORDINATES. HE HACKED A SURVEILLANCE SATELLITE--THAT'S WHAT WE'RE SEEING HERE.
I DON'T KNOW WHY IT WORKED. I'M JUST GLAD IT DID.
WE SHOULD BE CAREFUL. WE DON'T KNOW THAT THE LOGAN WHO CAME BACK IS THE LOGAN WHO DIED.
IN FACT, EVERYTHING WE'VE SEEN SUGGESTS HE'S NOT. HE'S WITH SOTEIRA NOW.
AND THAT WITCH PERSEPHONE.
IS THIS HER?
NO IDEA. WE DON'T KNOW WHAT PERSEPHONE LOOKS LIKE. ALL WE HAVE IS HER WARNING. IF WE GO AFTER HER OR SOTEIRA OR LOGAN, SHE'LL KILL X-GENE CARRIERS.
MUTANT KIDS, BEFORE THEIR POWERS MANIFEST.

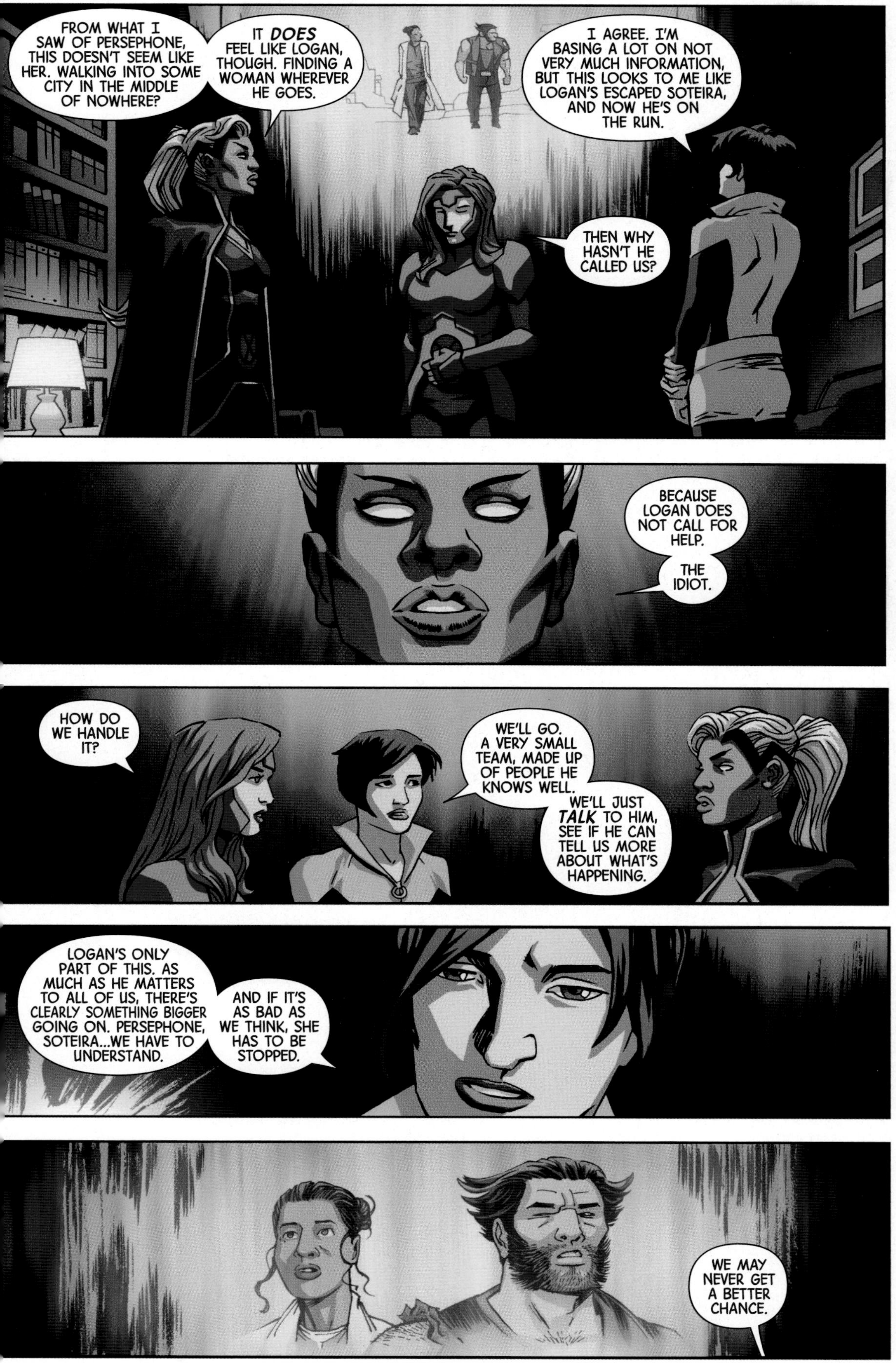
FROM WHAT I SAW OF PERSEPHONE, THIS DOESN'T SEEM LIKE HER. WALKING INTO SOME CITY IN THE MIDDLE OF NOWHERE?
IT *DOES* FEEL LIKE LOGAN, THOUGH. FINDING A WOMAN WHEREVER HE GOES.
I AGREE. I'M BASING A LOT ON NOT VERY MUCH INFORMATION, BUT THIS LOOKS TO ME LIKE LOGAN'S ESCAPED SOTEIRA, AND NOW HE'S ON THE RUN.
THEN WHY HASN'T HE CALLED US?
BECAUSE LOGAN DOES NOT CALL FOR HELP.
THE IDIOT.
HOW DO WE HANDLE IT?
WE'LL GO. A VERY SMALL TEAM, MADE UP OF PEOPLE HE KNOWS WELL.
WE'LL JUST *TALK* TO HIM, SEE IF HE CAN TELL US MORE ABOUT WHAT'S HAPPENING.
LOGAN'S ONLY PART OF THIS. AS MUCH AS HE MATTERS TO ALL OF US, THERE'S CLEARLY SOMETHING BIGGER GOING ON. PERSEPHONE, SOTEIRA...WE HAVE TO UNDERSTAND.
AND IF IT'S AS BAD AS WE THINK, SHE HAS TO BE STOPPED.
WE MAY NEVER GET A BETTER CHANCE.

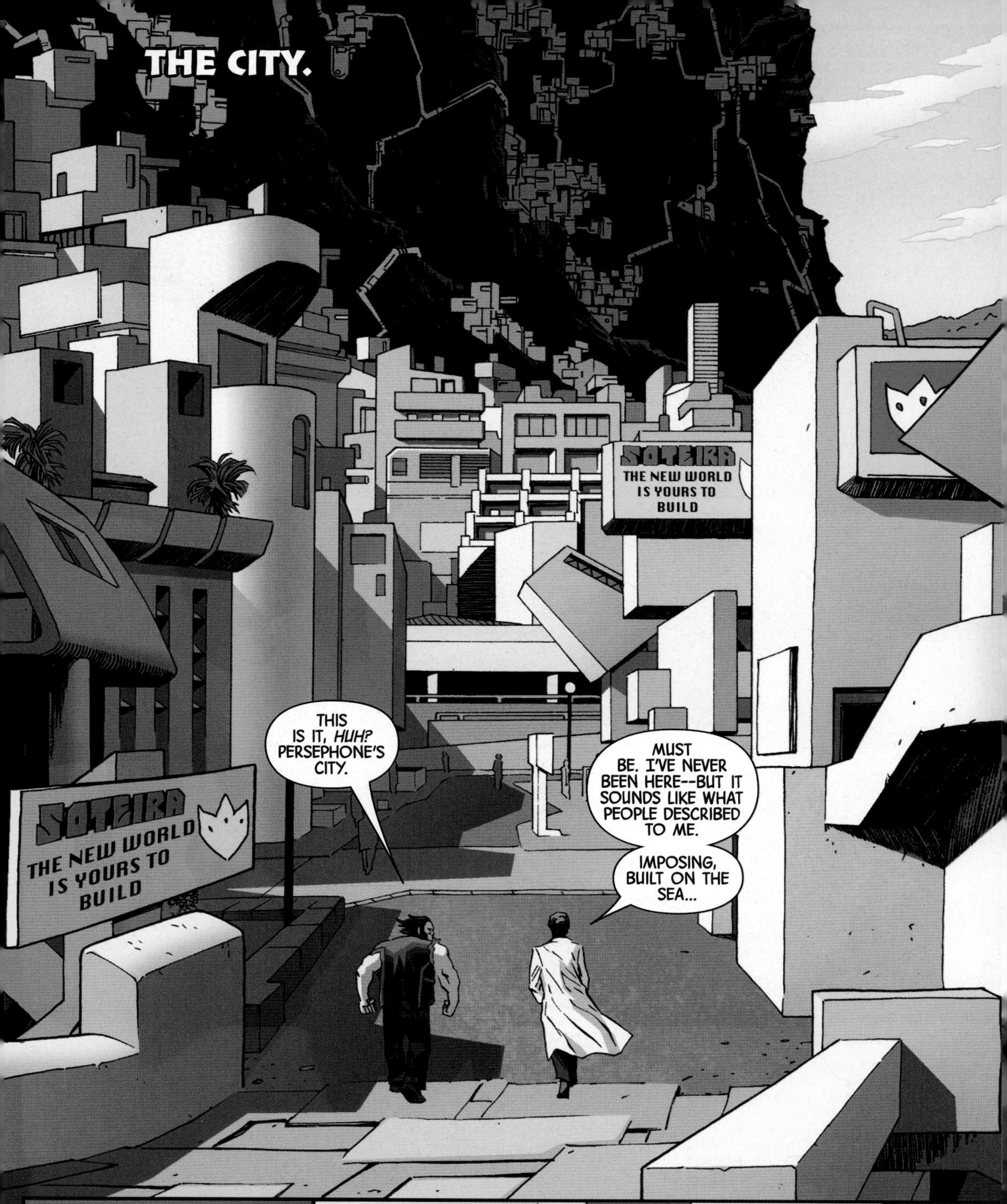
THE CITY.
SOTEIRA THE NEW WORLD IS YOURS TO BUILD
THIS IS IT, *HUH?* PERSEPHONE'S CITY.
SOTEIRA THE NEW WORLD IS YOURS TO BUILD
MUST BE. I'VE NEVER BEEN HERE--BUT IT SOUNDS LIKE WHAT PEOPLE DESCRIBED TO ME.
IMPOSING, BUILT ON THE SEA...

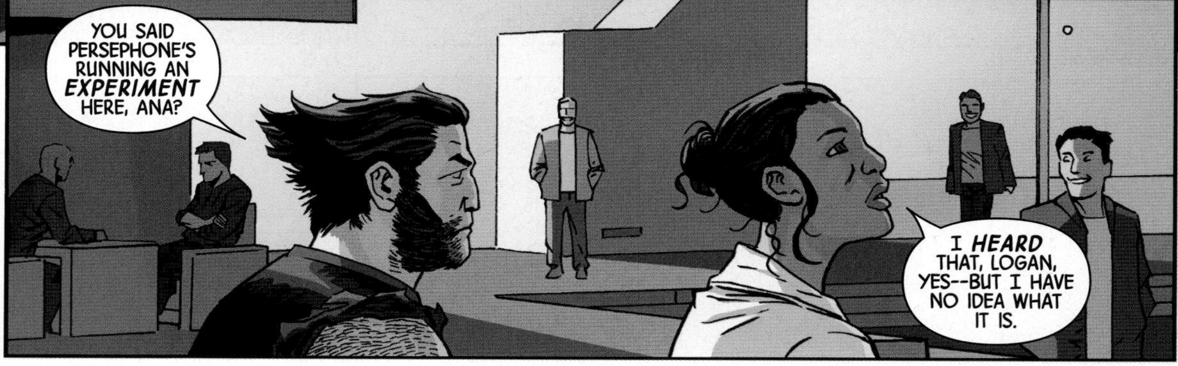
YOU SAID PERSEPHONE'S RUNNING AN ***EXPERIMENT*** HERE, ANA?
I ***HEARD*** THAT, LOGAN, YES--BUT I HAVE NO IDEA WHAT IT IS.

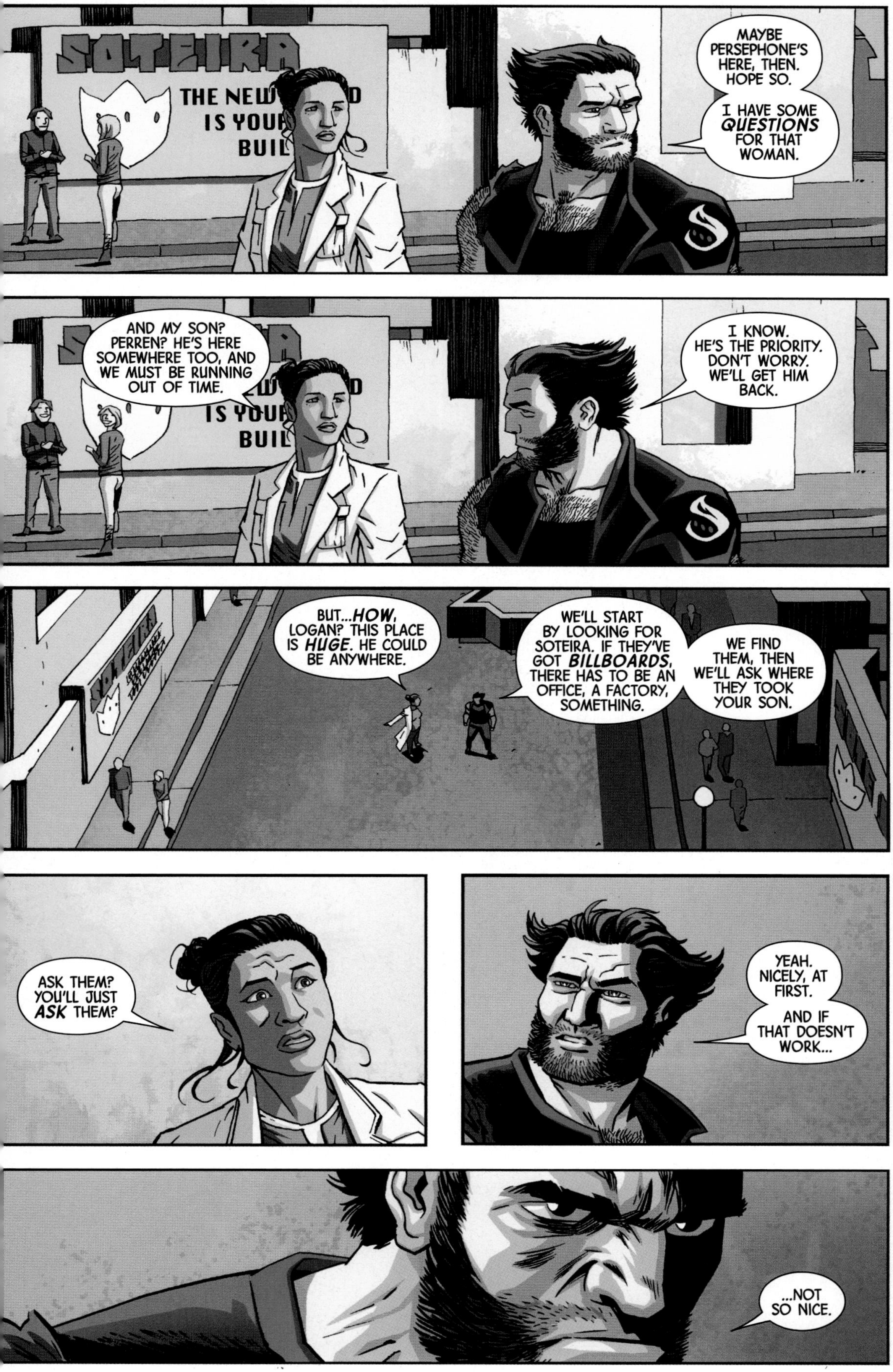
SOTEIRA
THE NEW D
IS YOUR
BUIL
MAYBE PERSEPHONE'S HERE, THEN. HOPE SO.
I HAVE SOME QUESTIONS FOR THAT WOMAN.
AND MY SON? PERREN? HE'S HERE SOMEWHERE TOO, AND WE MUST BE RUNNING OUT OF TIME.
I KNOW. HE'S THE PRIORITY. DON'T WORRY. WE'LL GET HIM BACK.
BUT...HOW, LOGAN? THIS PLACE IS HUGE. HE COULD BE ANYWHERE.
WE'LL START BY LOOKING FOR SOTEIRA. IF THEY'VE GOT BILLBOARDS, THERE HAS TO BE AN OFFICE, A FACTORY, SOMETHING.
WE FIND THEM, THEN WE'LL ASK WHERE THEY TOOK YOUR SON.
ASK THEM? YOU'LL JUST ASK THEM?
YEAH. NICELY, AT FIRST.
AND IF THAT DOESN'T WORK...
...NOT SO NICE.

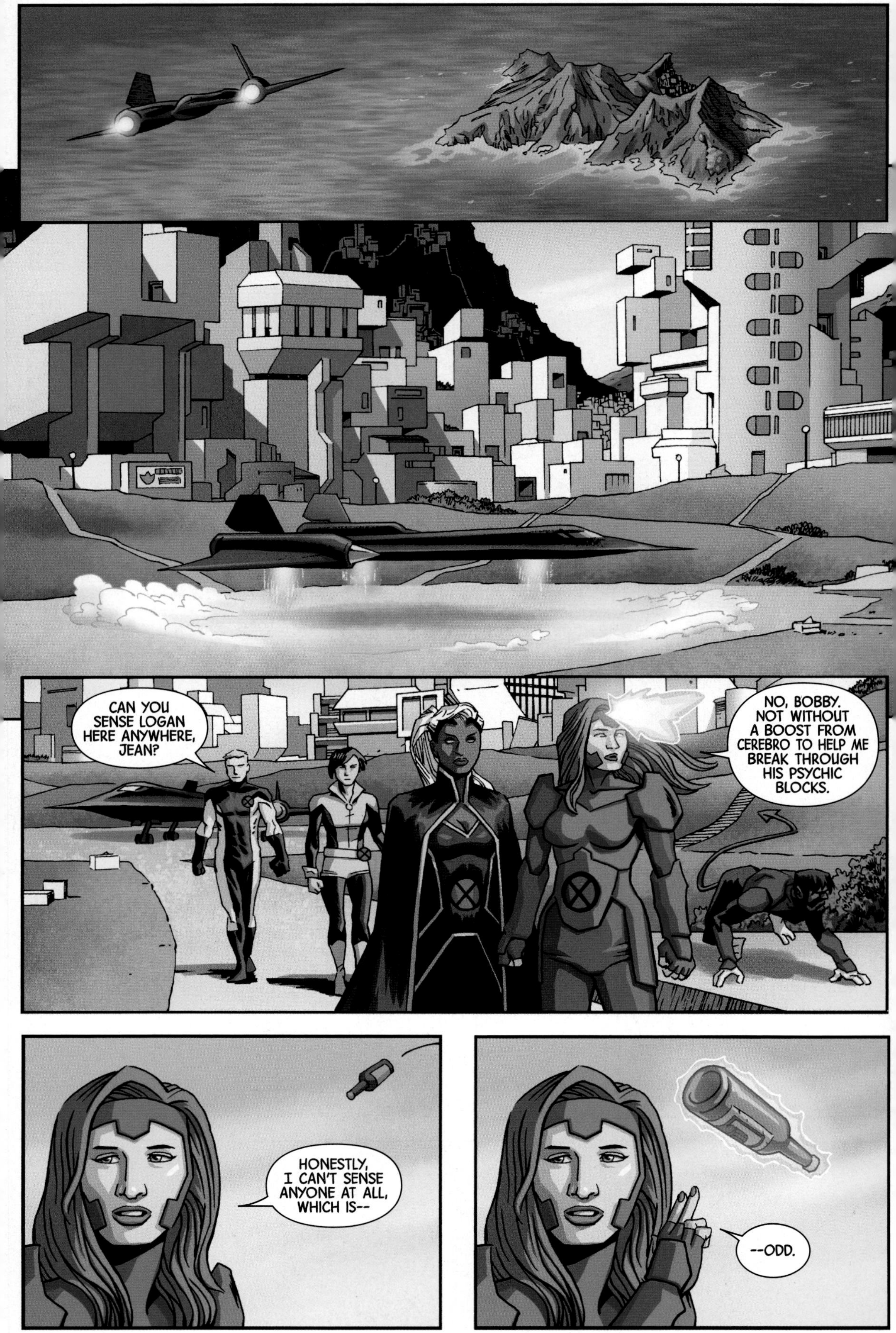
CAN YOU SENSE LOGAN HERE ANYWHERE, JEAN?
NO, BOBBY. NOT WITHOUT A BOOST FROM CEREBRO TO HELP ME BREAK THROUGH HIS PSYCHIC BLOCKS.
HONESTLY, I CAN'T SENSE ANYONE AT ALL, WHICH IS--
--ODD.

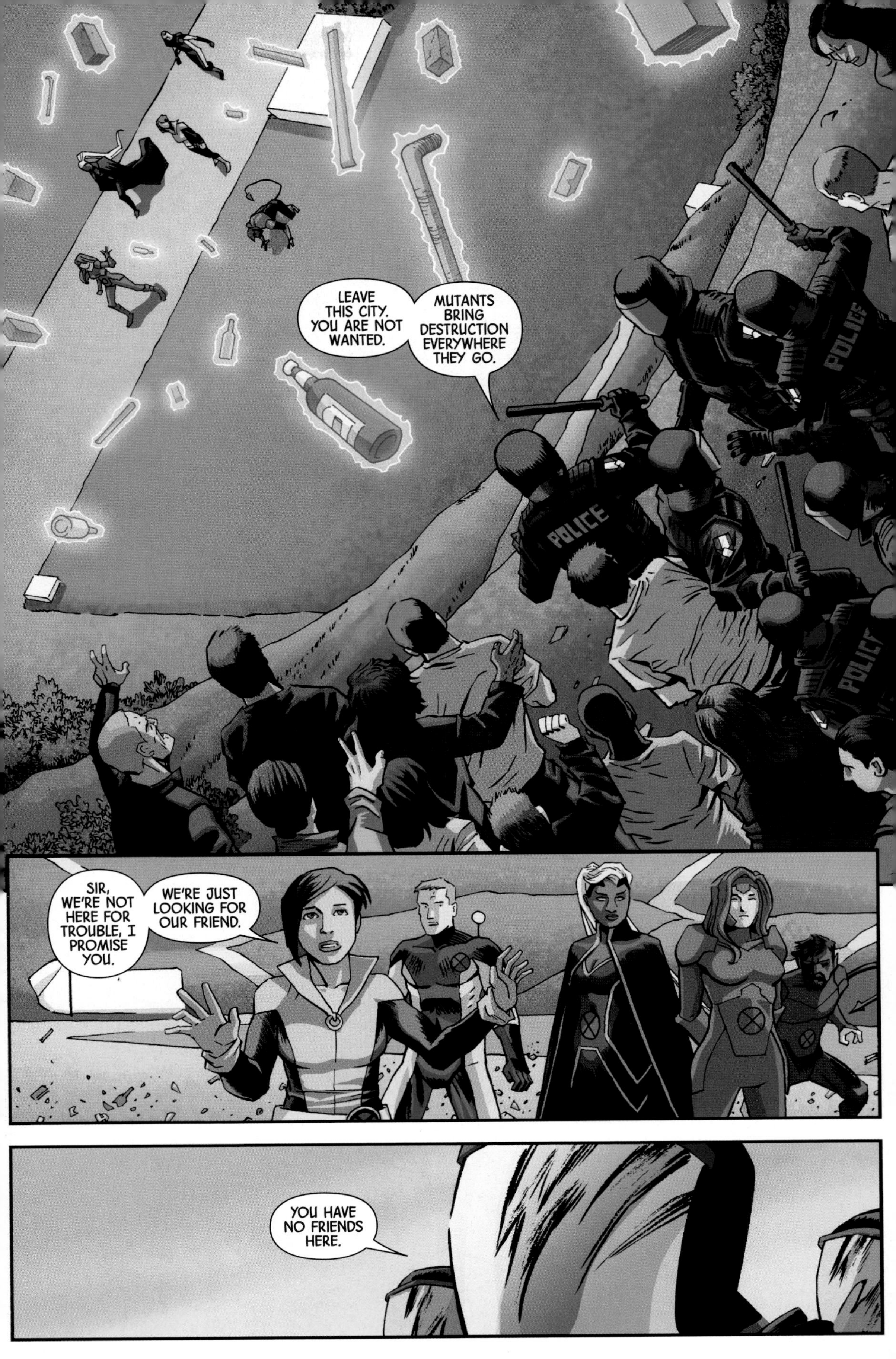
LEAVE THIS CITY. YOU ARE NOT WANTED.
MUTANTS BRING DESTRUCTION EVERYWHERE THEY GO.
POLICE
POLICE
POLICE
SIR, WE'RE NOT HERE FOR TROUBLE, I PROMISE YOU.
WE'RE JUST LOOKING FOR OUR FRIEND.
YOU HAVE NO FRIENDS HERE.

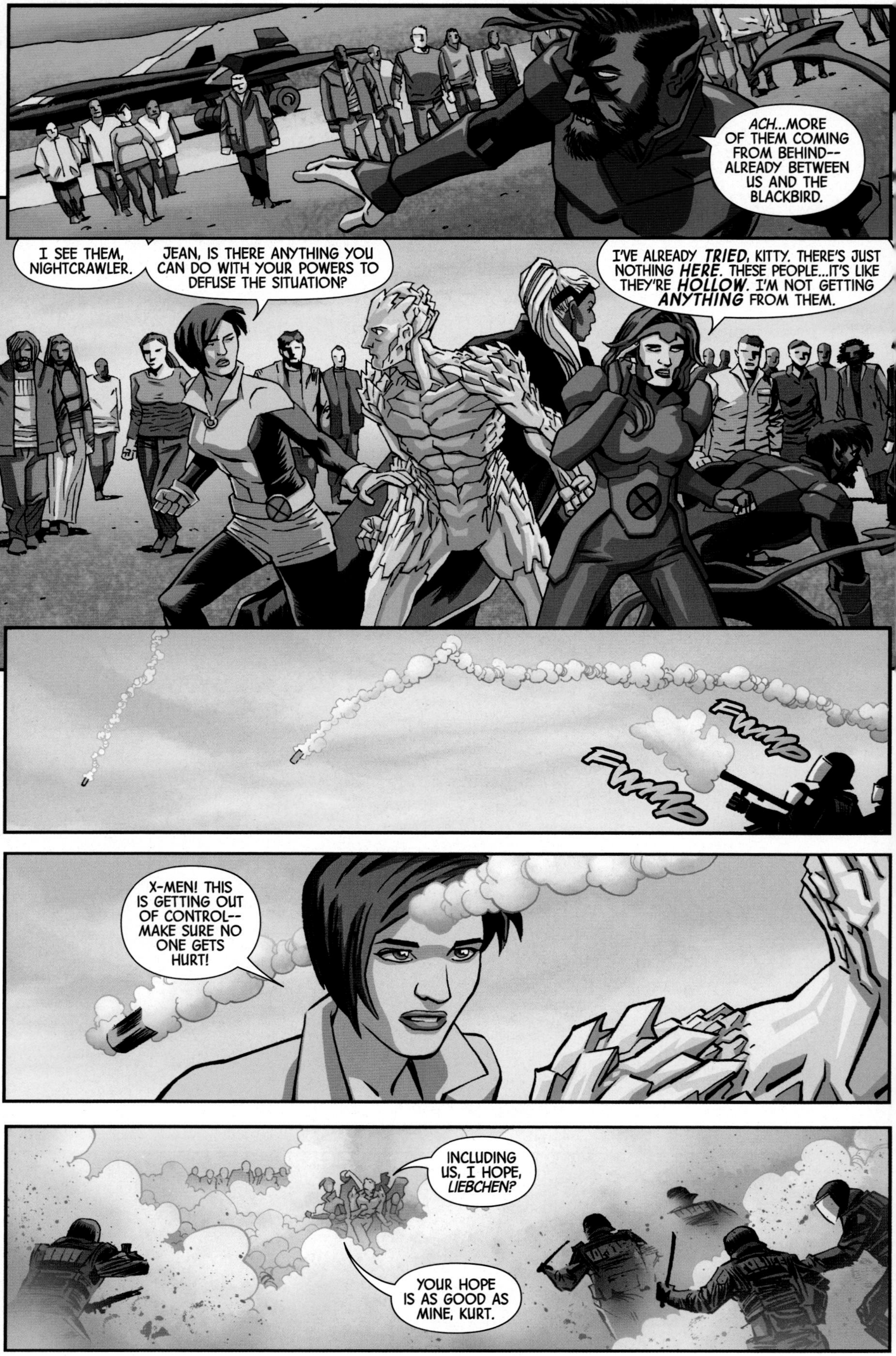
ACH...MORE OF THEM COMING FROM BEHIND-- ALREADY BETWEEN US AND THE BLACKBIRD.
I SEE THEM, NIGHTCRAWLER.
JEAN, IS THERE ANYTHING YOU CAN DO WITH YOUR POWERS TO DEFUSE THE SITUATION?
I'VE ALREADY TRIED, KITTY. THERE'S JUST NOTHING HERE. THESE PEOPLE...IT'S LIKE THEY'RE HOLLOW. I'M NOT GETTING ANYTHING FROM THEM.
FWMP
FWMP
X-MEN! THIS IS GETTING OUT OF CONTROL-- MAKE SURE NO ONE GETS HURT!
INCLUDING US, I HOPE, LIEBCHEN?
YOUR HOPE IS AS GOOD AS MINE, KURT.

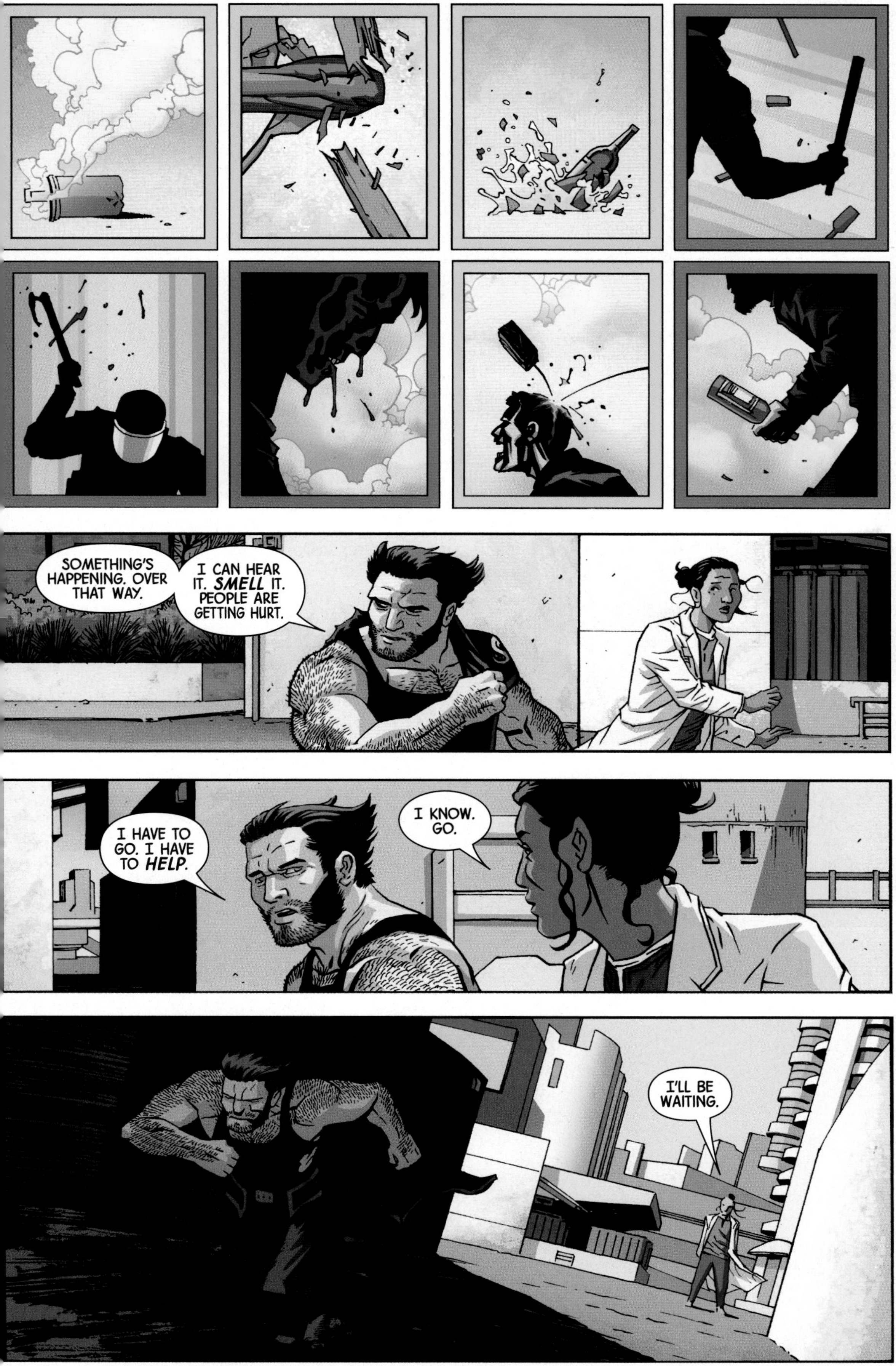
SOMETHING'S HAPPENING. OVER THAT WAY.
I CAN HEAR IT. SMELL IT. PEOPLE ARE GETTING HURT.
I HAVE TO GO. I HAVE TO HELP.
I KNOW. GO.
I'LL BE WAITING.

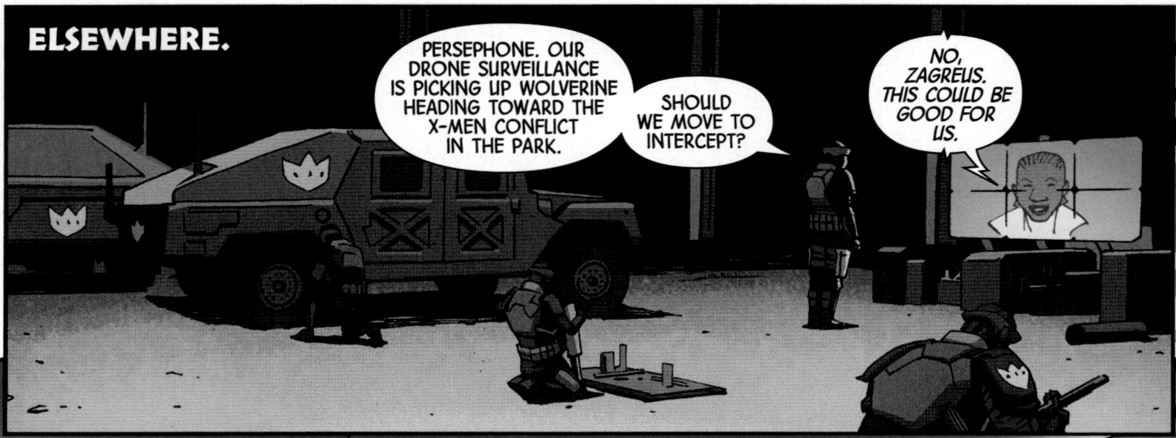
ELSEWHERE.
PERSEPHONE. OUR DRONE SURVEILLANCE IS PICKING UP WOLVERINE HEADING TOWARD THE X-MEN CONFLICT IN THE PARK.
SHOULD WE MOVE TO INTERCEPT?
NO, ZAGREUS. THIS COULD BE GOOD FOR US.

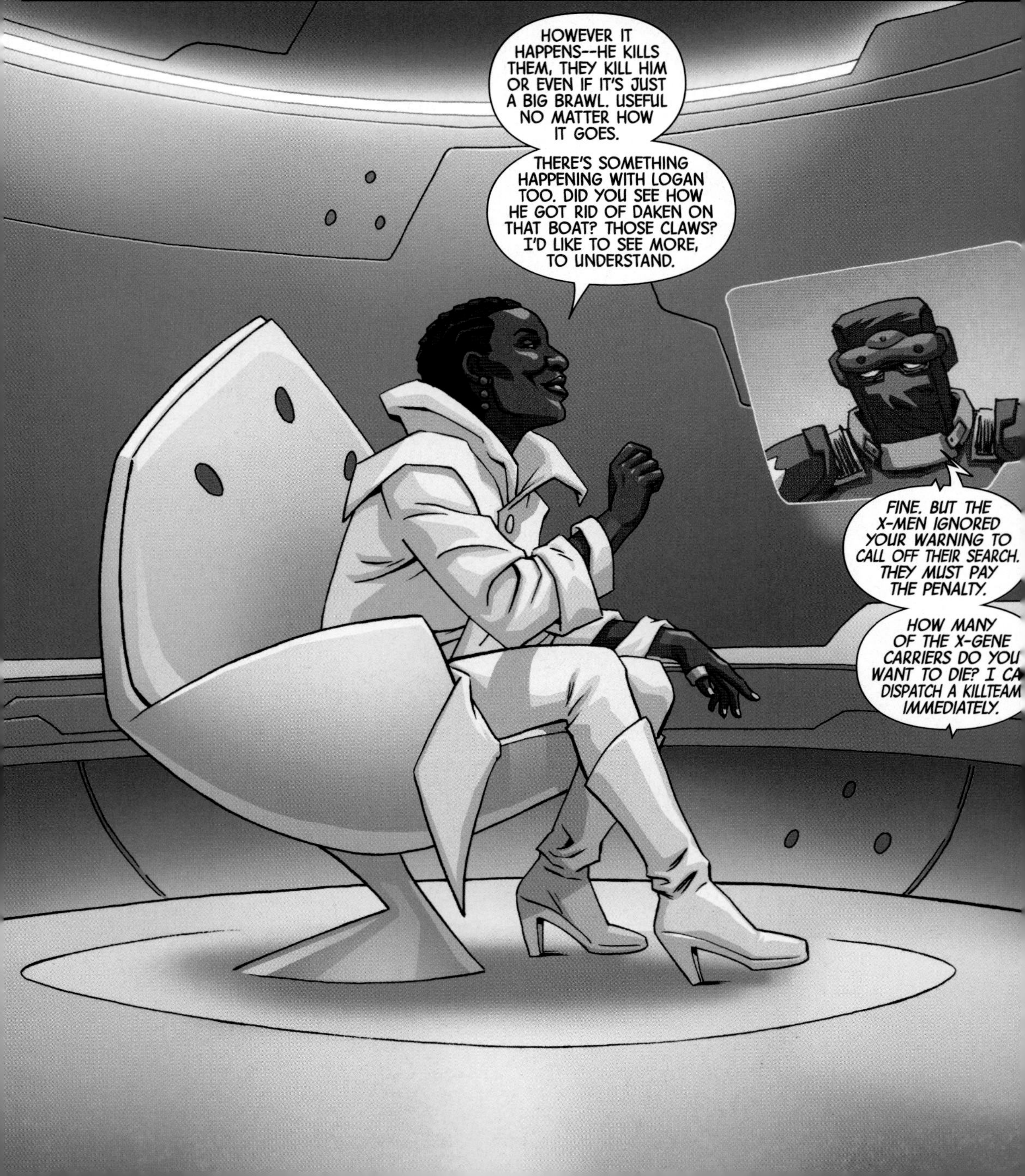
HOWEVER IT HAPPENS--HE KILLS THEM, THEY KILL HIM OR EVEN IF IT'S JUST A BIG BRAWL. USEFUL NO MATTER HOW IT GOES.
THERE'S SOMETHING HAPPENING WITH LOGAN TOO. DID YOU SEE HOW HE GOT RID OF DAKEN ON THAT BOAT? THOSE CLAWS? I'D LIKE TO SEE MORE, TO UNDERSTAND.
FINE. BUT THE X-MEN IGNORED YOUR WARNING TO CALL OFF THEIR SEARCH. THEY MUST PAY THE PENALTY.

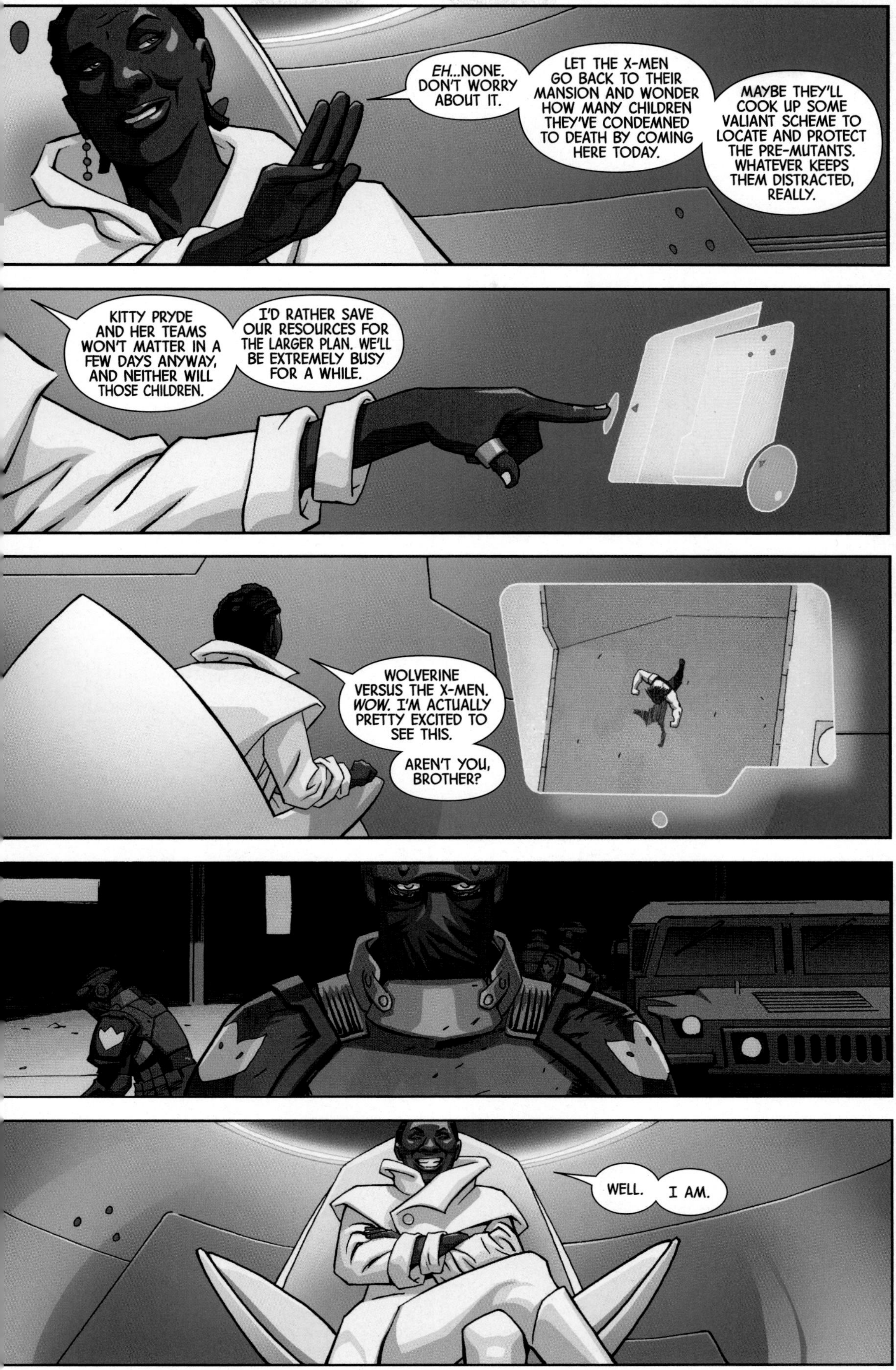
EH...NONE. DON'T WORRY ABOUT IT.
LET THE X-MEN GO BACK TO THEIR MANSION AND WONDER HOW MANY CHILDREN THEY'VE CONDEMNED TO DEATH BY COMING HERE TODAY.
MAYBE THEY'LL COOK UP SOME VALIANT SCHEME TO LOCATE AND PROTECT THE PRE-MUTANTS. WHATEVER KEEPS THEM DISTRACTED, REALLY.
KITTY PRYDE AND HER TEAMS WON'T MATTER IN A FEW DAYS ANYWAY, AND NEITHER WILL THOSE CHILDREN.
I'D RATHER SAVE OUR RESOURCES FOR THE LARGER PLAN. WE'LL BE EXTREMELY BUSY FOR A WHILE.
WOLVERINE VERSUS THE X-MEN. WOW. I'M ACTUALLY PRETTY EXCITED TO SEE THIS.
AREN'T YOU, BROTHER?
WELL.
I AM.

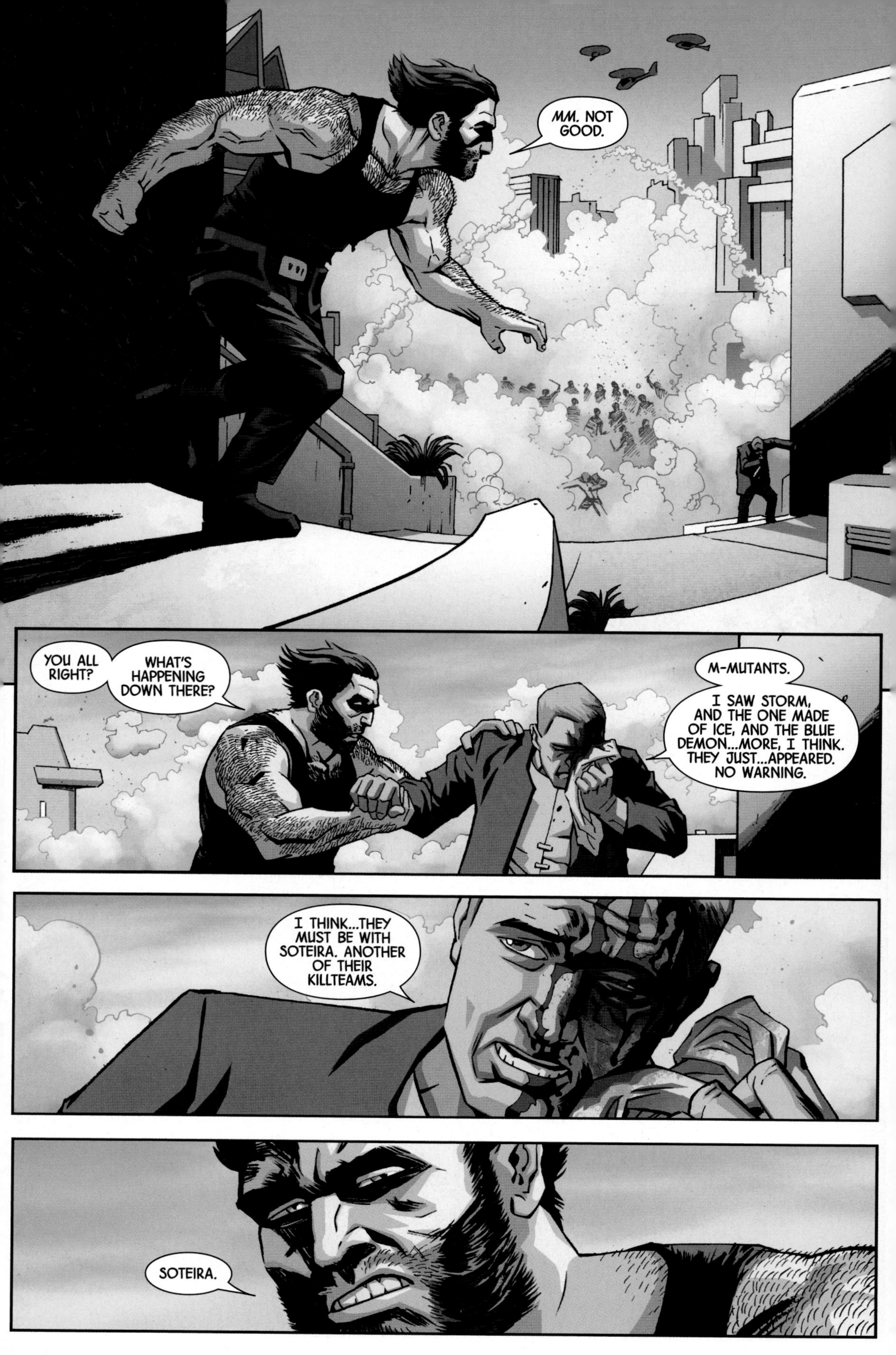
MM. NOT GOOD.
YOU ALL RIGHT?
WHAT'S HAPPENING DOWN THERE?
M-MUTANTS.
I SAW STORM, AND THE ONE MADE OF ICE, AND THE BLUE DEMON...MORE, I THINK. THEY JUST...APPEARED. NO WARNING.
I THINK...THEY MUST BE WITH SOTEIRA. ANOTHER OF THEIR KILLTEAMS.
SOTEIRA.

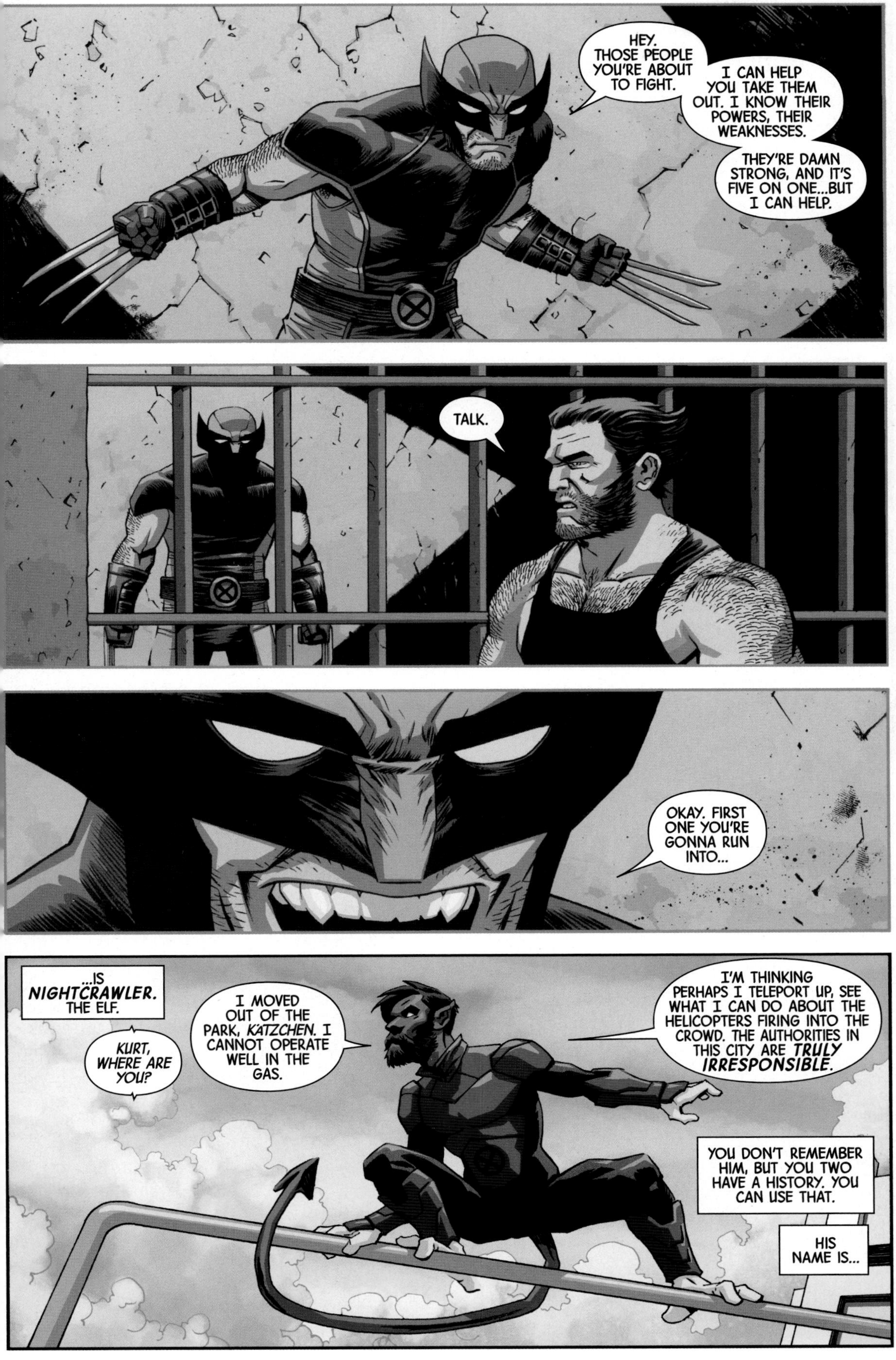
HEY. THOSE PEOPLE YOU'RE ABOUT TO FIGHT.
I CAN HELP YOU TAKE THEM OUT. I KNOW THEIR POWERS, THEIR WEAKNESSES.
THEY'RE DAMN STRONG, AND IT'S FIVE ON ONE...BUT I CAN HELP.
TALK.
OKAY. FIRST ONE YOU'RE GONNA RUN INTO...
...IS *NIGHTCRAWLER.* THE ELF.
KURT, WHERE ARE YOU?
I MOVED OUT OF THE PARK, *KÄTZCHEN.* I CANNOT OPERATE WELL IN THE GAS.
I'M THINKING PERHAPS I TELEPORT UP, SEE WHAT I CAN DO ABOUT THE HELICOPTERS FIRING INTO THE CROWD. THE AUTHORITIES IN THIS CITY ARE ***TRULY IRRESPONSIBLE.***
YOU DON'T REMEMBER HIM, BUT YOU TWO HAVE A HISTORY. YOU CAN USE THAT.
HIS NAME IS...

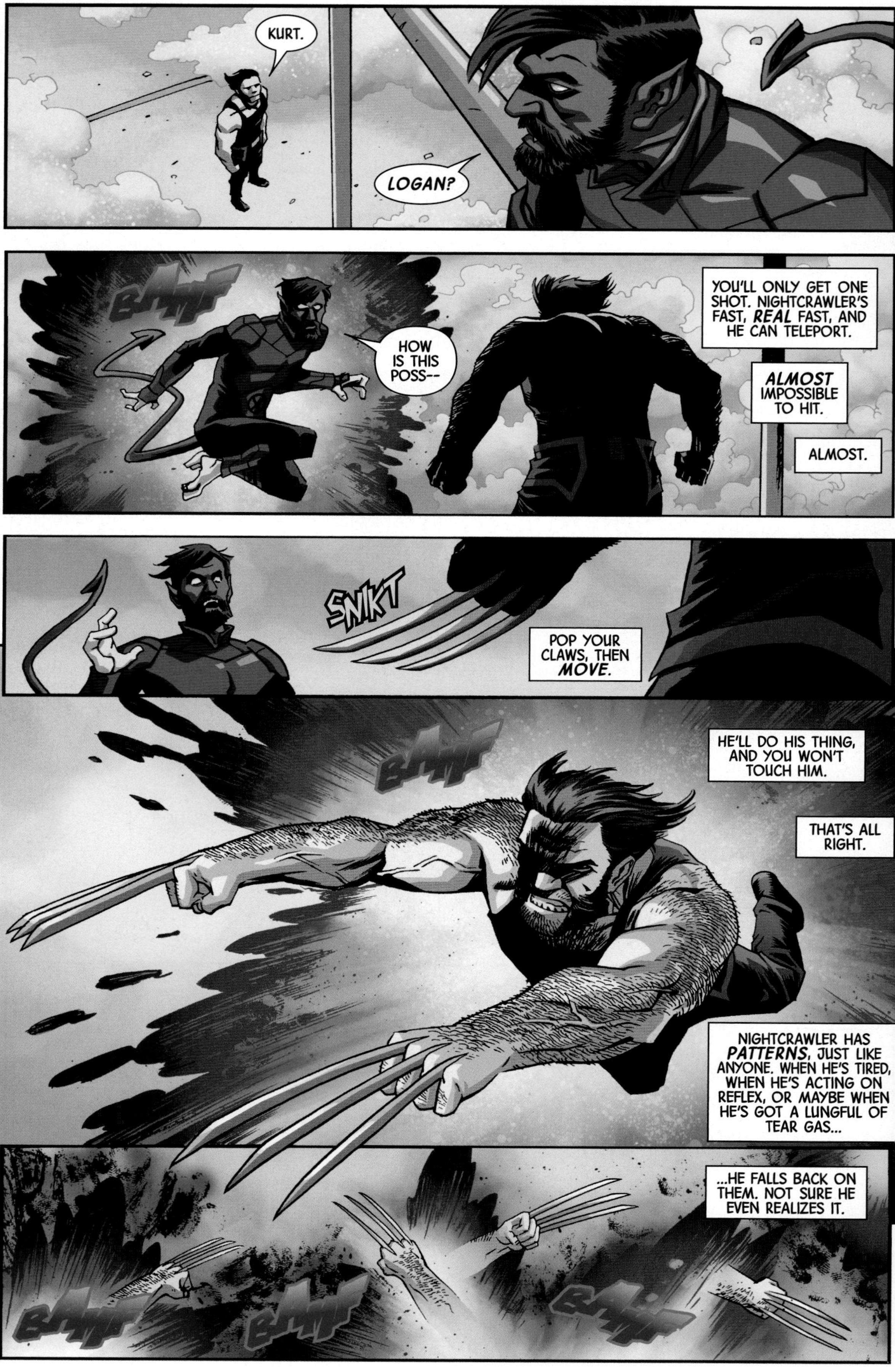

KURT.
LOGAN?
BAMF
HOW IS THIS POSS--
YOU'LL ONLY GET ONE SHOT. NIGHTCRAWLER'S FAST, REAL FAST, AND HE CAN TELEPORT.
ALMOST IMPOSSIBLE TO HIT.
ALMOST.
SNIKT
POP YOUR CLAWS, THEN MOVE.
BAMF
HE'LL DO HIS THING, AND YOU WON'T TOUCH HIM.
THAT'S ALL RIGHT.
NIGHTCRAWLER HAS PATTERNS, JUST LIKE ANYONE. WHEN HE'S TIRED, WHEN HE'S ACTING ON REFLEX, OR MAYBE WHEN HE'S GOT A LUNGFUL OF TEAR GAS...
...HE FALLS BACK ON THEM. NOT SURE HE EVEN REALIZES IT.
BAMF
BAMF
BAMF

BUT *YOU* DO. YOU NOTICED THEM YEARS AGO.

UP, DOWN, BACK, LEFT...

...UP AGAIN.

MEIN G--

BAMF

SHHHK

YOU NOTICED THEM, AND YOU MEMORIZED THEM.

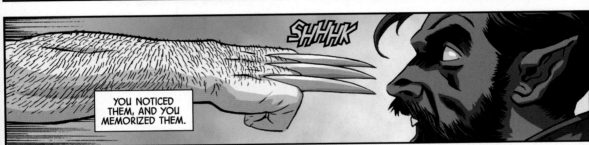

YOU KNOW...

KRRCK

...JUST IN CASE.

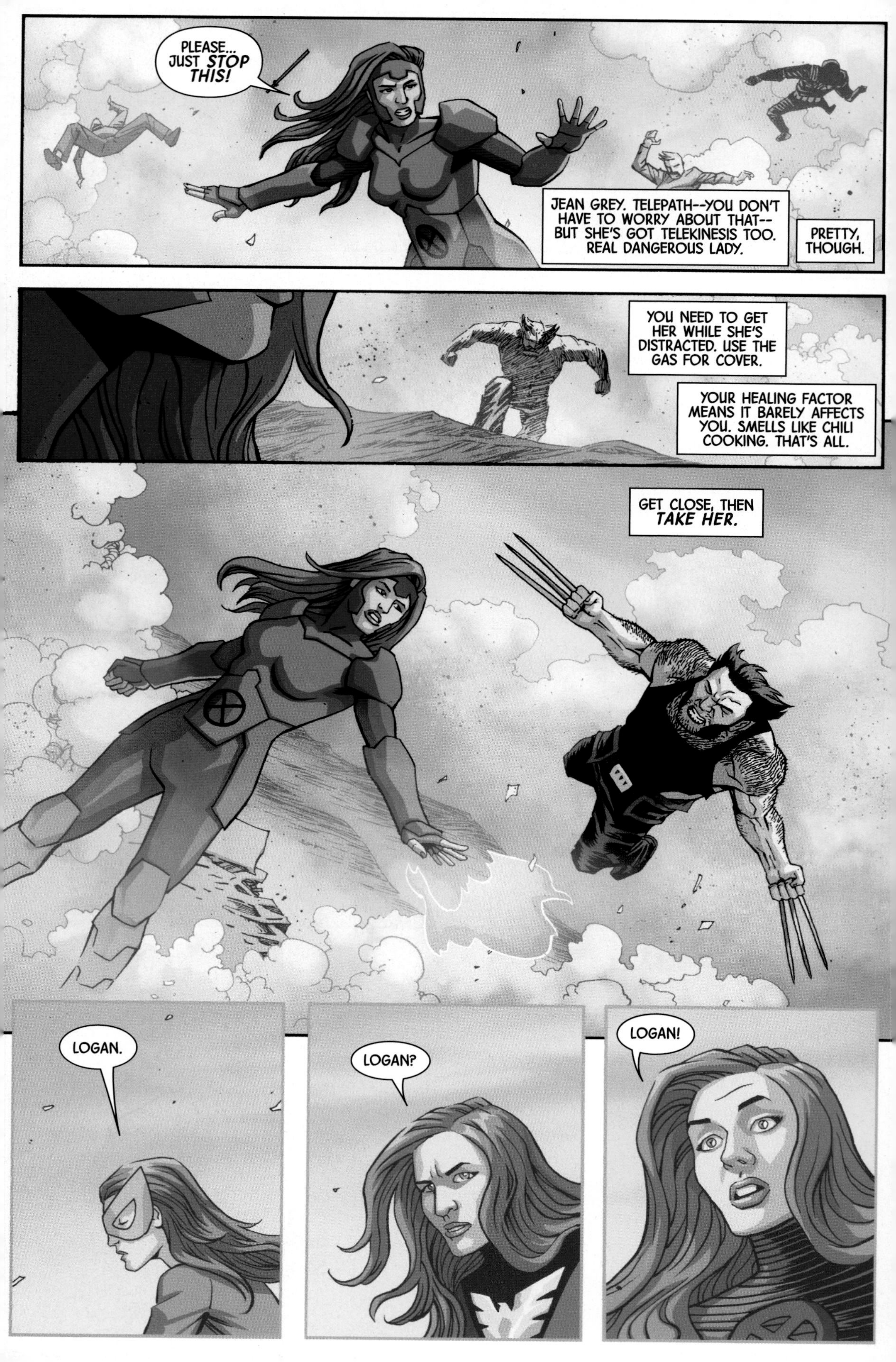

PLEASE... JUST STOP THIS!
JEAN GREY. TELEPATH--YOU DON'T HAVE TO WORRY ABOUT THAT--BUT SHE'S GOT TELEKINESIS TOO. REAL DANGEROUS LADY.
PRETTY, THOUGH.
YOU NEED TO GET HER WHILE SHE'S DISTRACTED. USE THE GAS FOR COVER.
YOUR HEALING FACTOR MEANS IT BARELY AFFECTS YOU. SMELLS LIKE CHILI COOKING. THAT'S ALL.
GET CLOSE, THEN TAKE HER.
LOGAN.
LOGAN?
LOGAN!

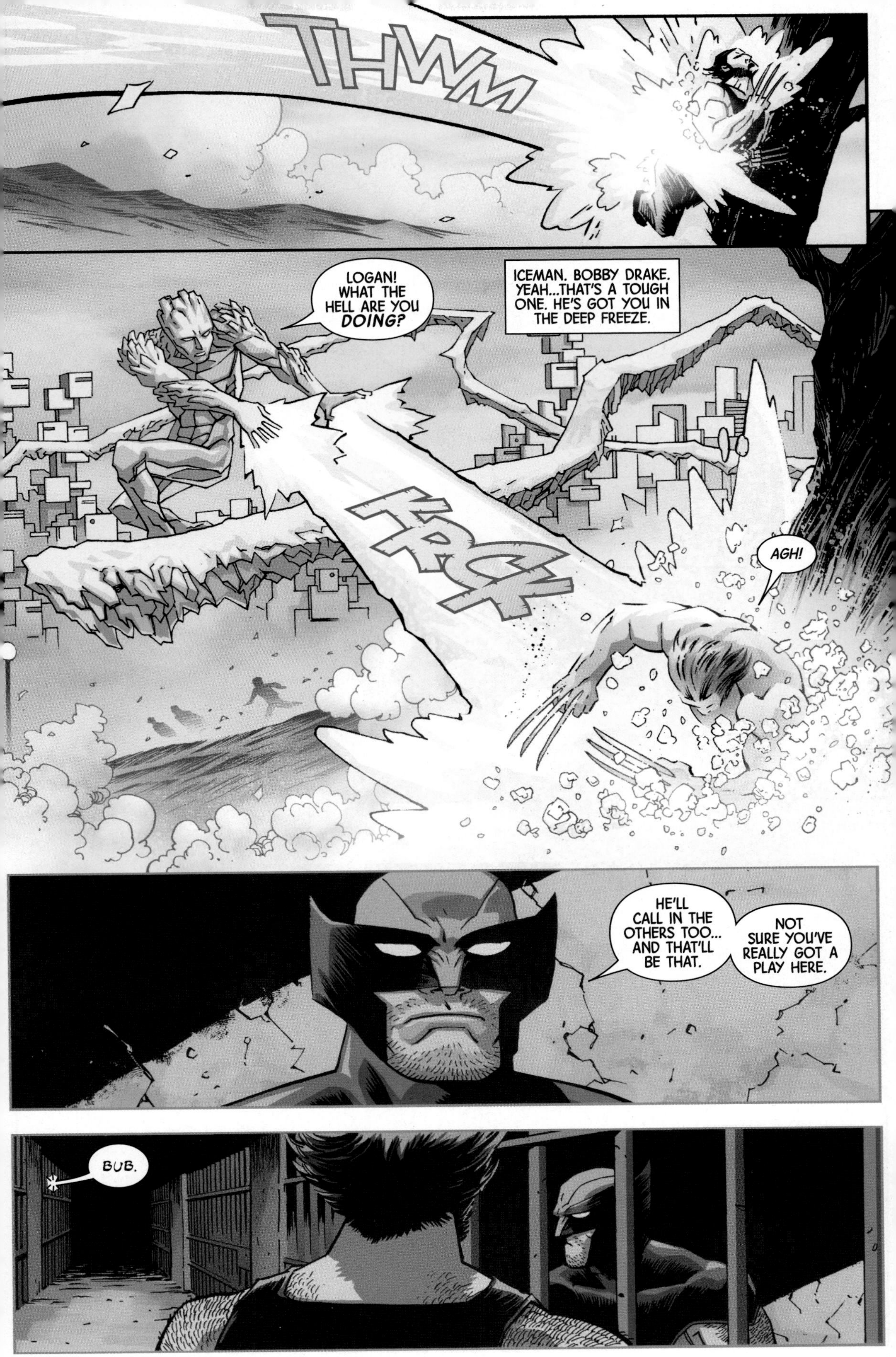
THWM
LOGAN! WHAT THE HELL ARE YOU DOING?
ICEMAN. BOBBY DRAKE. YEAH...THAT'S A TOUGH ONE. HE'S GOT YOU IN THE DEEP FREEZE.
K'RCK
AGH!
HE'LL CALL IN THE OTHERS TOO... AND THAT'LL BE THAT.
NOT SURE YOU'VE REALLY GOT A PLAY HERE.
BUB.

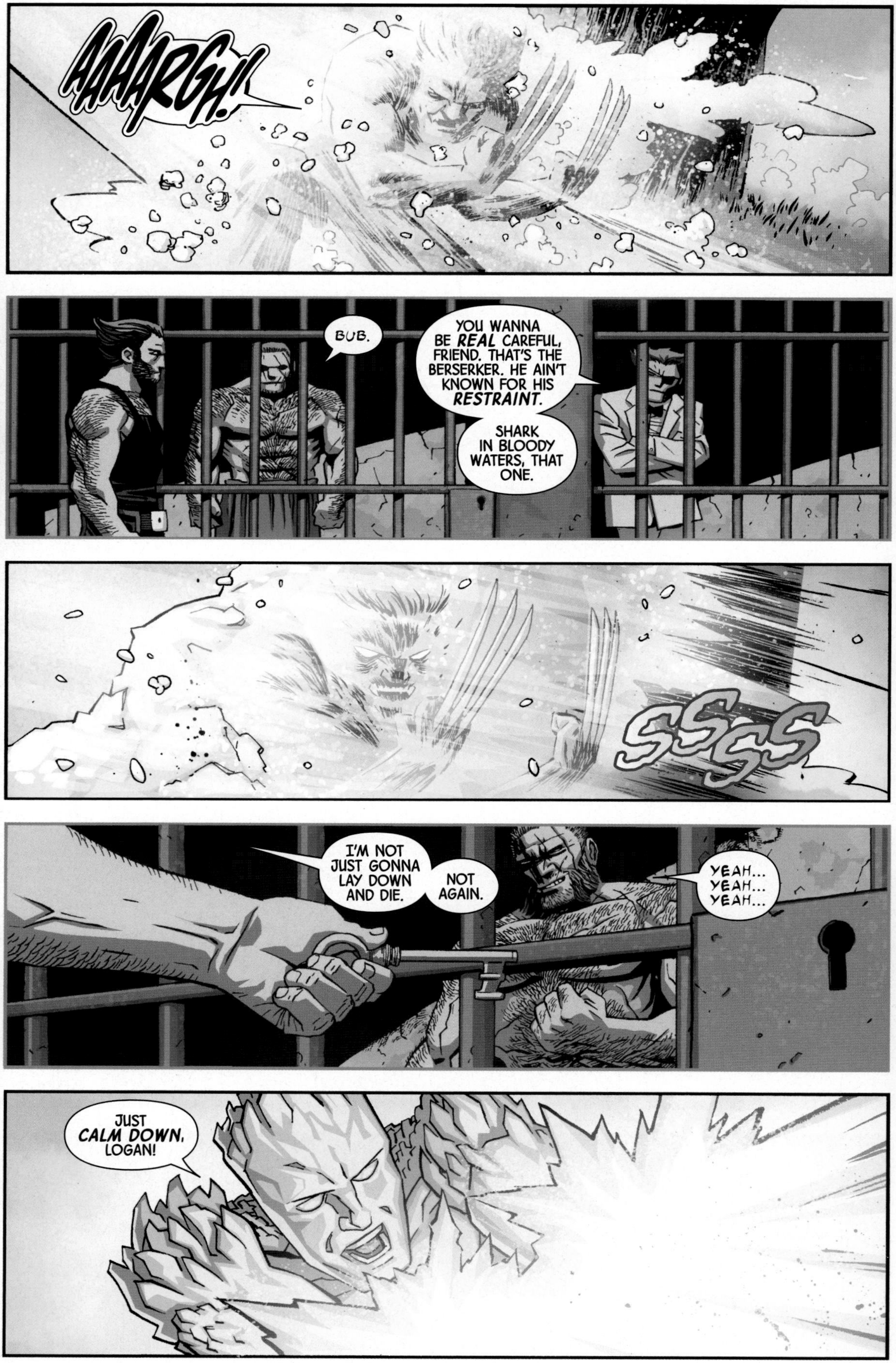
AAAARGH!!
BUB.
YOU WANNA BE REAL CAREFUL, FRIEND. THAT'S THE BERSERKER. HE AIN'T KNOWN FOR HIS RESTRAINT.
SHARK IN BLOODY WATERS, THAT ONE.
SSSS
I'M NOT JUST GONNA LAY DOWN AND DIE.
NOT AGAIN.
YEAH... YEAH... YEAH...
JUST CALM DOWN, LOGAN!

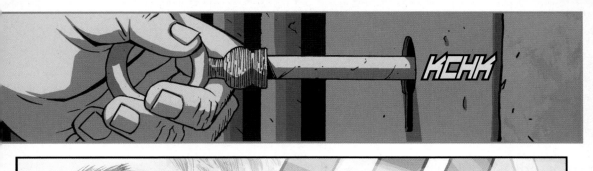

KCHK

SSSSSS

SSSSSSSNIKT

YEAH.

SSSSSSSSS

BEEN WAITIN' FOR THIS.

AAGH!

SSSK

KRRCKK

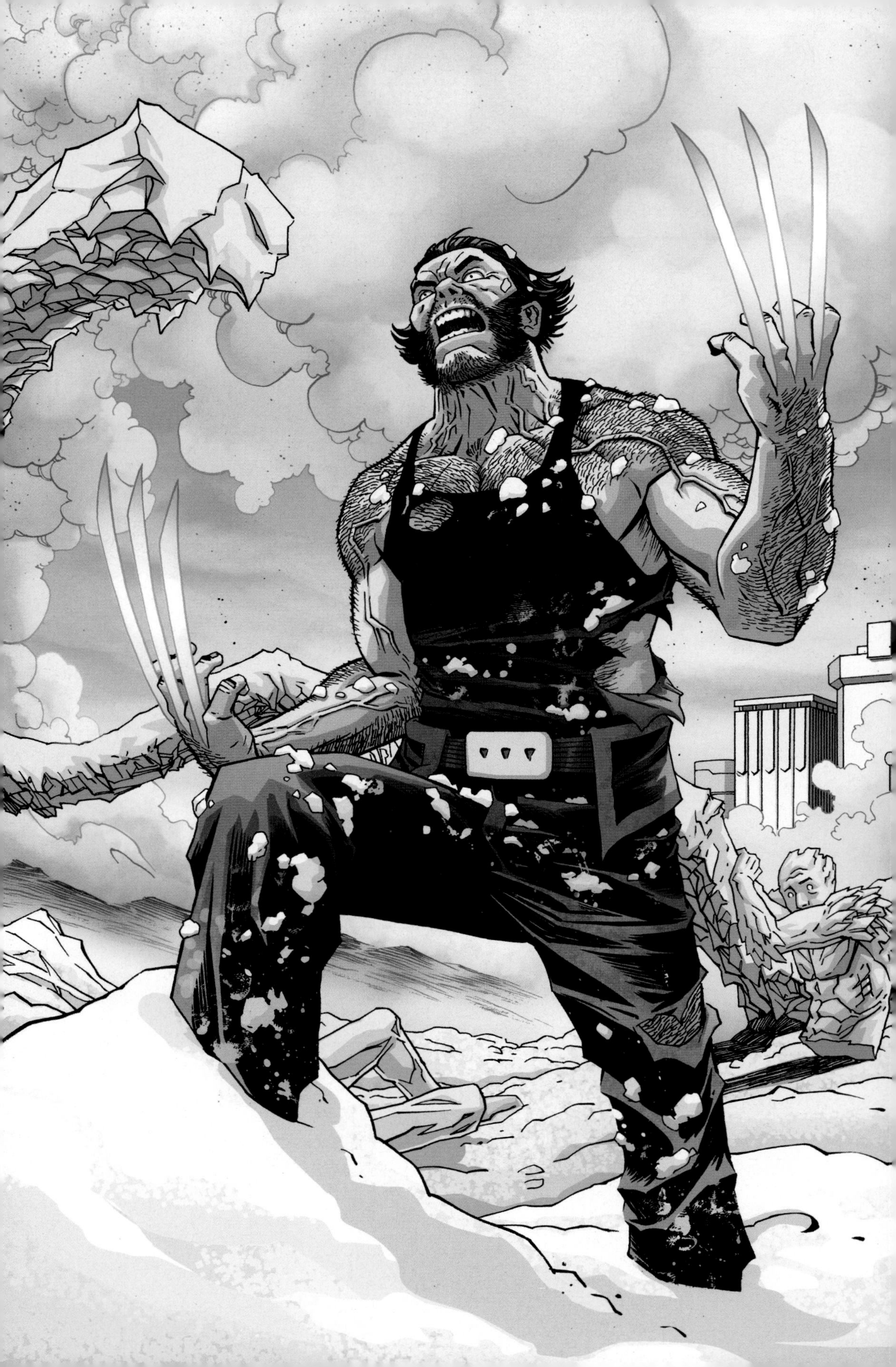

4

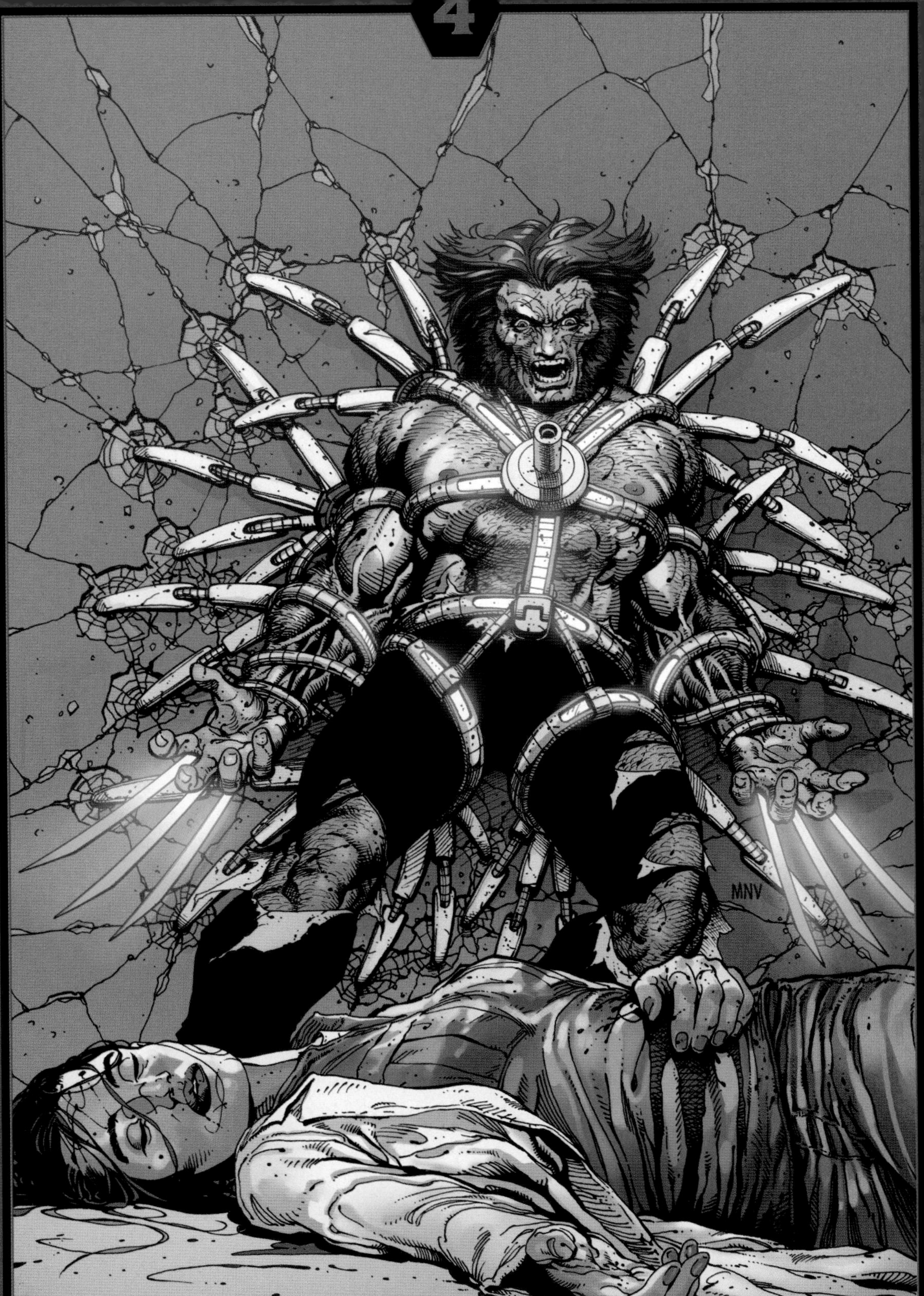
MNV

CHAPTER FOUR
JUDGMENT

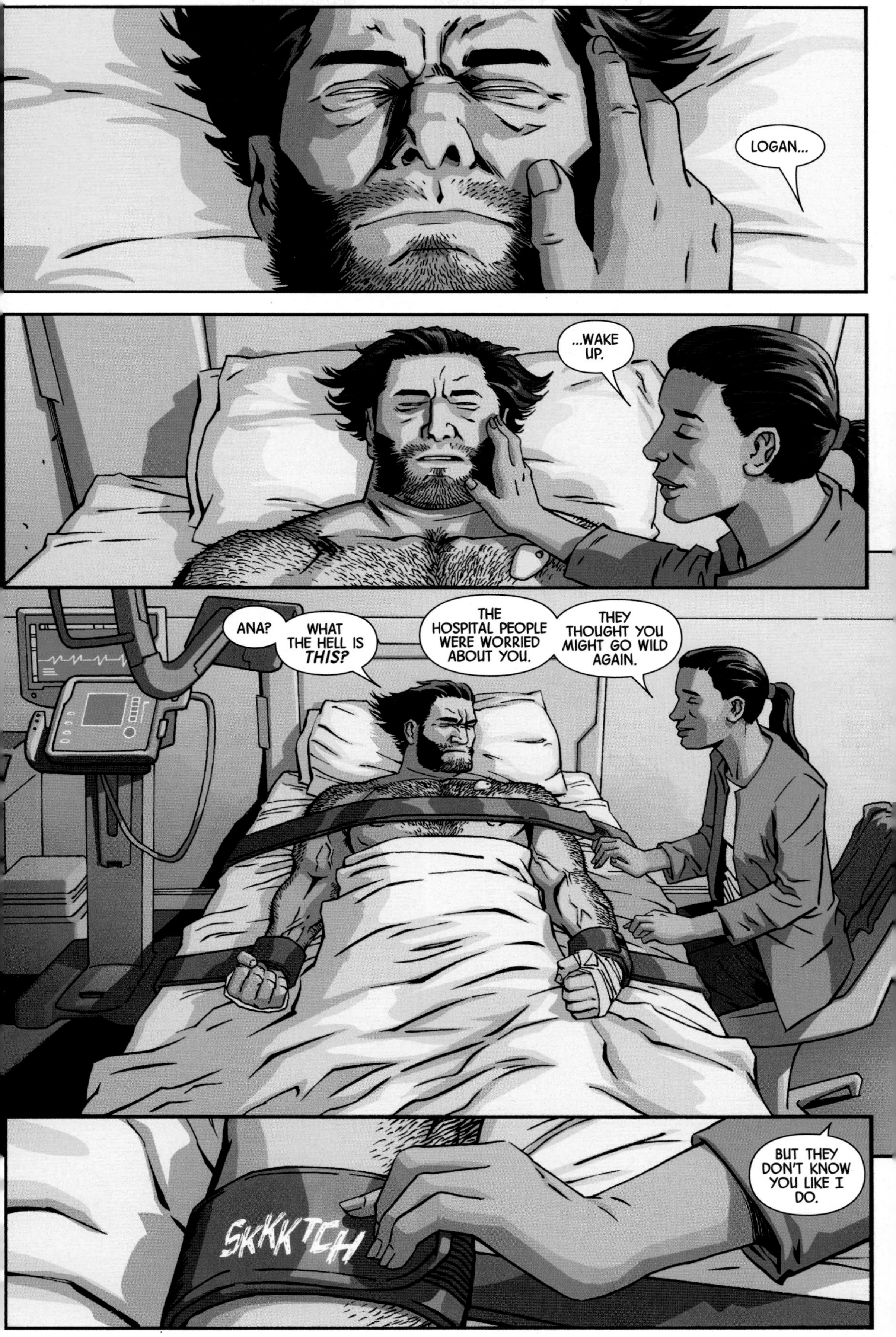
LOGAN...
...WAKE UP.
ANA?
WHAT THE HELL IS THIS?
THE HOSPITAL PEOPLE WERE WORRIED ABOUT YOU.
THEY THOUGHT YOU MIGHT GO WILD AGAIN.
BUT THEY DON'T KNOW YOU LIKE I DO.
SKKKTCH

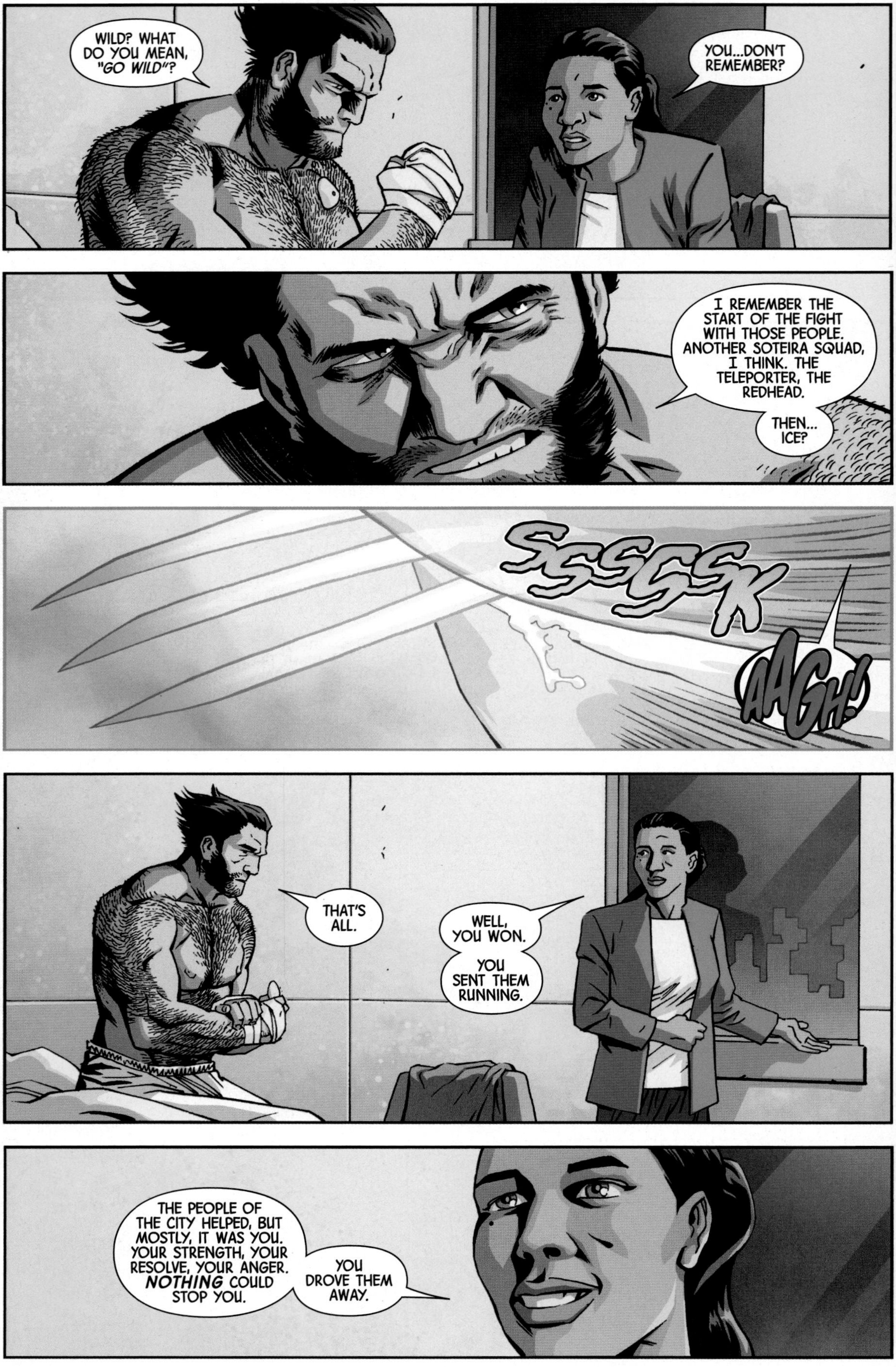
WILD? WHAT DO YOU MEAN, "GO WILD"?
YOU...DON'T REMEMBER?
I REMEMBER THE START OF THE FIGHT WITH THOSE PEOPLE. ANOTHER SOTEIRA SQUAD, I THINK. THE TELEPORTER, THE REDHEAD.
THEN... ICE?
SSSSSK
AAGH!
THAT'S ALL.
WELL, YOU WON.
YOU SENT THEM RUNNING.
THE PEOPLE OF THE CITY HELPED, BUT MOSTLY, IT WAS YOU. YOUR STRENGTH, YOUR RESOLVE, YOUR ANGER. NOTHING COULD STOP YOU.
YOU DROVE THEM AWAY.

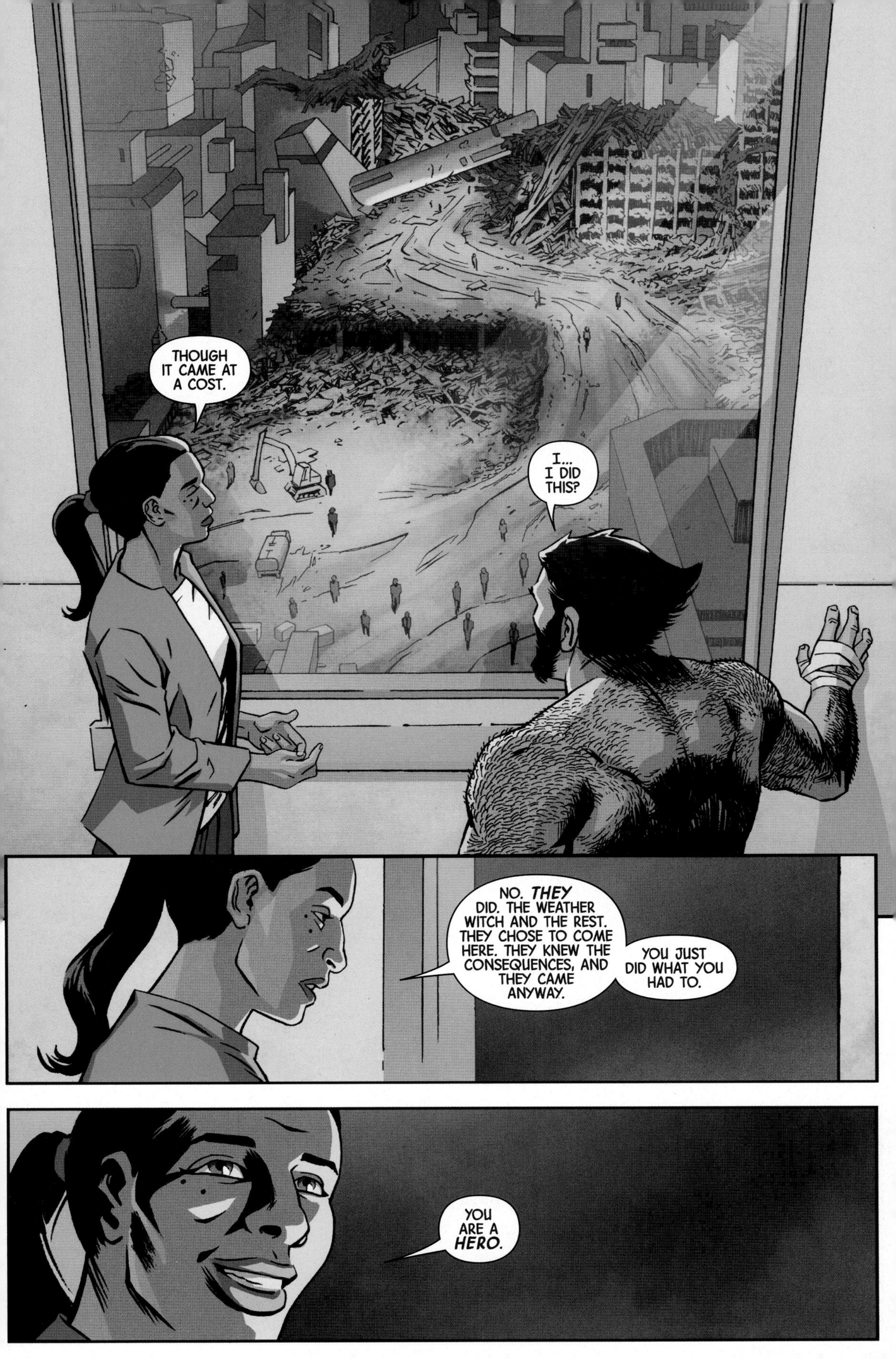
THOUGH IT CAME AT A COST.
I... I DID THIS?
NO. *THEY* DID. THE WEATHER WITCH AND THE REST. THEY CHOSE TO COME HERE. THEY KNEW THE CONSEQUENCES, AND THEY CAME ANYWAY.
YOU JUST DID WHAT YOU HAD TO.
YOU ARE A *HERO*.

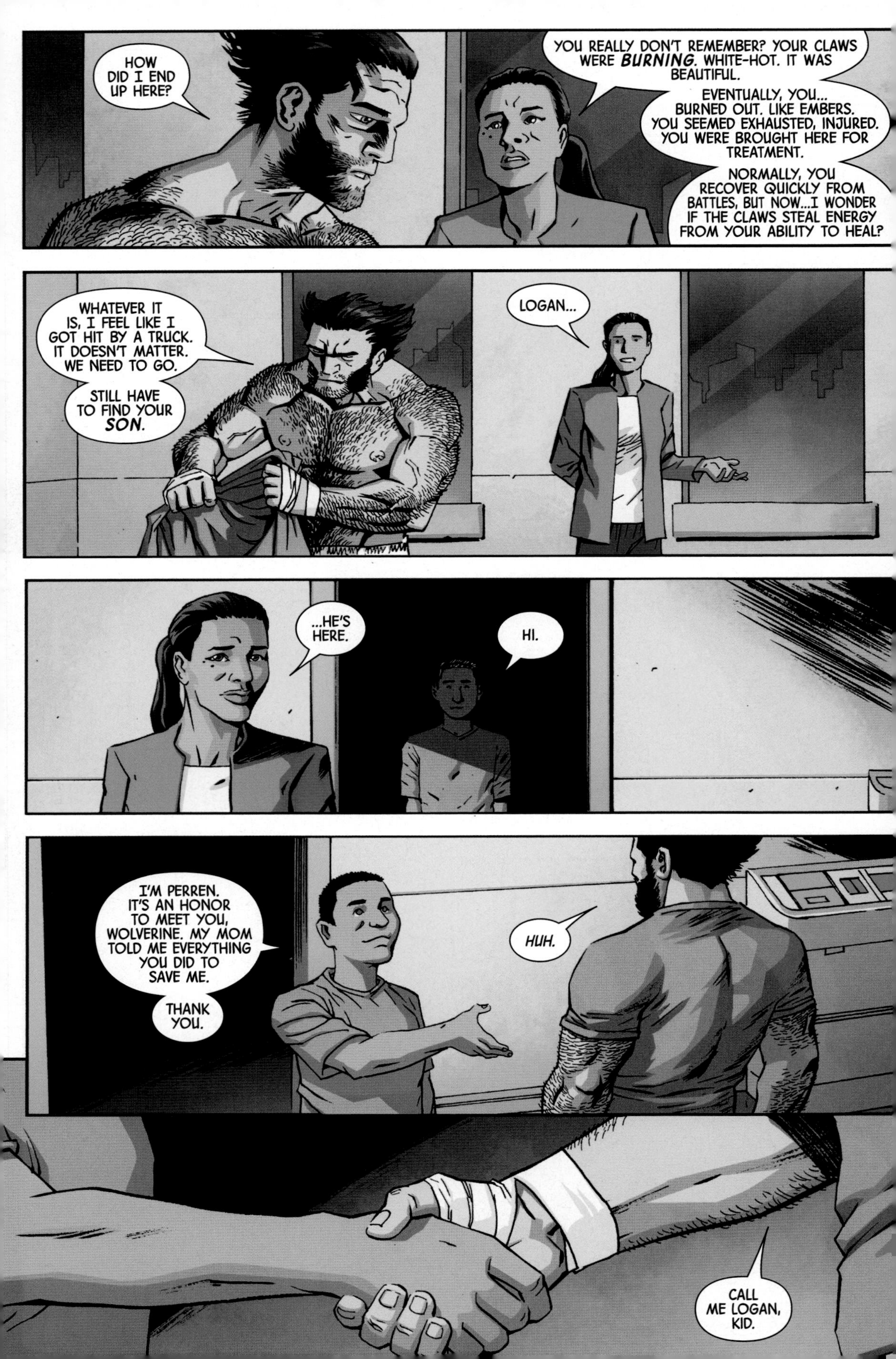
HOW DID I END UP HERE?
YOU REALLY DON'T REMEMBER? YOUR CLAWS WERE BURNING. WHITE-HOT. IT WAS BEAUTIFUL.
EVENTUALLY, YOU... BURNED OUT. LIKE EMBERS. YOU SEEMED EXHAUSTED, INJURED. YOU WERE BROUGHT HERE FOR TREATMENT.
NORMALLY, YOU RECOVER QUICKLY FROM BATTLES, BUT NOW...I WONDER IF THE CLAWS STEAL ENERGY FROM YOUR ABILITY TO HEAL?
WHATEVER IT IS, I FEEL LIKE I GOT HIT BY A TRUCK. IT DOESN'T MATTER. WE NEED TO GO.
STILL HAVE TO FIND YOUR SON.
LOGAN...
...HE'S HERE.
HI.
I'M PERREN. IT'S AN HONOR TO MEET YOU, WOLVERINE. MY MOM TOLD ME EVERYTHING YOU DID TO SAVE ME.
THANK YOU.
HUH.
CALL ME LOGAN, KID.

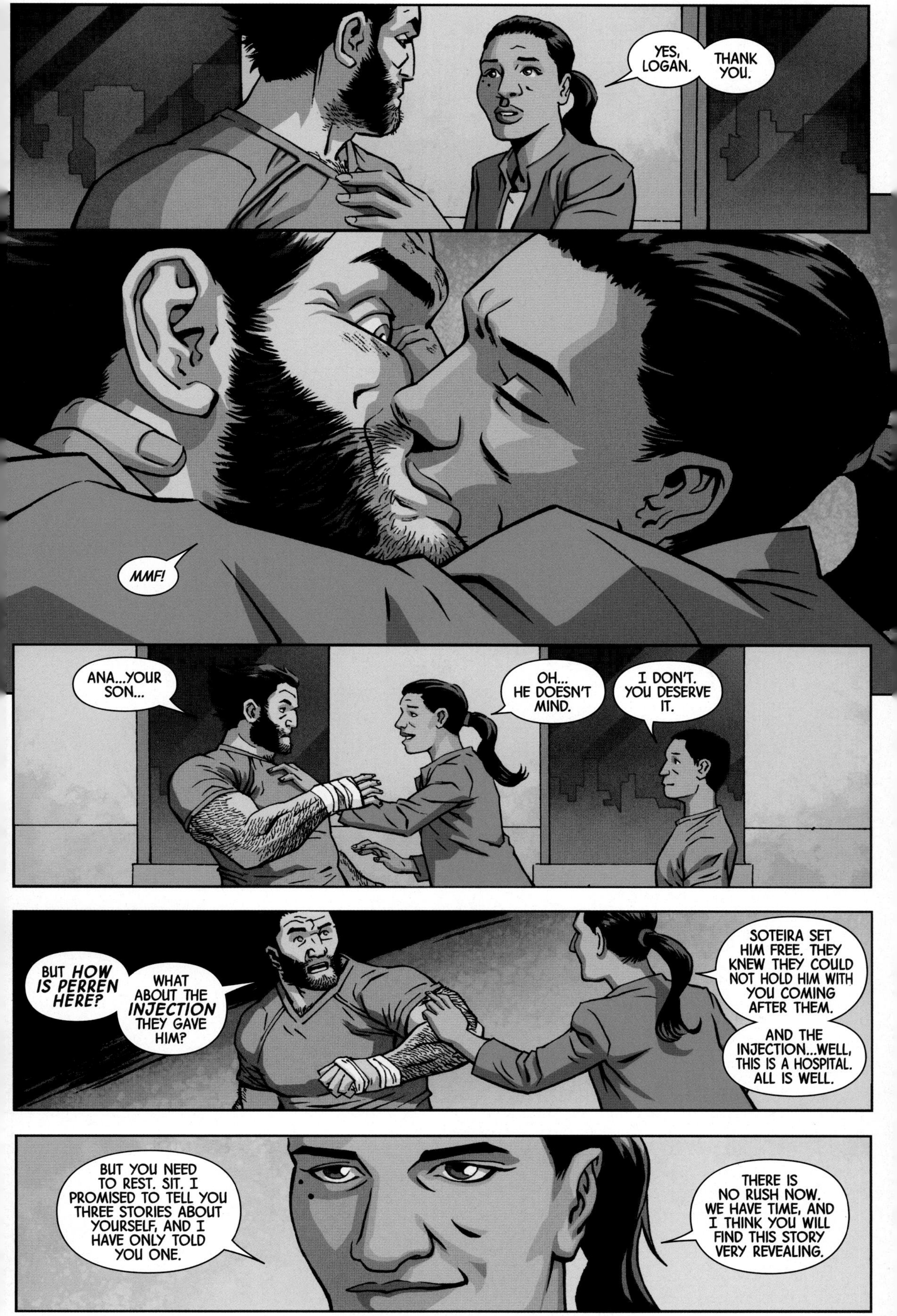

YES, LOGAN.
THANK YOU.
MMF!
ANA...YOUR SON...
OH... HE DOESN'T MIND.
I DON'T. YOU DESERVE IT.
BUT *HOW IS PERREN HERE?*
WHAT ABOUT THE *INJECTION* THEY GAVE HIM?
SOTEIRA SET HIM FREE. THEY KNEW THEY COULD NOT HOLD HIM WITH YOU COMING AFTER THEM.
AND THE INJECTION...WELL, THIS IS A HOSPITAL. ALL IS WELL.
BUT YOU NEED TO REST. SIT. I PROMISED TO TELL YOU THREE STORIES ABOUT YOURSELF, AND I HAVE ONLY TOLD YOU ONE.
THERE IS NO RUSH NOW. WE HAVE TIME, AND I THINK YOU WILL FIND THIS STORY VERY REVEALING.

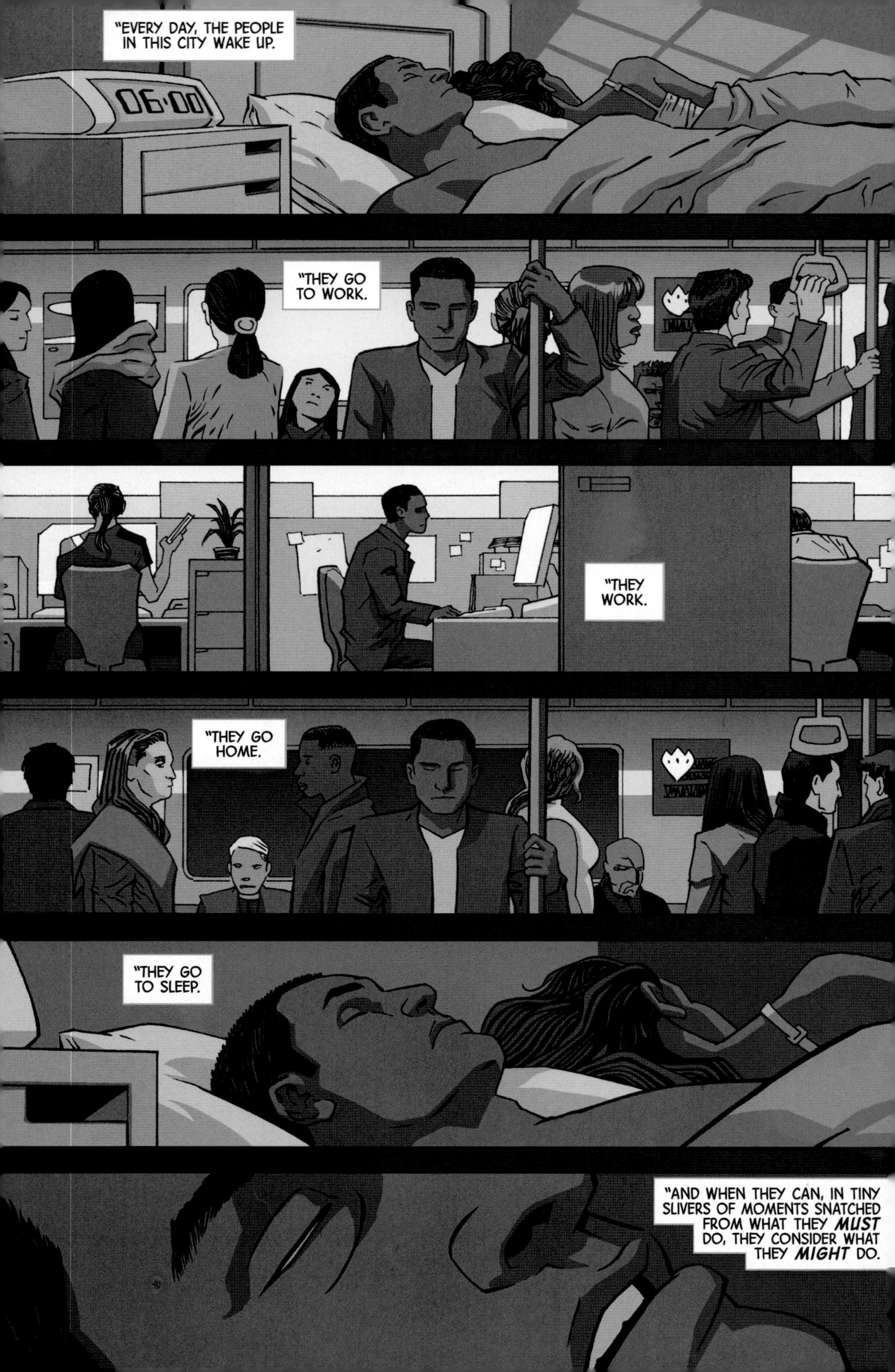

"EVERY DAY, THE PEOPLE IN THIS CITY WAKE UP.
06:00
"THEY GO TO WORK.
"THEY WORK.
"THEY GO HOME.
"THEY GO TO SLEEP.
"AND WHEN THEY CAN, IN TINY SLIVERS OF MOMENTS SNATCHED FROM WHAT THEY *MUST* DO, THEY CONSIDER WHAT THEY *MIGHT* DO.

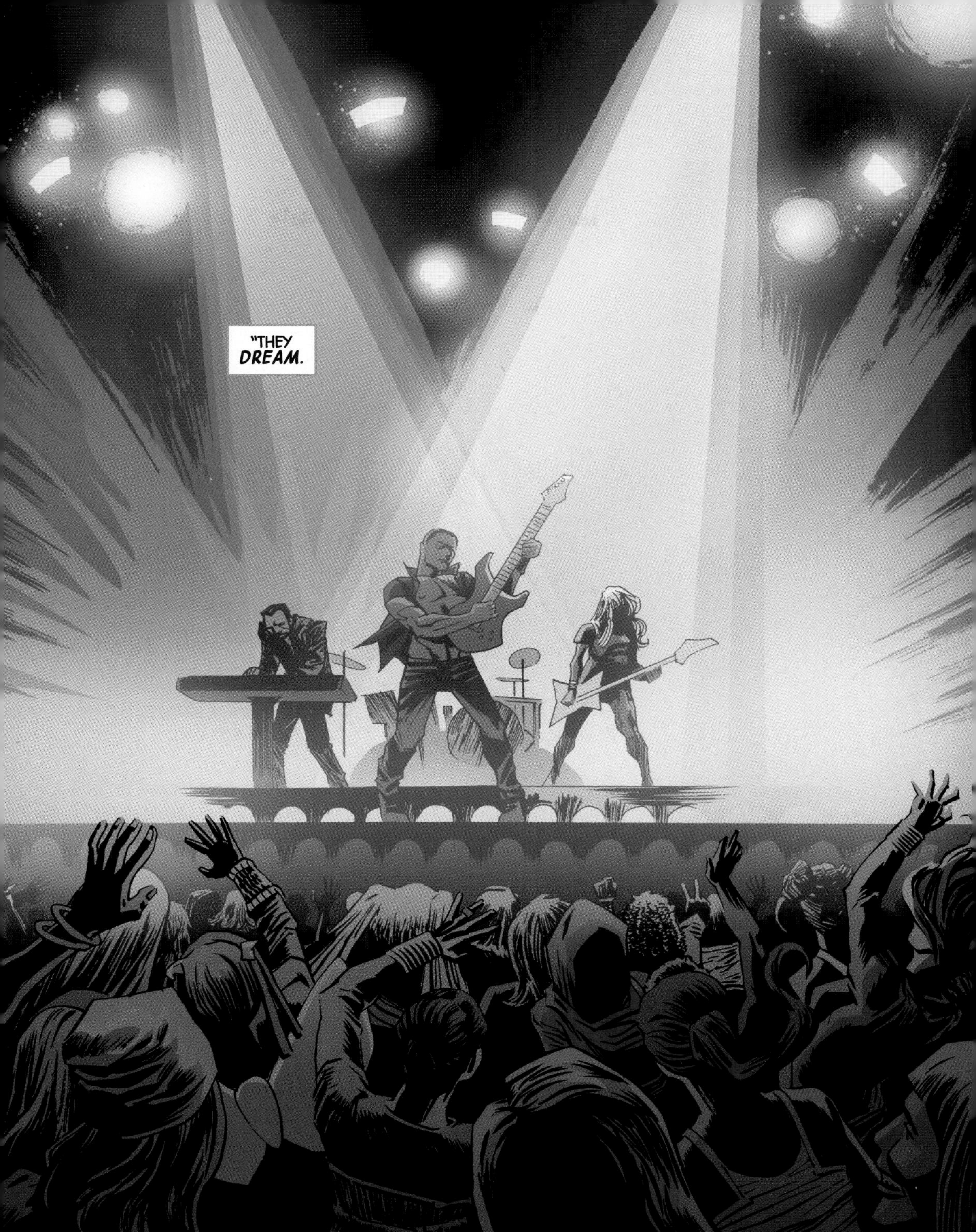
"THEY DREAM.

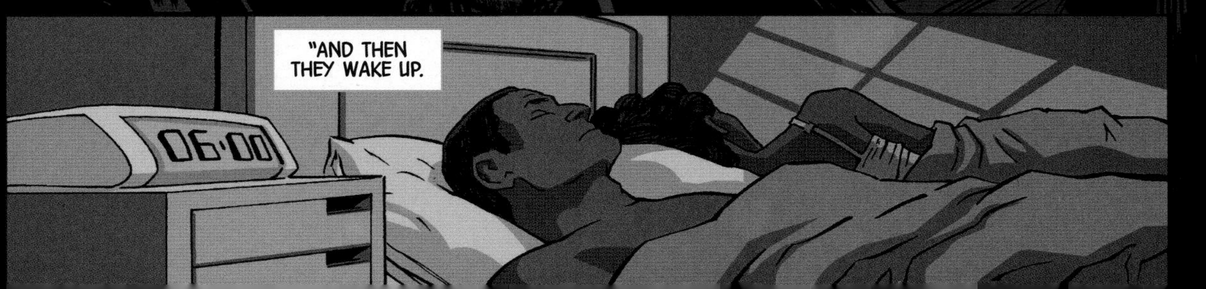
"AND THEN THEY WAKE UP.
06:00

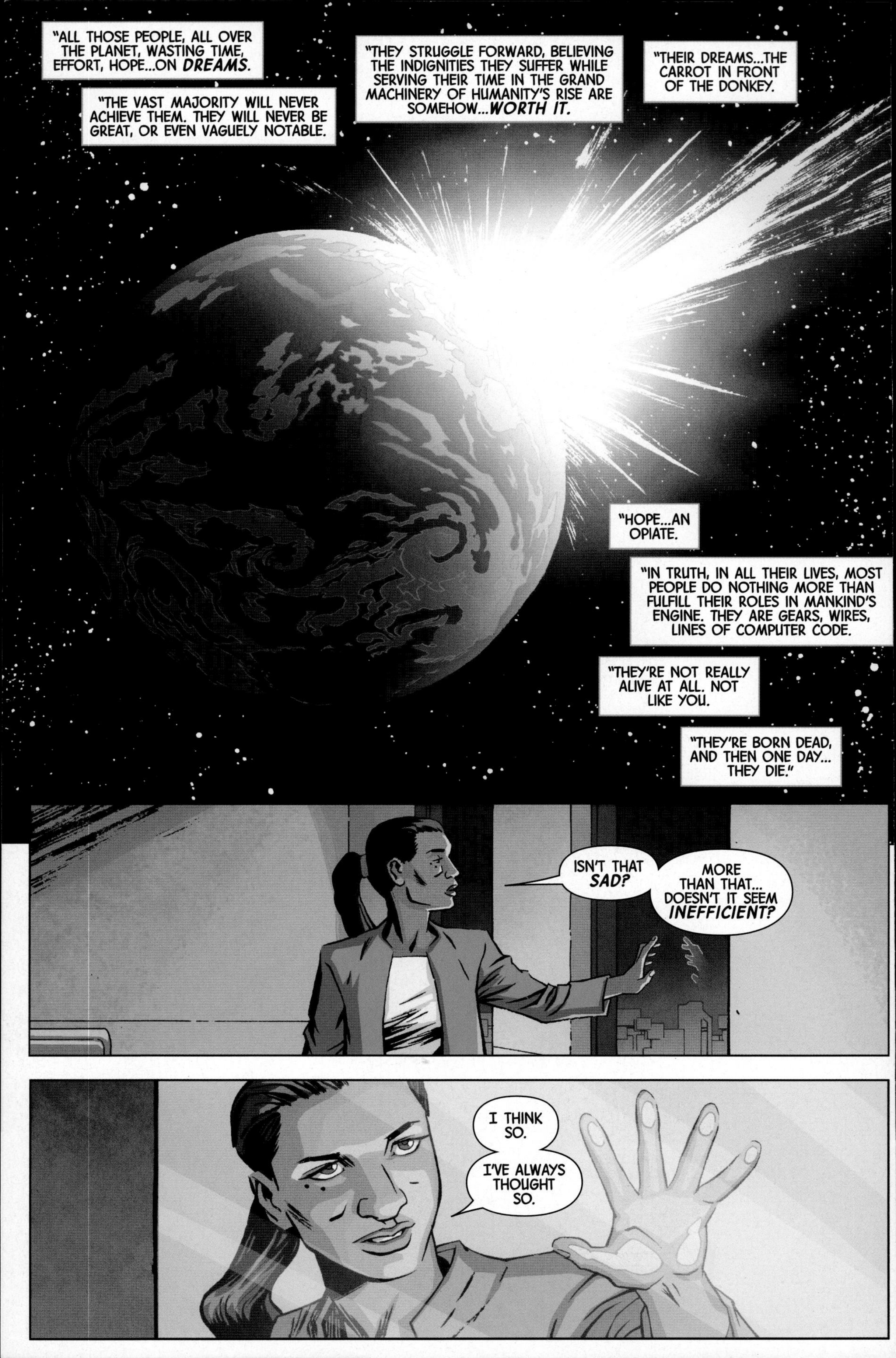
"ALL THOSE PEOPLE, ALL OVER THE PLANET, WASTING TIME, EFFORT, HOPE...ON DREAMS.
"THE VAST MAJORITY WILL NEVER ACHIEVE THEM. THEY WILL NEVER BE GREAT, OR EVEN VAGUELY NOTABLE.
"THEY STRUGGLE FORWARD, BELIEVING THE INDIGNITIES THEY SUFFER WHILE SERVING THEIR TIME IN THE GRAND MACHINERY OF HUMANITY'S RISE ARE SOMEHOW...WORTH IT.
"THEIR DREAMS...THE CARROT IN FRONT OF THE DONKEY.
"HOPE...AN OPIATE.
"IN TRUTH, IN ALL THEIR LIVES, MOST PEOPLE DO NOTHING MORE THAN FULFILL THEIR ROLES IN MANKIND'S ENGINE. THEY ARE GEARS, WIRES, LINES OF COMPUTER CODE.
"THEY'RE NOT REALLY ALIVE AT ALL. NOT LIKE YOU.
"THEY'RE BORN DEAD, AND THEN ONE DAY... THEY DIE."
ISN'T THAT SAD?
MORE THAN THAT... DOESN'T IT SEEM INEFFICIENT?
I THINK SO.
I'VE ALWAYS THOUGHT SO.

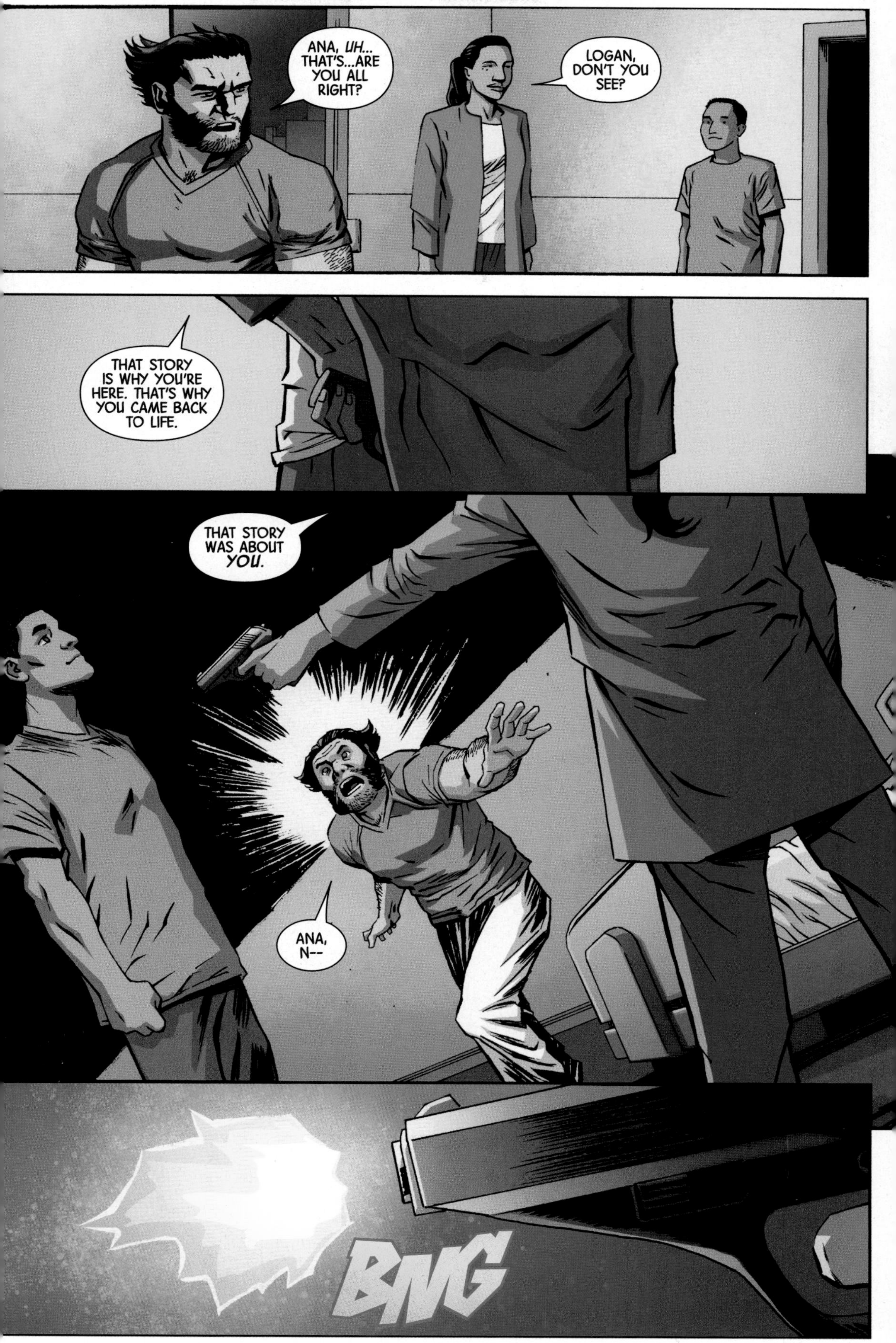
ANA, UH... THAT'S...ARE YOU ALL RIGHT?
LOGAN, DON'T YOU SEE?
THAT STORY IS WHY YOU'RE HERE. THAT'S WHY YOU CAME BACK TO LIFE.
THAT STORY WAS ABOUT YOU.
ANA, N--
BMG

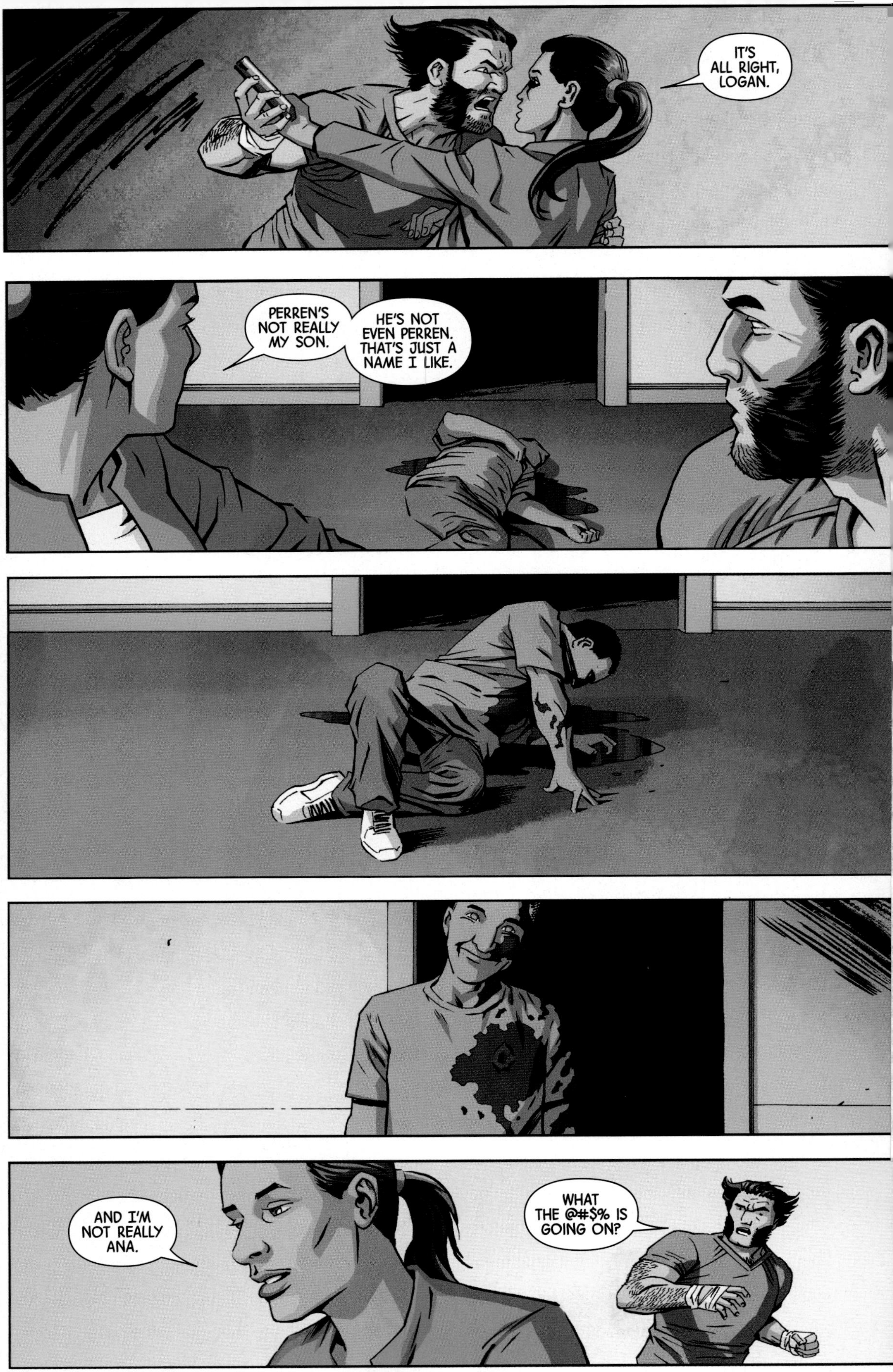
IT'S ALL RIGHT, LOGAN.
PERREN'S NOT REALLY MY SON.
HE'S NOT EVEN PERREN. THAT'S JUST A NAME I LIKE.
AND I'M NOT REALLY ANA.
WHAT THE @#$% IS GOING ON?

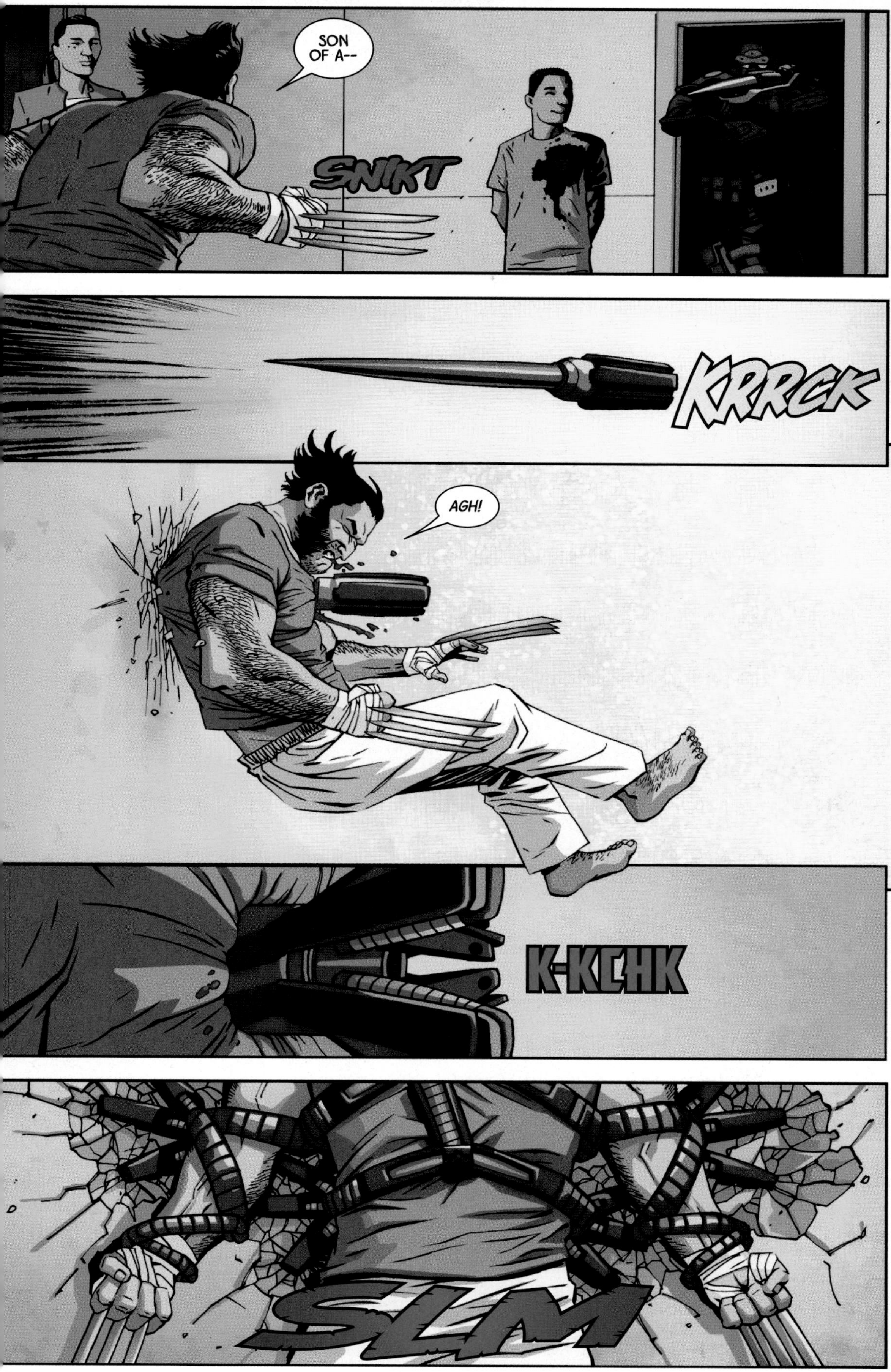

SON OF A--
SNIKT
KRRCK
AGH!
K-KCHK
SLM

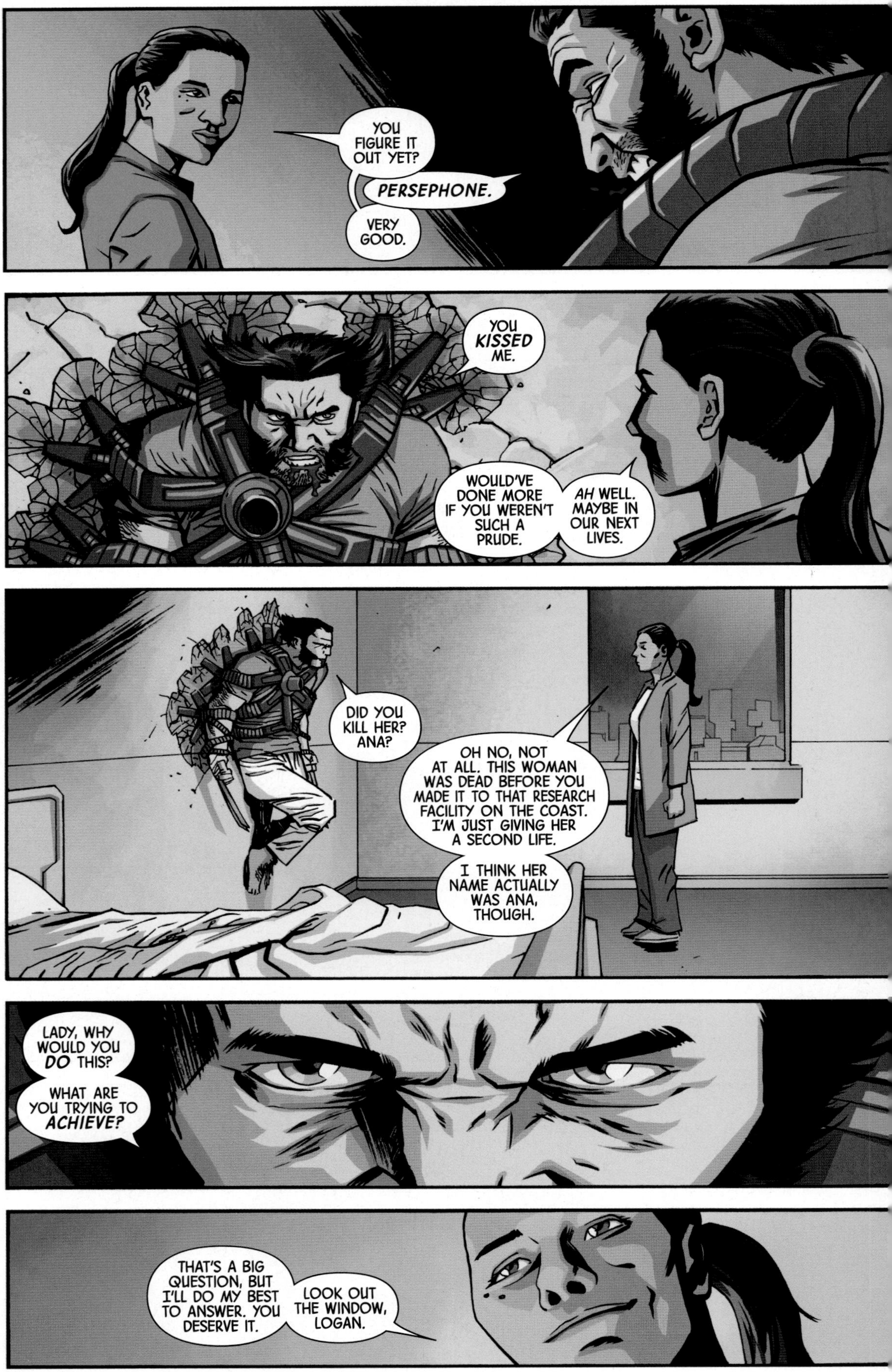
YOU FIGURE IT OUT YET?
PERSEPHONE.
VERY GOOD.
YOU *KISSED* ME.
WOULD'VE DONE MORE IF YOU WEREN'T SUCH A PRUDE.
AH WELL. MAYBE IN OUR NEXT LIVES.
DID YOU KILL HER? ANA?
OH NO, NOT AT ALL. THIS WOMAN WAS DEAD BEFORE YOU MADE IT TO THAT RESEARCH FACILITY ON THE COAST. I'M JUST GIVING HER A SECOND LIFE.
I THINK HER NAME ACTUALLY WAS ANA, THOUGH.
LADY, WHY WOULD YOU *DO* THIS?
WHAT ARE YOU TRYING TO *ACHIEVE?*
THAT'S A BIG QUESTION, BUT I'LL DO MY BEST TO ANSWER. YOU DESERVE IT.
LOOK OUT THE WINDOW, LOGAN.

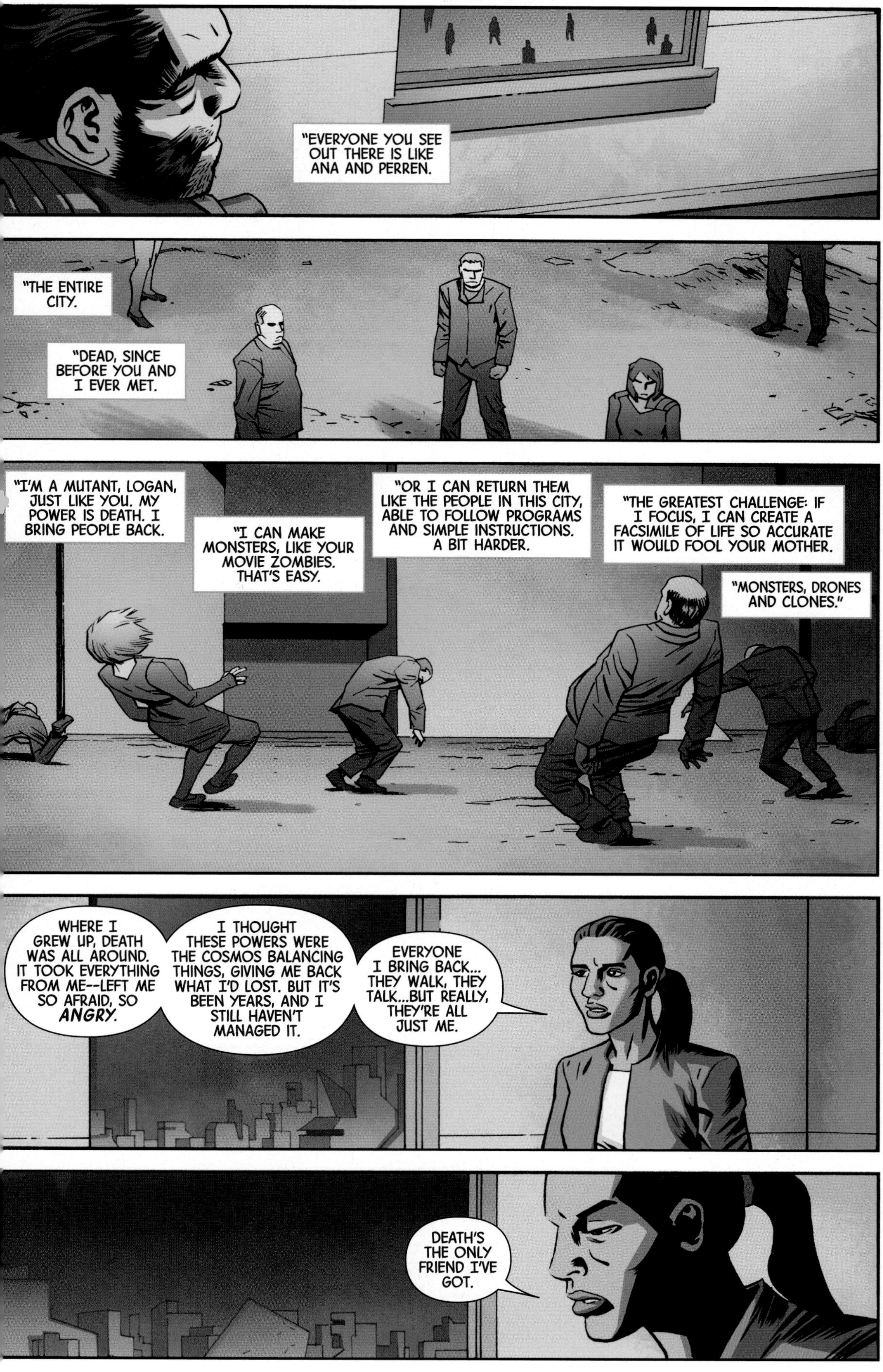
"EVERYONE YOU SEE OUT THERE IS LIKE ANA AND PERREN.
"THE ENTIRE CITY.
"DEAD, SINCE BEFORE YOU AND I EVER MET.
"I'M A MUTANT, LOGAN, JUST LIKE YOU. MY POWER IS DEATH. I BRING PEOPLE BACK.
"I CAN MAKE MONSTERS, LIKE YOUR MOVIE ZOMBIES. THAT'S EASY.
"OR I CAN RETURN THEM LIKE THE PEOPLE IN THIS CITY, ABLE TO FOLLOW PROGRAMS AND SIMPLE INSTRUCTIONS. A BIT HARDER.
"THE GREATEST CHALLENGE: IF I FOCUS, I CAN CREATE A FACSIMILE OF LIFE SO ACCURATE IT WOULD FOOL YOUR MOTHER.
"MONSTERS, DRONES AND CLONES."
WHERE I GREW UP, DEATH WAS ALL AROUND. IT TOOK EVERYTHING FROM ME--LEFT ME SO AFRAID, SO *ANGRY*.
I THOUGHT THESE POWERS WERE THE COSMOS BALANCING THINGS, GIVING ME BACK WHAT I'D LOST. BUT IT'S BEEN YEARS, AND I STILL HAVEN'T MANAGED IT.
EVERYONE I BRING BACK... THEY WALK, THEY TALK...BUT REALLY, THEY'RE ALL JUST ME.
DEATH'S THE ONLY FRIEND I'VE GOT.

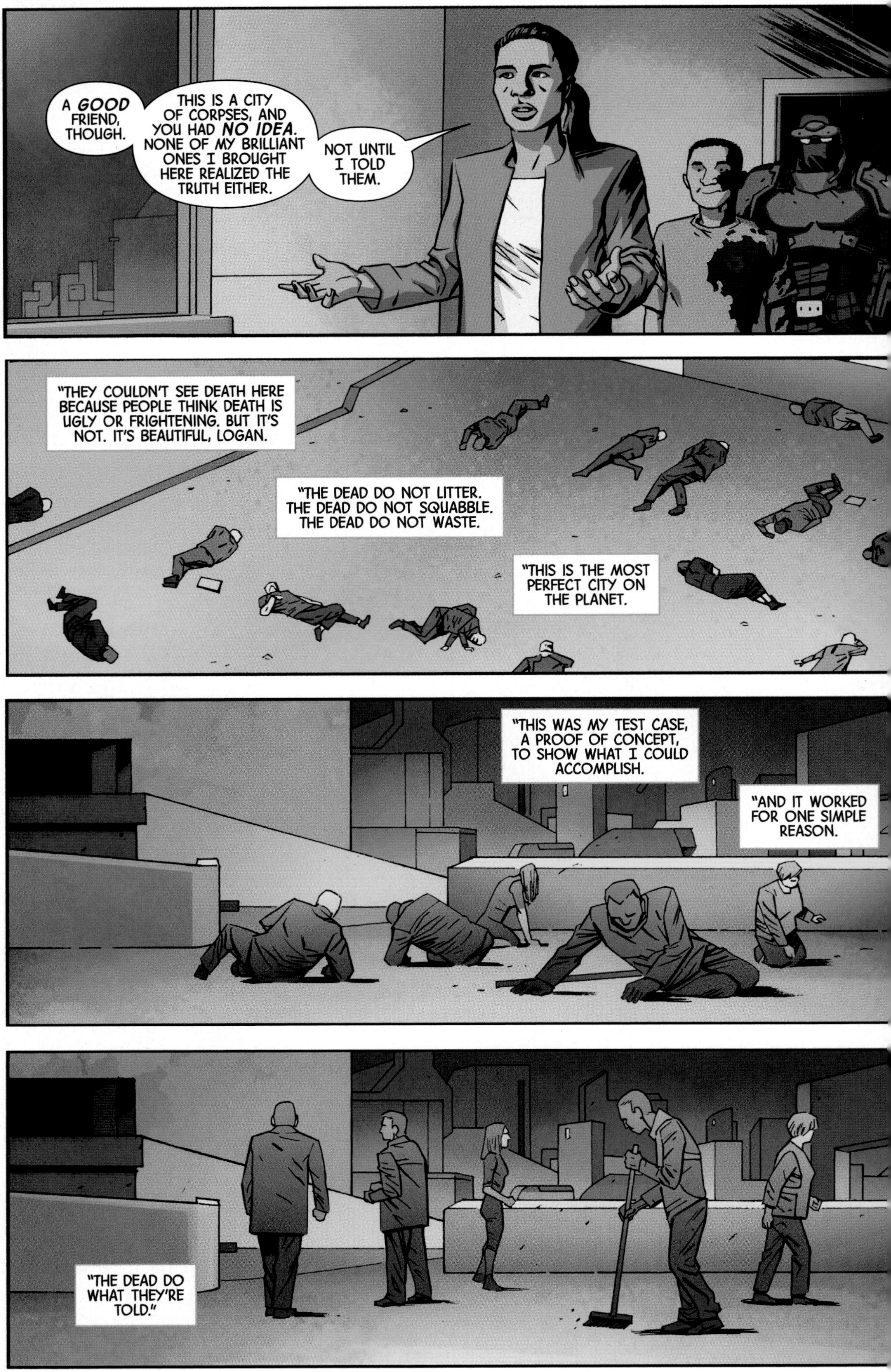
A GOOD FRIEND, THOUGH.
THIS IS A CITY OF CORPSES, AND YOU HAD NO IDEA. NONE OF MY BRILLIANT ONES I BROUGHT HERE REALIZED THE TRUTH EITHER.
NOT UNTIL I TOLD THEM.
"THEY COULDN'T SEE DEATH HERE BECAUSE PEOPLE THINK DEATH IS UGLY OR FRIGHTENING. BUT IT'S NOT. IT'S BEAUTIFUL, LOGAN.
"THE DEAD DO NOT LITTER. THE DEAD DO NOT SQUABBLE. THE DEAD DO NOT WASTE.
"THIS IS THE MOST PERFECT CITY ON THE PLANET.
"THIS WAS MY TEST CASE, A PROOF OF CONCEPT, TO SHOW WHAT I COULD ACCOMPLISH.
"AND IT WORKED FOR ONE SIMPLE REASON.
"THE DEAD DO WHAT THEY'RE TOLD."

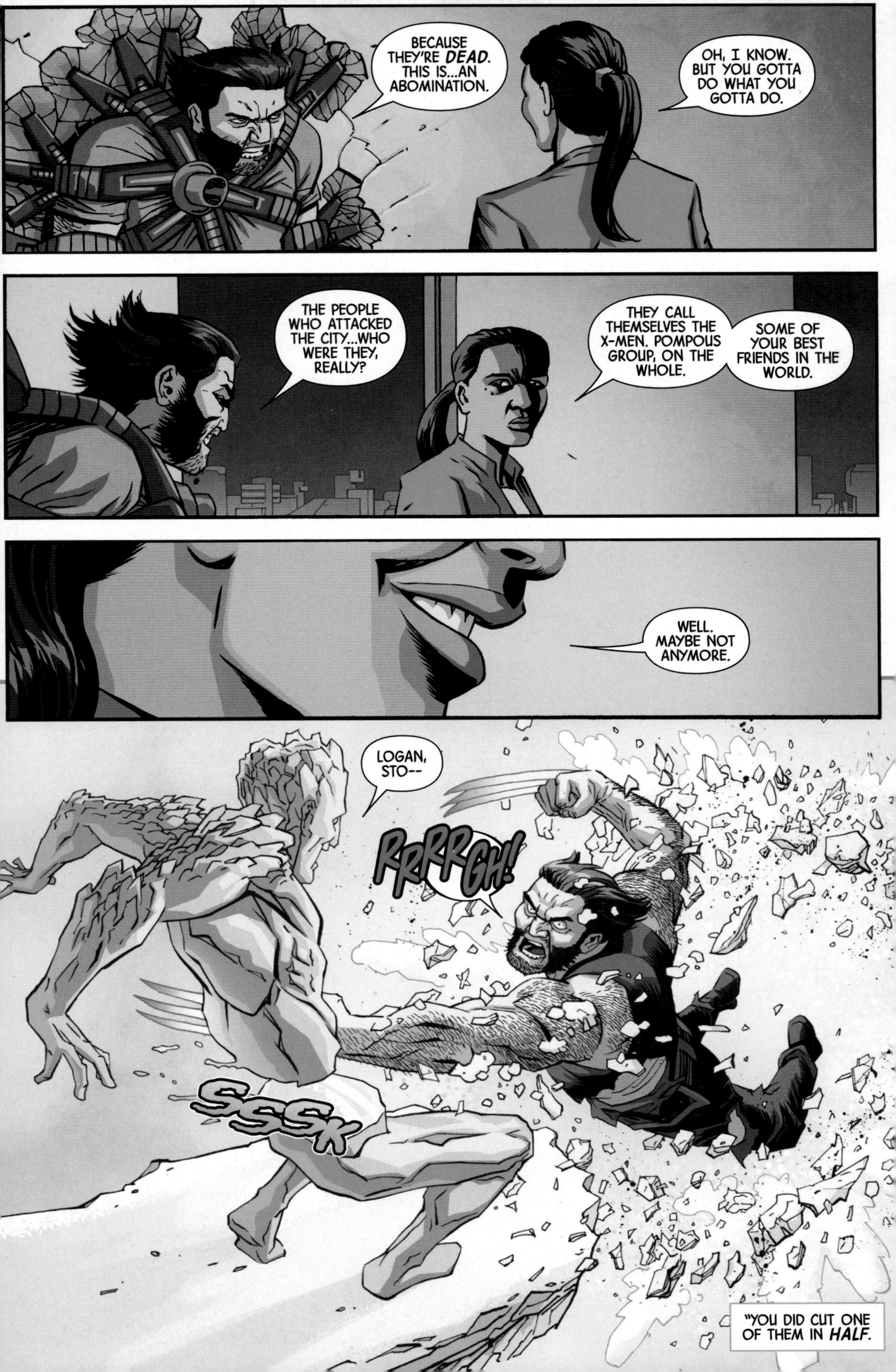
BECAUSE THEY'RE DEAD. THIS IS...AN ABOMINATION.
OH, I KNOW. BUT YOU GOTTA DO WHAT YOU GOTTA DO.
THE PEOPLE WHO ATTACKED THE CITY...WHO WERE THEY, REALLY?
THEY CALL THEMSELVES THE X-MEN. POMPOUS GROUP, ON THE WHOLE.
SOME OF YOUR BEST FRIENDS IN THE WORLD.
WELL. MAYBE NOT ANYMORE.
LOGAN, STO--
RRRRGH!
SSSK
"YOU DID CUT ONE OF THEM IN HALF.

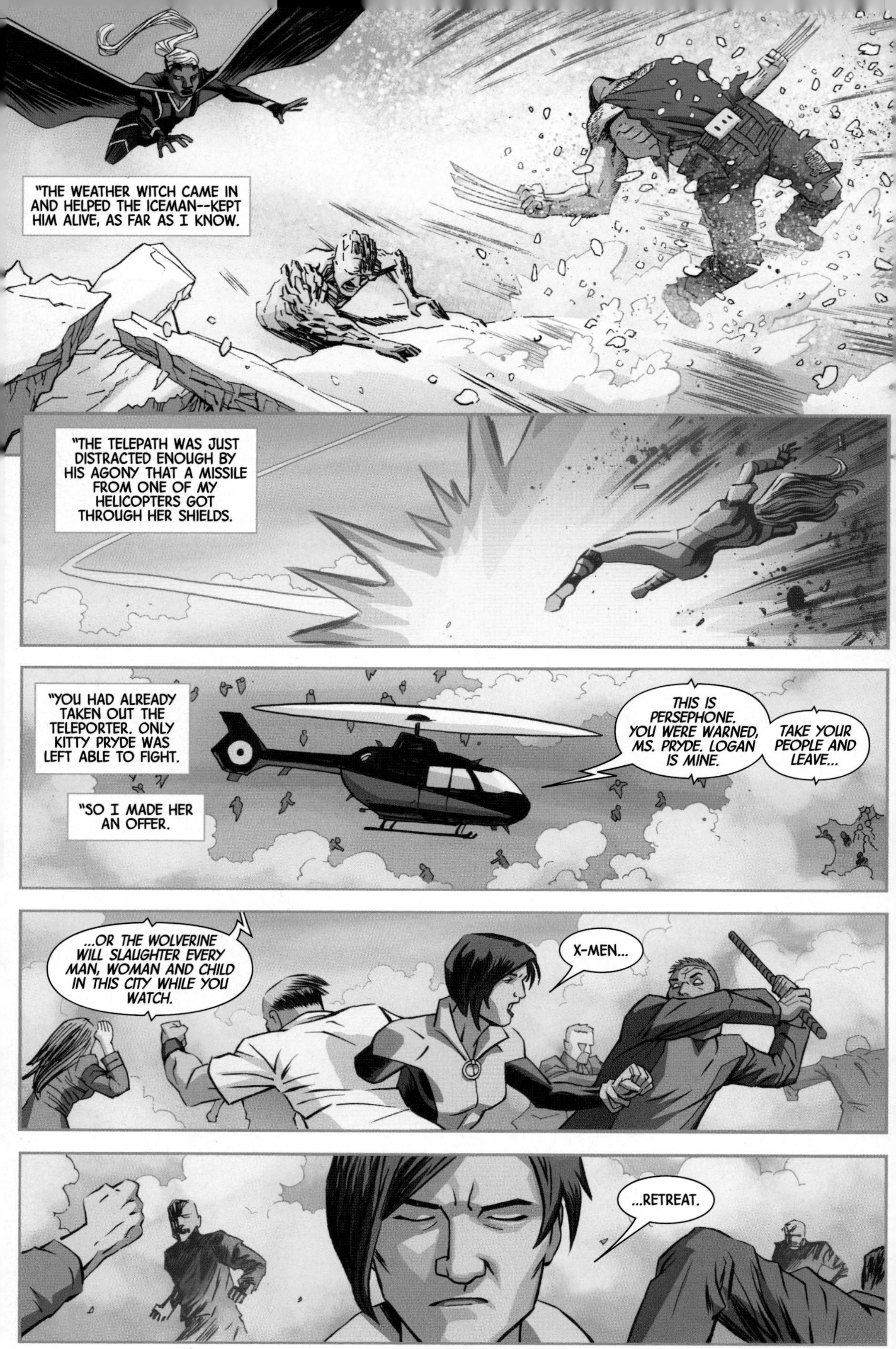
"THE WEATHER WITCH CAME IN AND HELPED THE ICEMAN--KEPT HIM ALIVE, AS FAR AS I KNOW.
"THE TELEPATH WAS JUST DISTRACTED ENOUGH BY HIS AGONY THAT A MISSILE FROM ONE OF MY HELICOPTERS GOT THROUGH HER SHIELDS.
"YOU HAD ALREADY TAKEN OUT THE TELEPORTER. ONLY KITTY PRYDE WAS LEFT ABLE TO FIGHT.
"SO I MADE HER AN OFFER.
THIS IS PERSEPHONE. YOU WERE WARNED, MS. PRYDE. LOGAN IS MINE.
TAKE YOUR PEOPLE AND LEAVE...
...OR THE WOLVERINE WILL SLAUGHTER EVERY MAN, WOMAN AND CHILD IN THIS CITY WHILE YOU WATCH.
X-MEN...
...RETREAT.

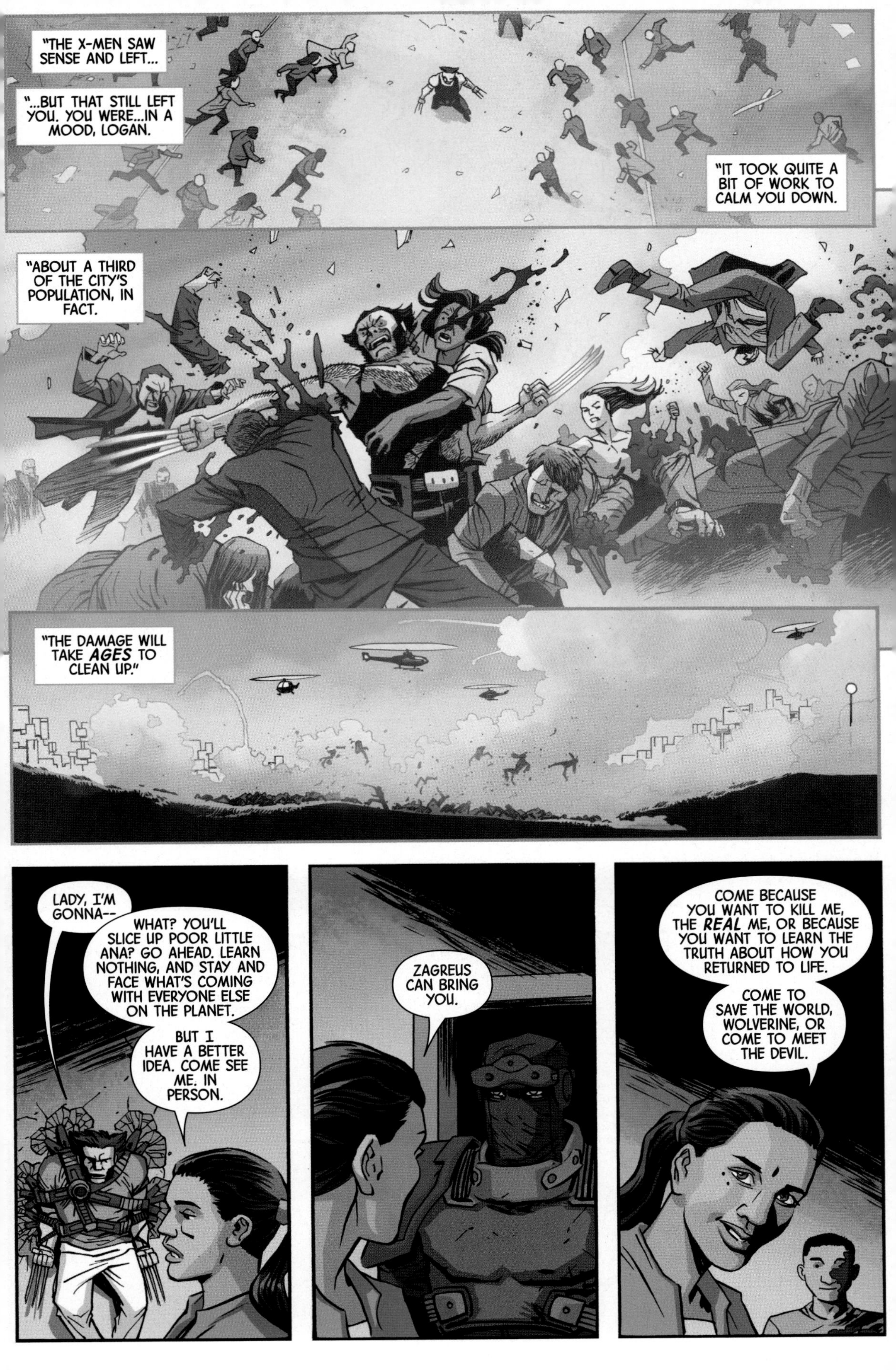
"THE X-MEN SAW SENSE AND LEFT...
"...BUT THAT STILL LEFT YOU. YOU WERE...IN A MOOD, LOGAN.
"IT TOOK QUITE A BIT OF WORK TO CALM YOU DOWN.
"ABOUT A THIRD OF THE CITY'S POPULATION, IN FACT.
"THE DAMAGE WILL TAKE *AGES* TO CLEAN UP."
LADY, I'M GONNA--
WHAT? YOU'LL SLICE UP POOR LITTLE ANA? GO AHEAD. LEARN NOTHING, AND STAY AND FACE WHAT'S COMING WITH EVERYONE ELSE ON THE PLANET.
BUT I HAVE A BETTER IDEA. COME SEE ME. IN PERSON.
ZAGREUS CAN BRING YOU.
COME BECAUSE YOU WANT TO KILL ME, THE *REAL* ME, OR BECAUSE YOU WANT TO LEARN THE TRUTH ABOUT HOW YOU RETURNED TO LIFE.
COME TO SAVE THE WORLD, WOLVERINE, OR COME TO MEET THE DEVIL.

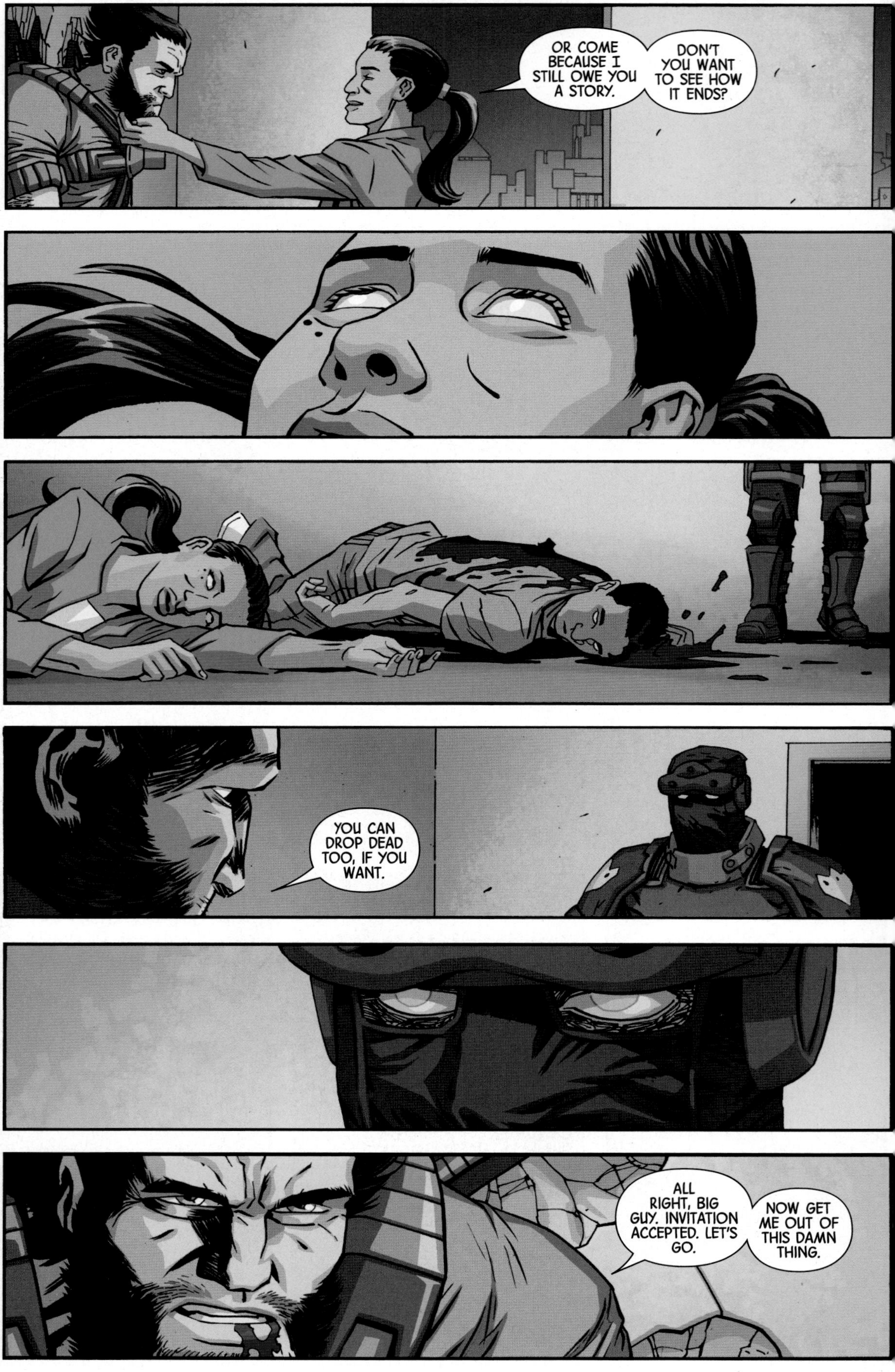
OR COME BECAUSE I STILL OWE YOU A STORY.
DON'T YOU WANT TO SEE HOW IT ENDS?
YOU CAN DROP DEAD TOO, IF YOU WANT.
ALL RIGHT, BIG GUY. INVITATION ACCEPTED. LET'S GO.
NOW GET ME OUT OF THIS DAMN THING.

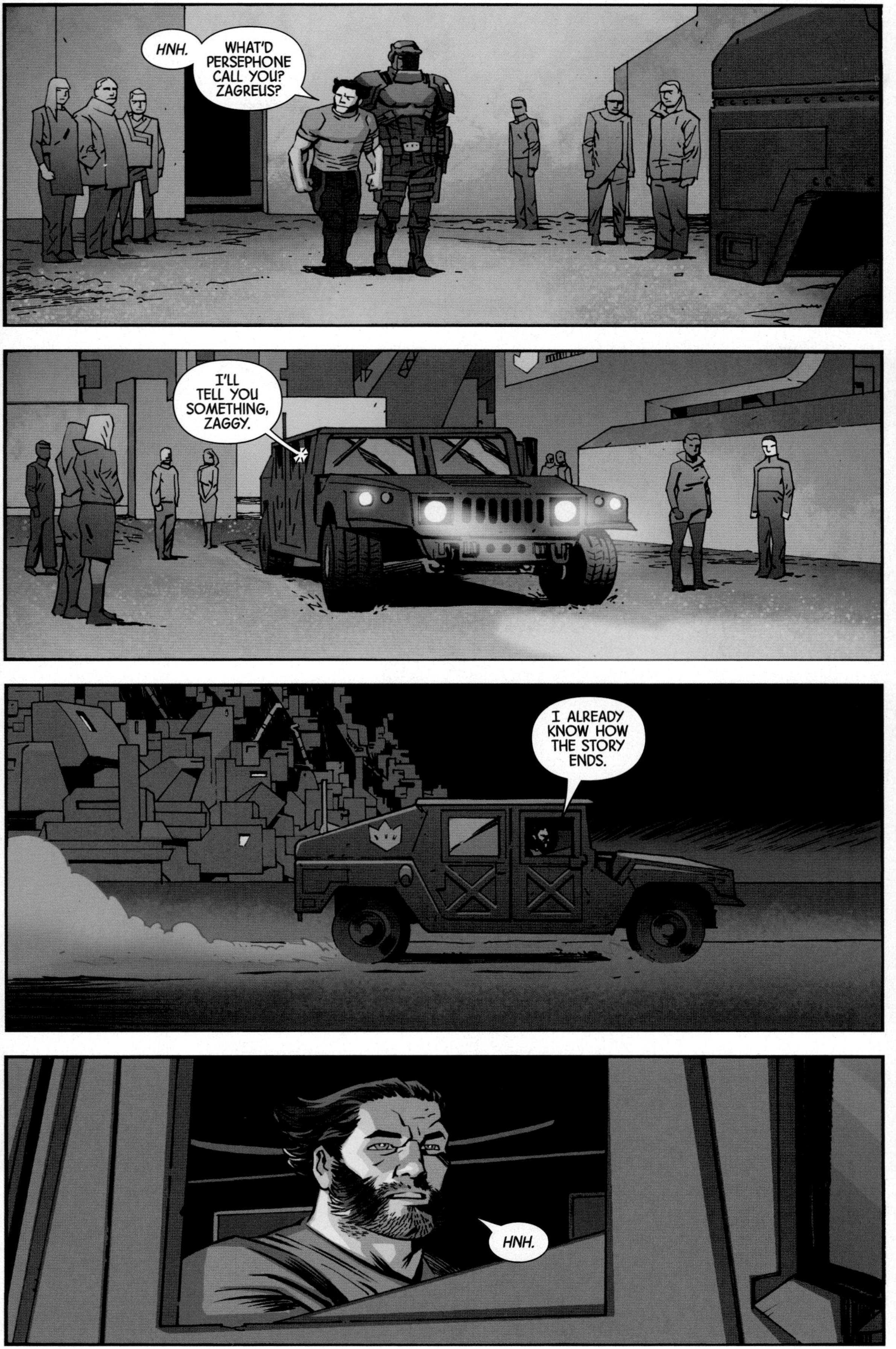
HNH.
WHAT'D PERSEPHONE CALL YOU? ZAGREUS?
I'LL TELL YOU SOMETHING, ZAGGY.
I ALREADY KNOW HOW THE STORY ENDS.
HNH.

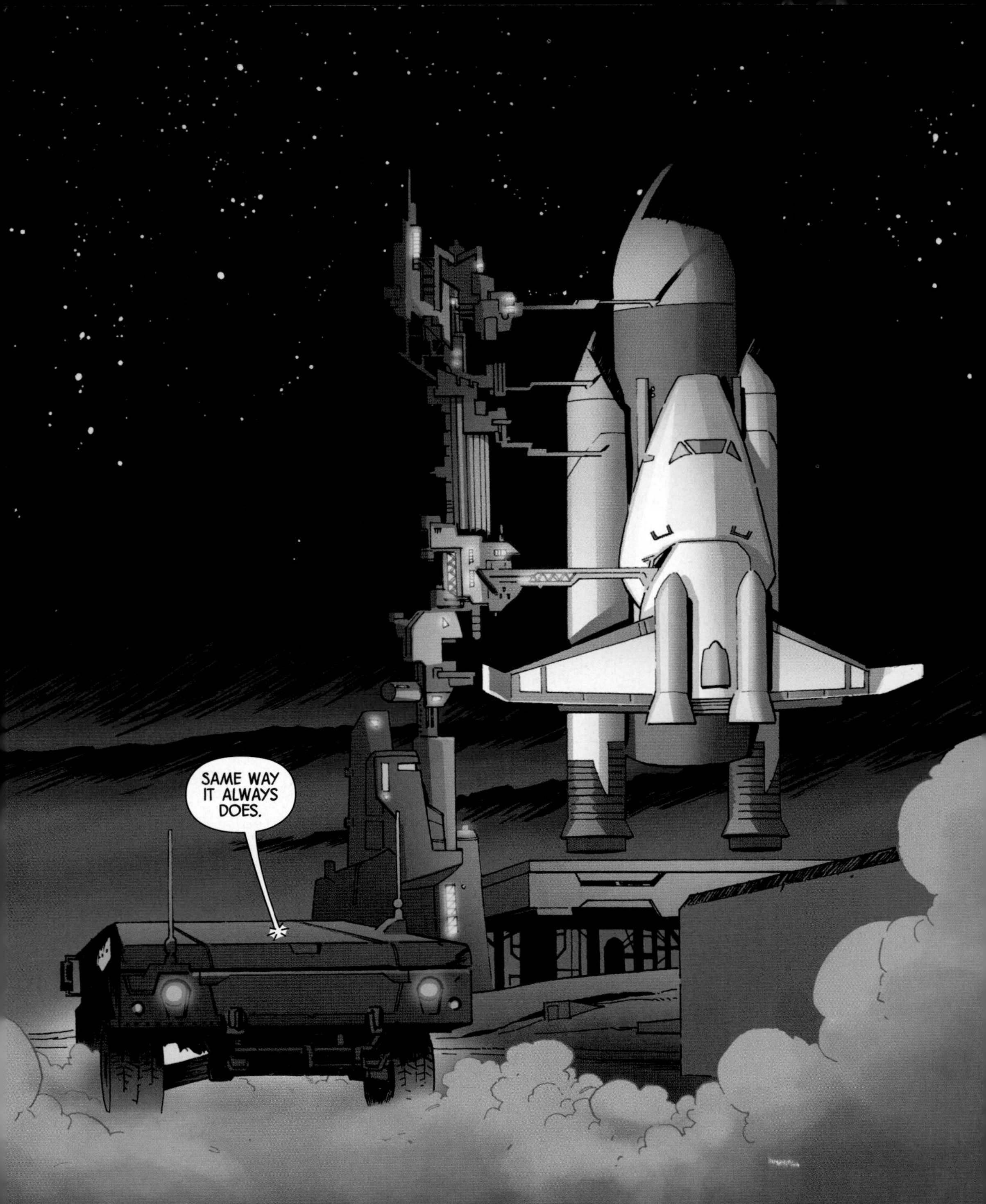
SAME WAY IT ALWAYS DOES.

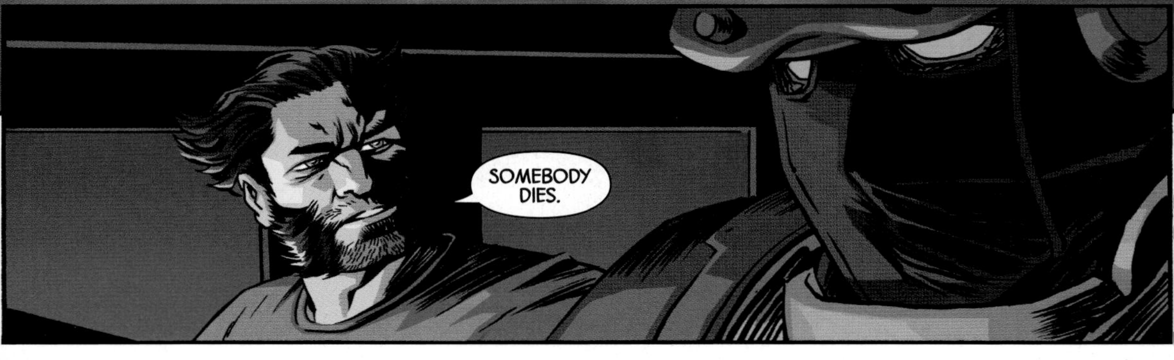
SOMEBODY DIES.

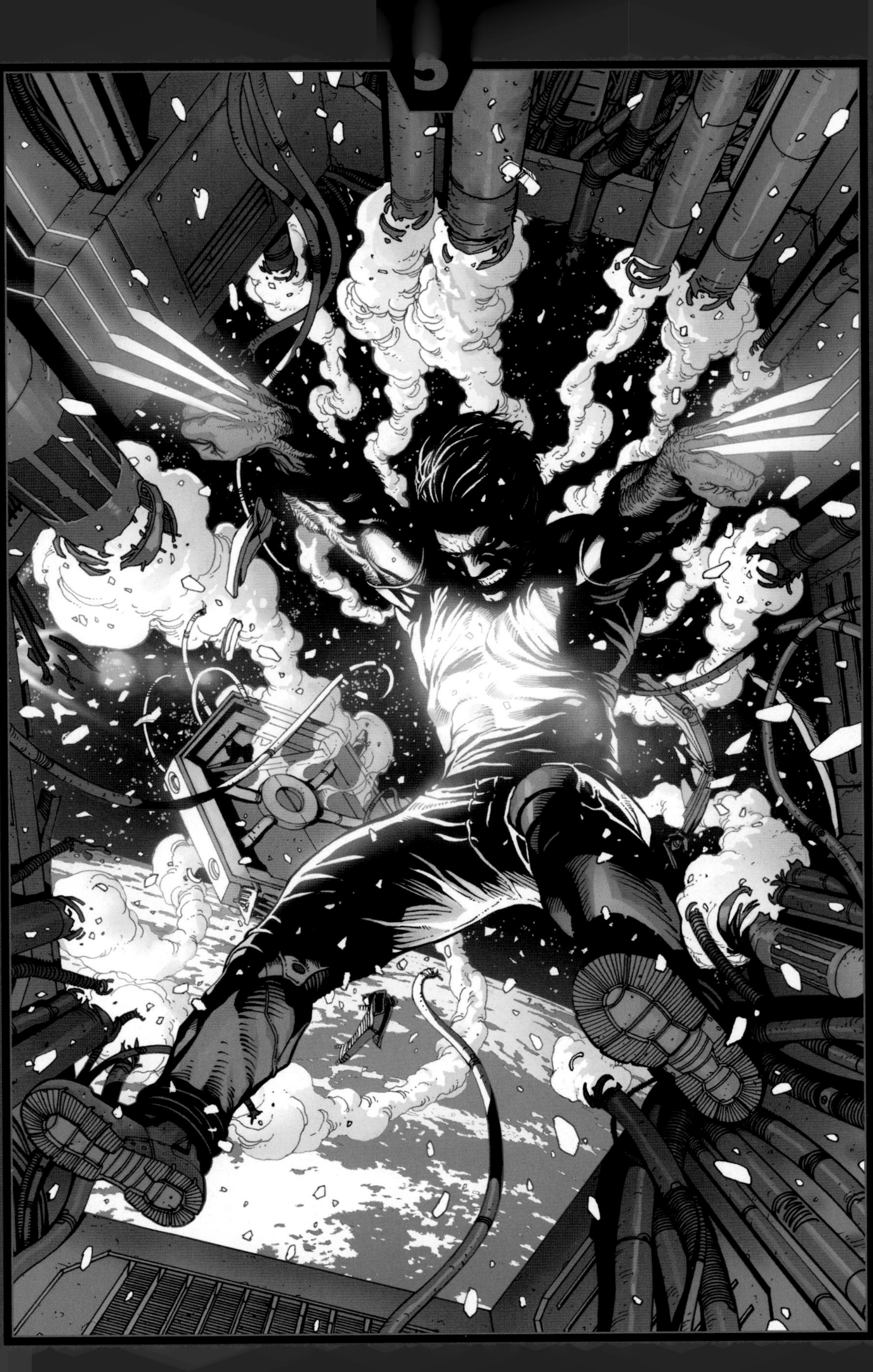

CHAPTER FIVE
HEAVEN

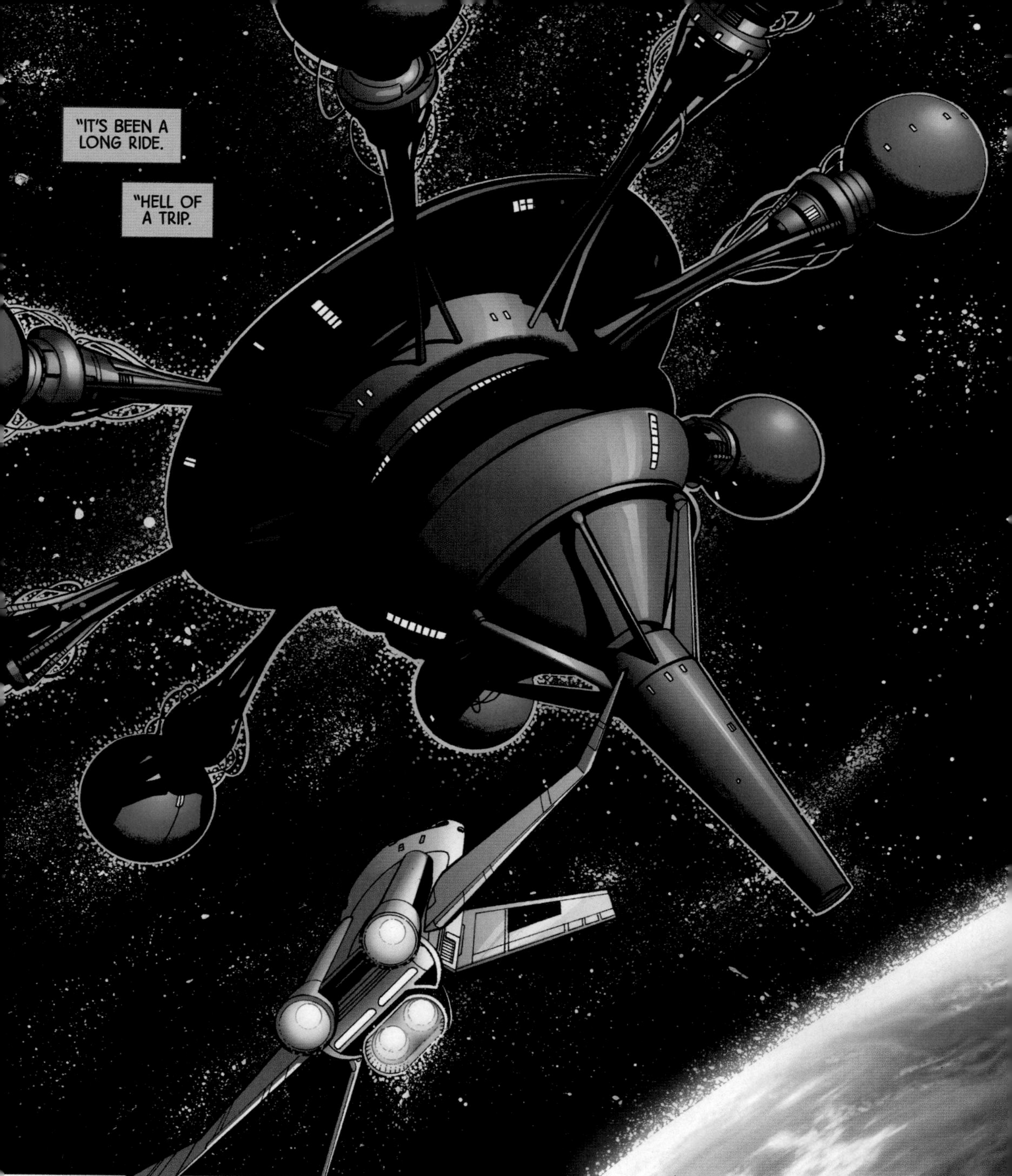
"IT'S BEEN A LONG RIDE.
"HELL OF A TRIP.

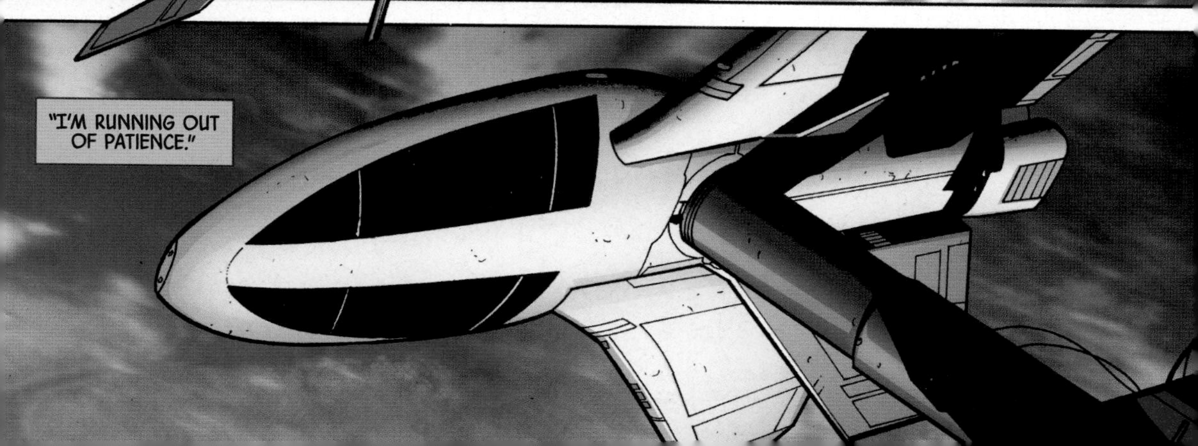
"I'M RUNNING OUT OF PATIENCE."

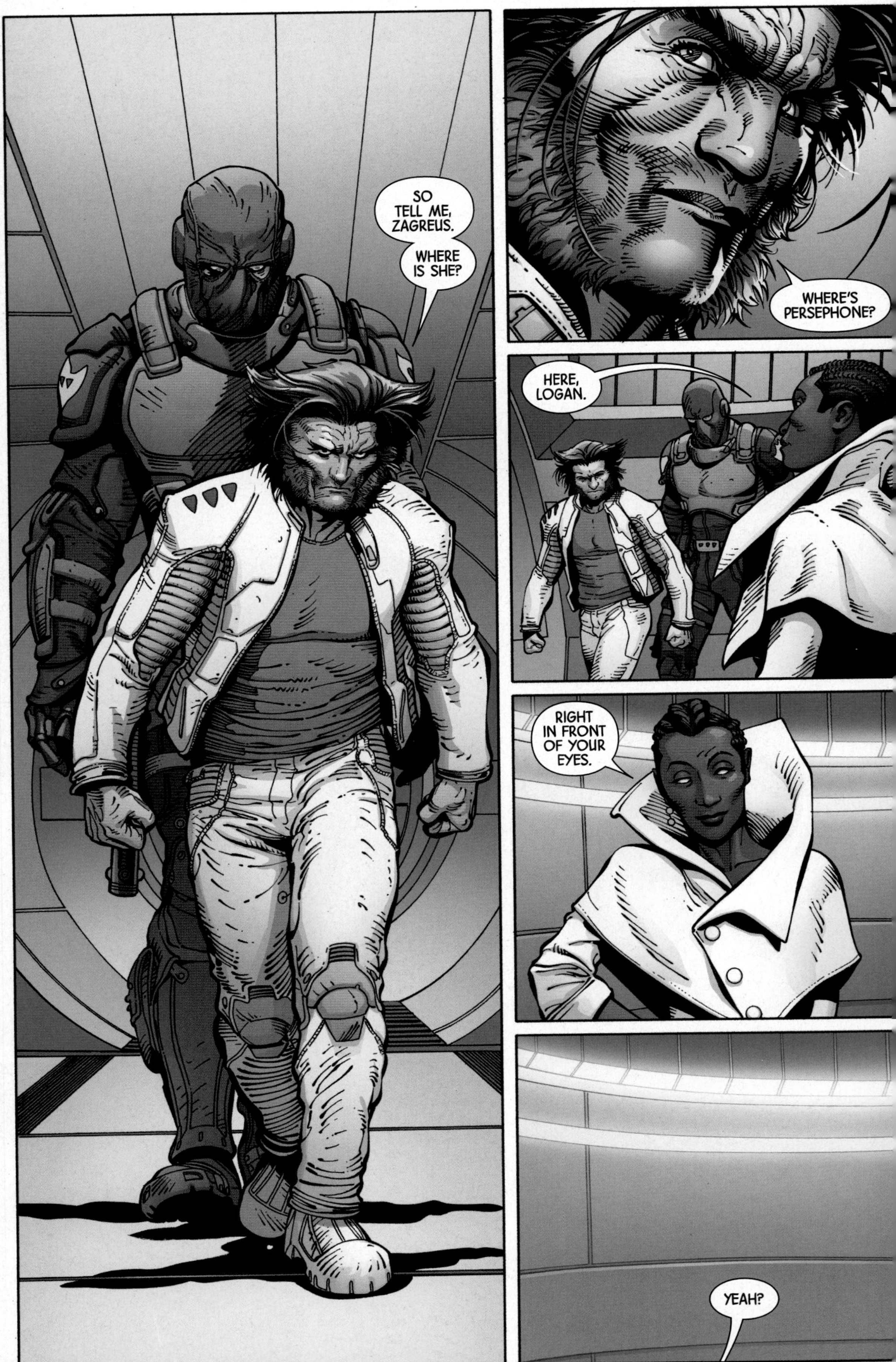
SO TELL ME, ZAGREUS.
WHERE IS SHE?
WHERE'S PERSEPHONE?
HERE, LOGAN.
RIGHT IN FRONT OF YOUR EYES.
YEAH?

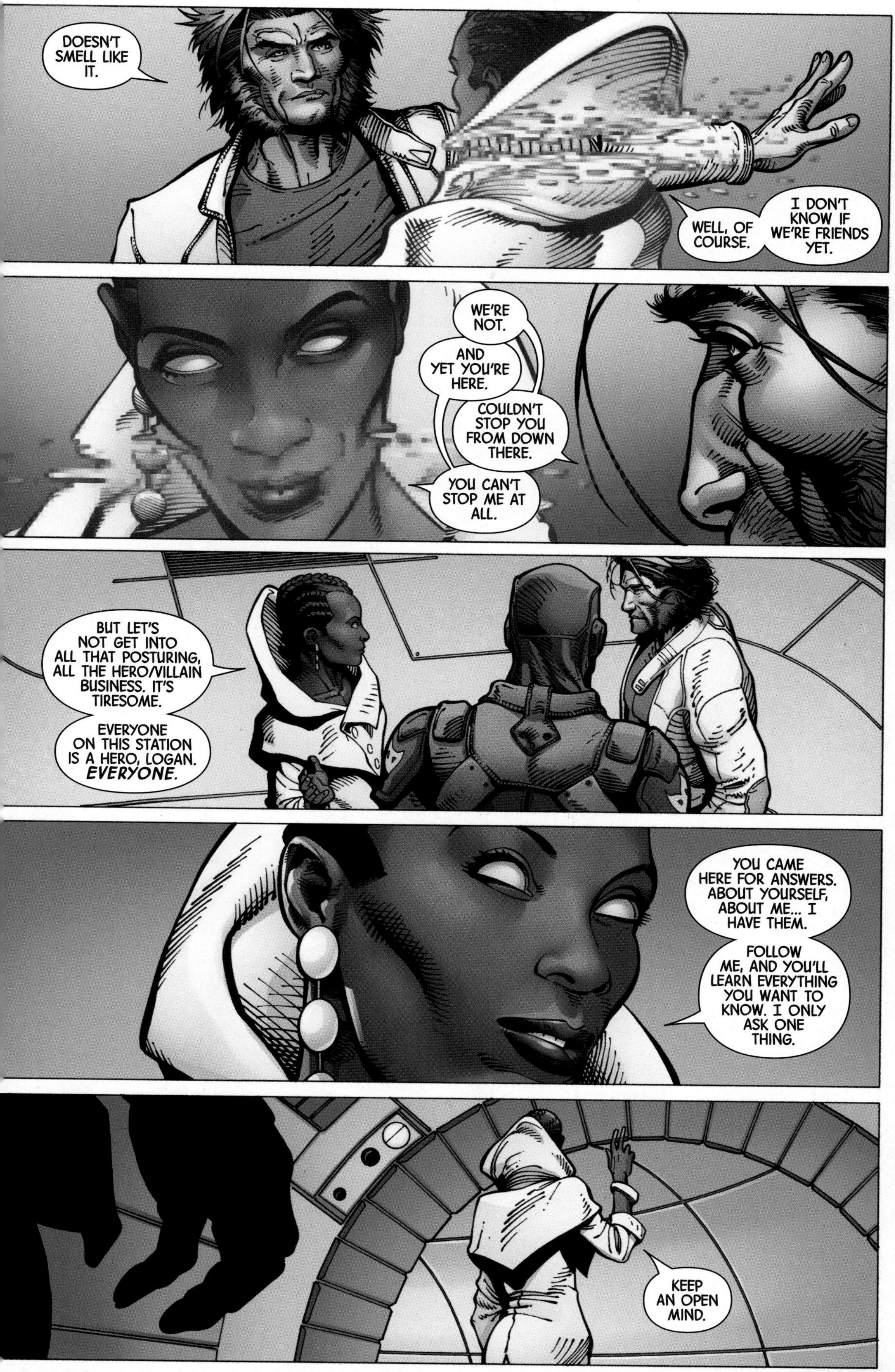
DOESN'T SMELL LIKE IT.
WELL, OF COURSE.
I DON'T KNOW IF WE'RE FRIENDS YET.
WE'RE NOT.
AND YET YOU'RE HERE.
COULDN'T STOP YOU FROM DOWN THERE.
YOU CAN'T STOP ME AT ALL.
BUT LET'S NOT GET INTO ALL THAT POSTURING, ALL THE HERO/VILLAIN BUSINESS. IT'S TIRESOME.
EVERYONE ON THIS STATION IS A HERO, LOGAN. *EVERYONE.*
YOU CAME HERE FOR ANSWERS. ABOUT YOURSELF, ABOUT ME... I HAVE THEM.
FOLLOW ME, AND YOU'LL LEARN EVERYTHING YOU WANT TO KNOW. I ONLY ASK ONE THING.
KEEP AN OPEN MIND.

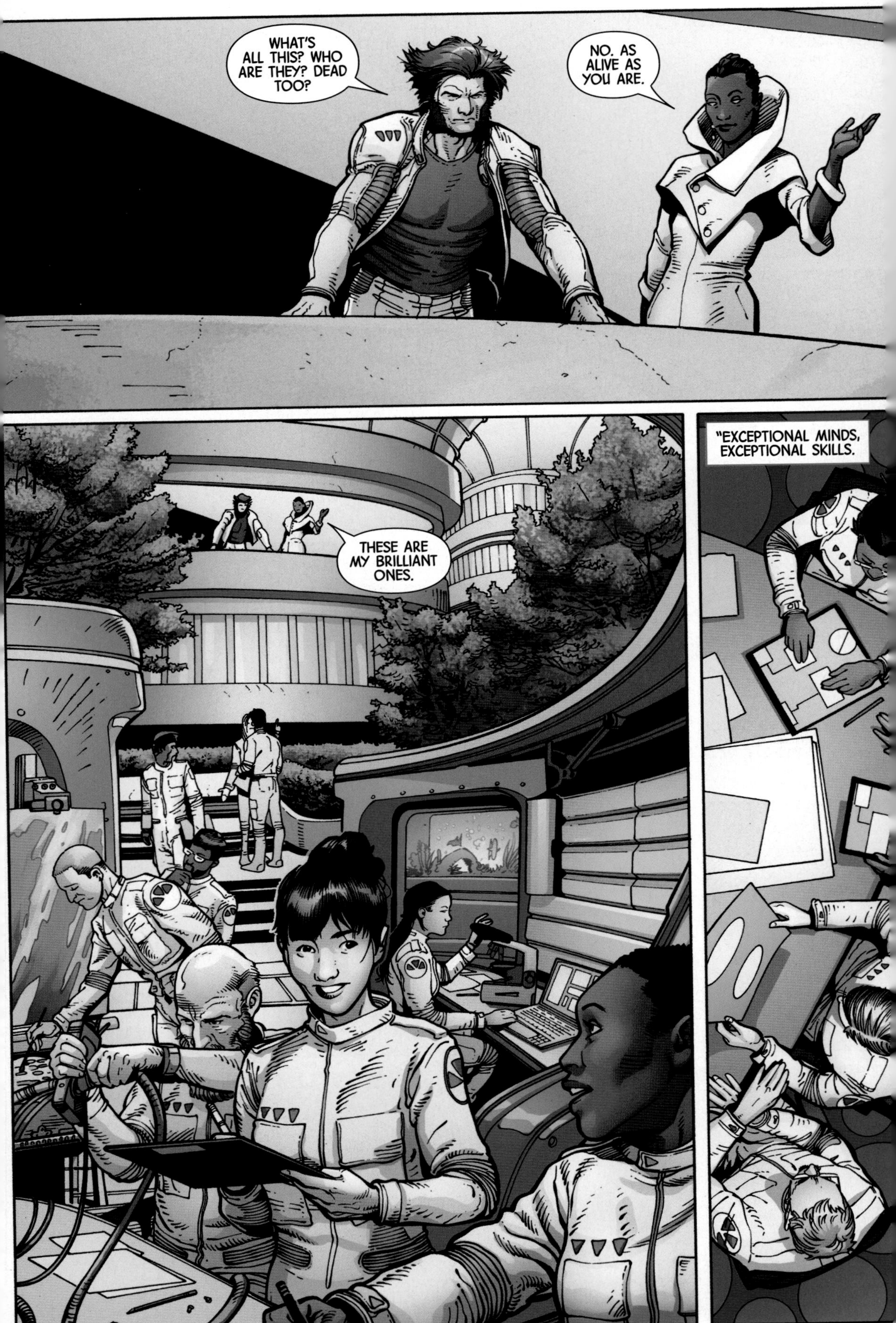
WHAT'S ALL THIS? WHO ARE THEY? DEAD TOO?
NO. AS ALIVE AS YOU ARE.
THESE ARE MY BRILLIANT ONES.
"EXCEPTIONAL MINDS, EXCEPTIONAL SKILLS.

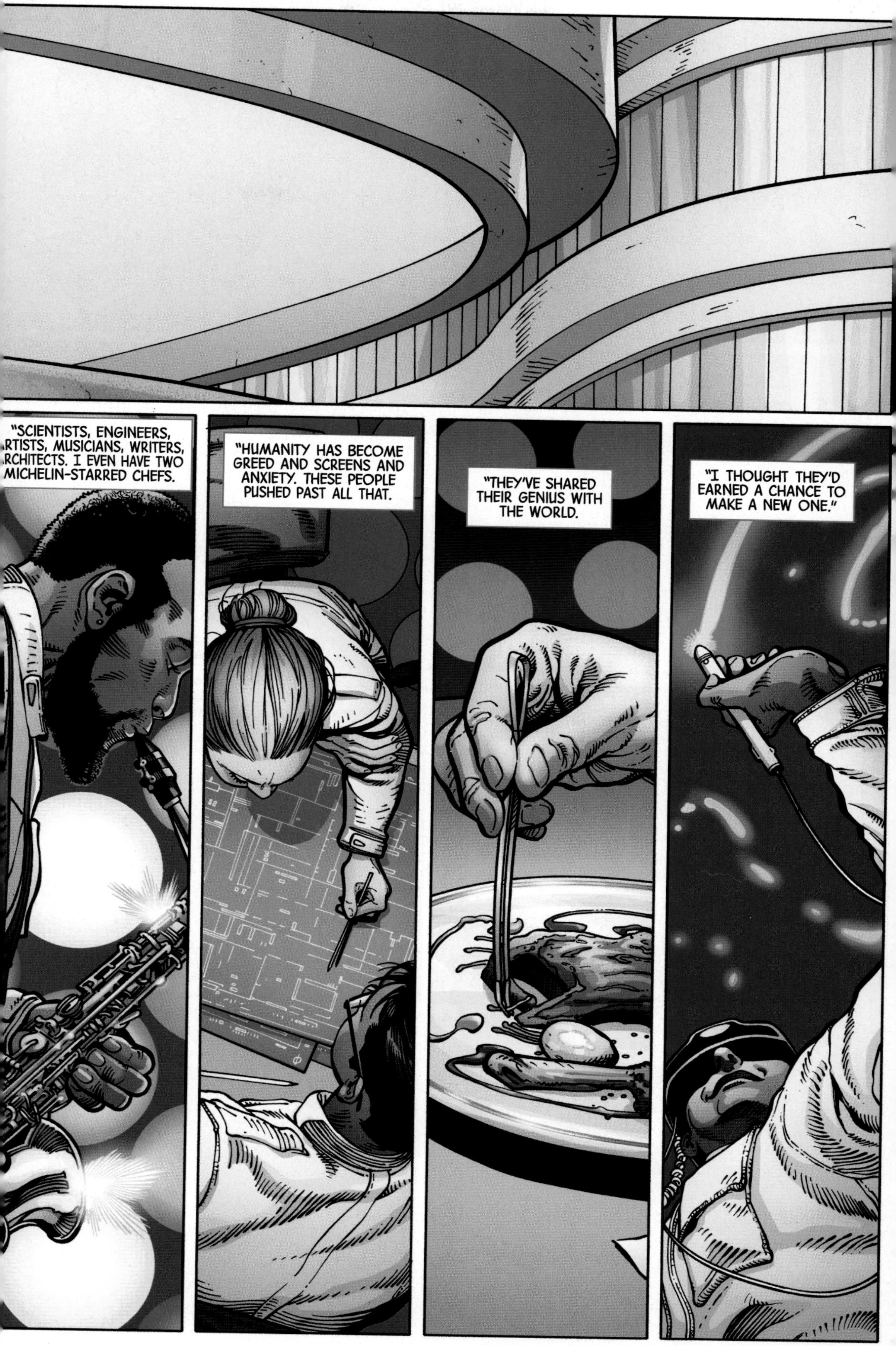
"SCIENTISTS, ENGINEERS, RTISTS, MUSICIANS, WRITERS, RCHITECTS. I EVEN HAVE TWO MICHELIN-STARRED CHEFS.
"HUMANITY HAS BECOME GREED AND SCREENS AND ANXIETY. THESE PEOPLE PUSHED PAST ALL THAT.
"THEY'VE SHARED THEIR GENIUS WITH THE WORLD.
"I THOUGHT THEY'D EARNED A CHANCE TO MAKE A NEW ONE."

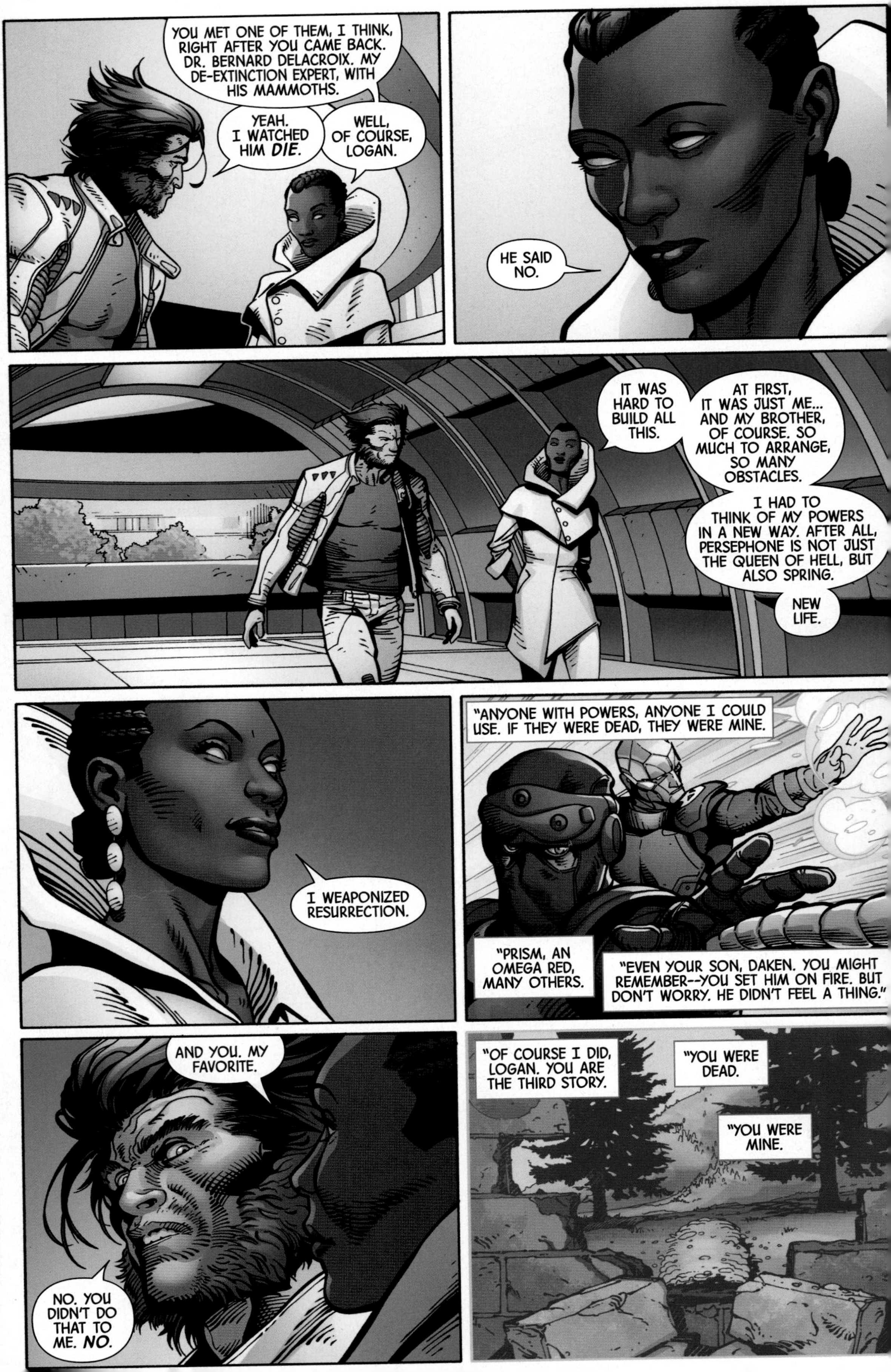
YOU MET ONE OF THEM, I THINK, RIGHT AFTER YOU CAME BACK. DR. BERNARD DELACROIX. MY DE-EXTINCTION EXPERT, WITH HIS MAMMOTHS.
YEAH. I WATCHED HIM *DIE*.
WELL, OF COURSE, LOGAN.
HE SAID NO.
IT WAS HARD TO BUILD ALL THIS.
AT FIRST, IT WAS JUST ME... AND MY BROTHER, OF COURSE. SO MUCH TO ARRANGE, SO MANY OBSTACLES.
I HAD TO THINK OF MY POWERS IN A NEW WAY. AFTER ALL, PERSEPHONE IS NOT JUST THE QUEEN OF HELL, BUT ALSO SPRING.
NEW LIFE.
I WEAPONIZED RESURRECTION.
"ANYONE WITH POWERS, ANYONE I COULD USE. IF THEY WERE DEAD, THEY WERE MINE.
"PRISM, AN OMEGA RED, MANY OTHERS.
"EVEN YOUR SON, DAKEN. YOU MIGHT REMEMBER--YOU SET HIM ON FIRE. BUT DON'T WORRY. HE DIDN'T FEEL A THING."
AND YOU. MY FAVORITE.
NO. YOU DIDN'T DO THAT TO ME. ***NO***.
"OF COURSE I DID, LOGAN. YOU ARE THE THIRD STORY.
"YOU WERE DEAD.
"YOU WERE MINE.

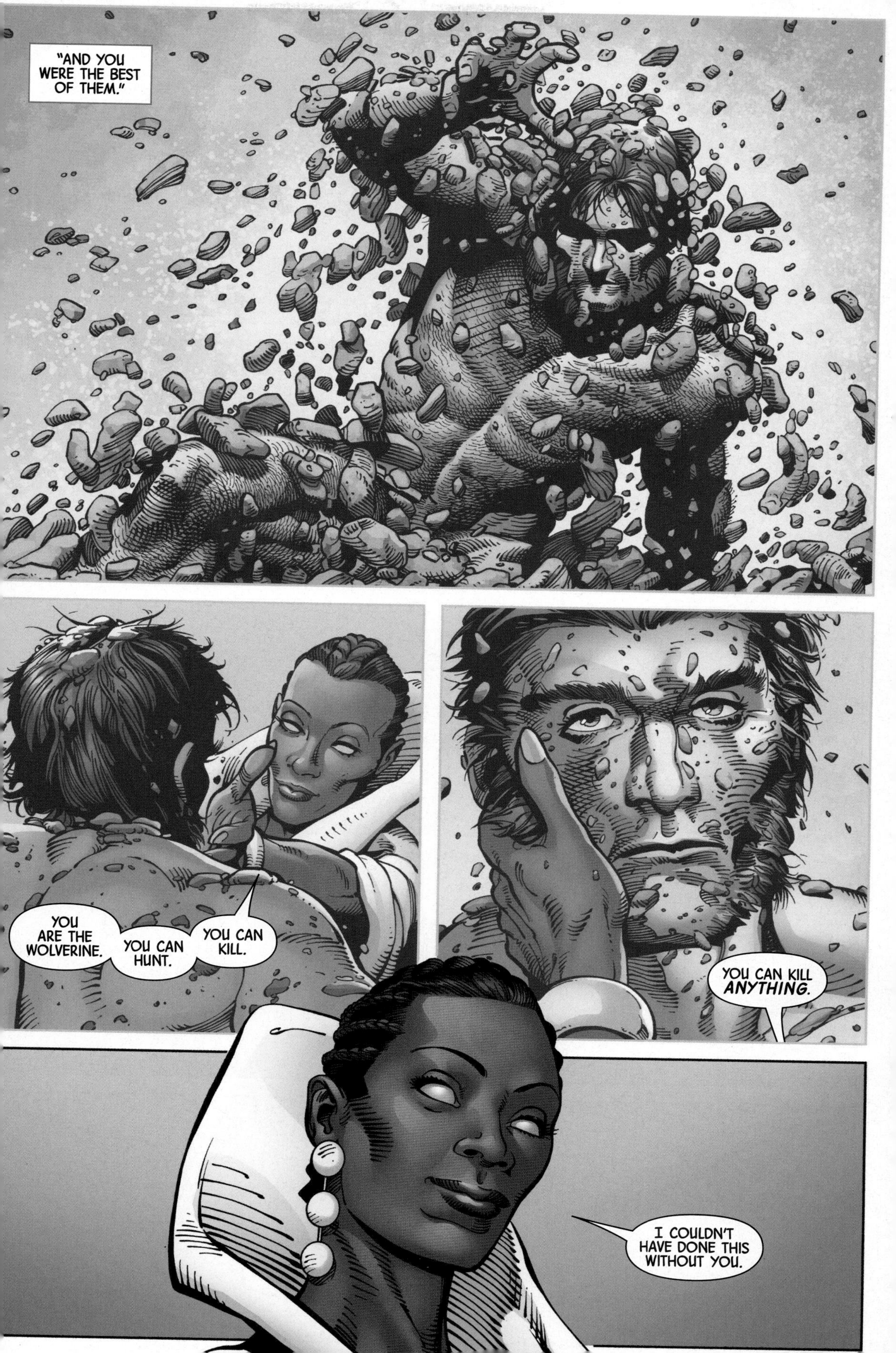
"AND YOU WERE THE BEST OF THEM."
YOU ARE THE WOLVERINE.
YOU CAN HUNT.
YOU CAN KILL.
YOU CAN KILL *ANYTHING*.
I COULDN'T HAVE DONE THIS WITHOUT YOU.

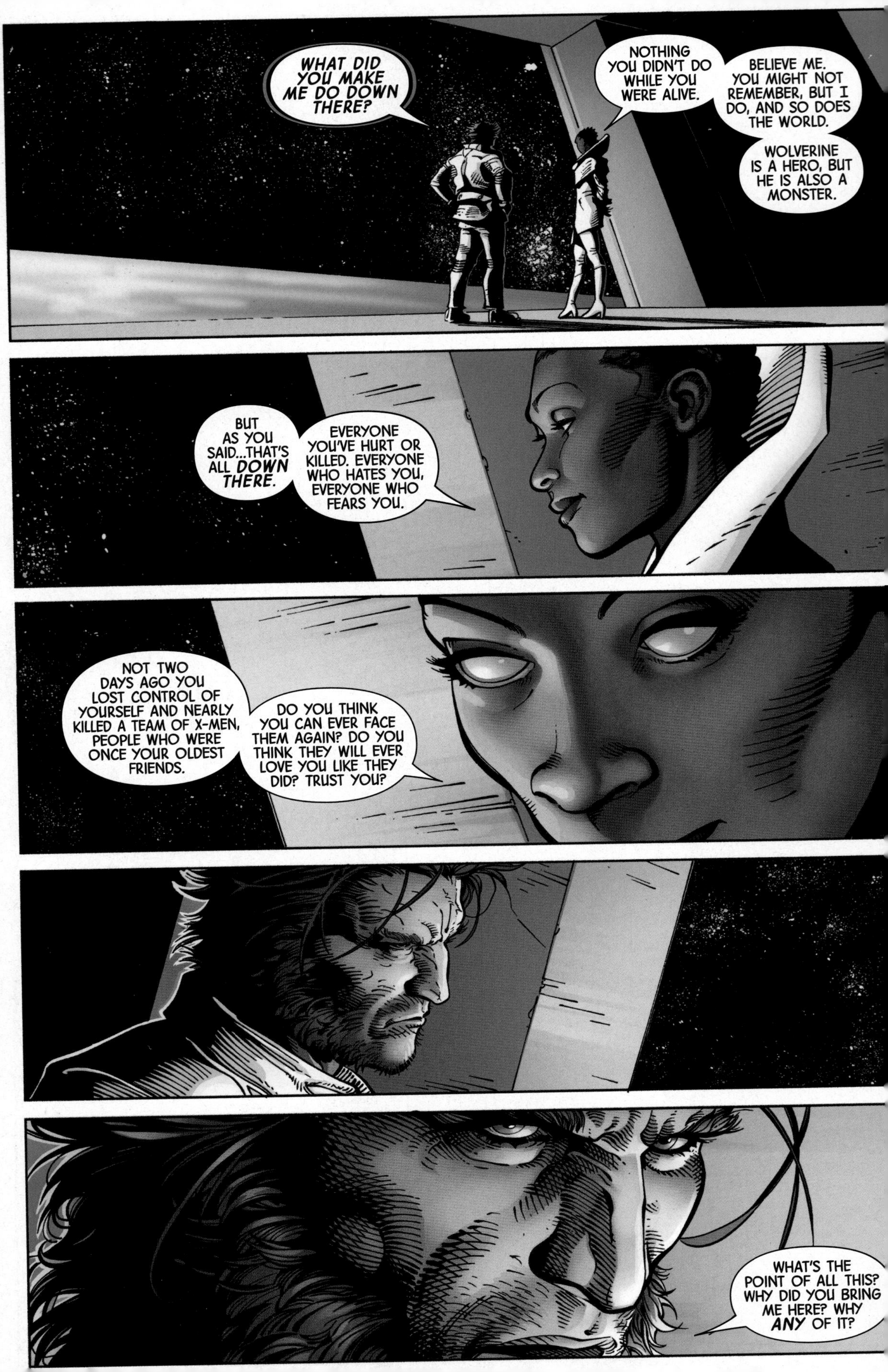
WHAT DID YOU MAKE ME DO DOWN THERE?
NOTHING YOU DIDN'T DO WHILE YOU WERE ALIVE.
BELIEVE ME. YOU MIGHT NOT REMEMBER, BUT I DO, AND SO DOES THE WORLD.
WOLVERINE IS A HERO, BUT HE IS ALSO A MONSTER.
BUT AS YOU SAID...THAT'S ALL DOWN THERE.
EVERYONE YOU'VE HURT OR KILLED. EVERYONE WHO HATES YOU, EVERYONE WHO FEARS YOU.
NOT TWO DAYS AGO YOU LOST CONTROL OF YOURSELF AND NEARLY KILLED A TEAM OF X-MEN, PEOPLE WHO WERE ONCE YOUR OLDEST FRIENDS.
DO YOU THINK YOU CAN EVER FACE THEM AGAIN? DO YOU THINK THEY WILL EVER LOVE YOU LIKE THEY DID? TRUST YOU?
WHAT'S THE POINT OF ALL THIS? WHY DID YOU BRING ME HERE? WHY ANY OF IT?

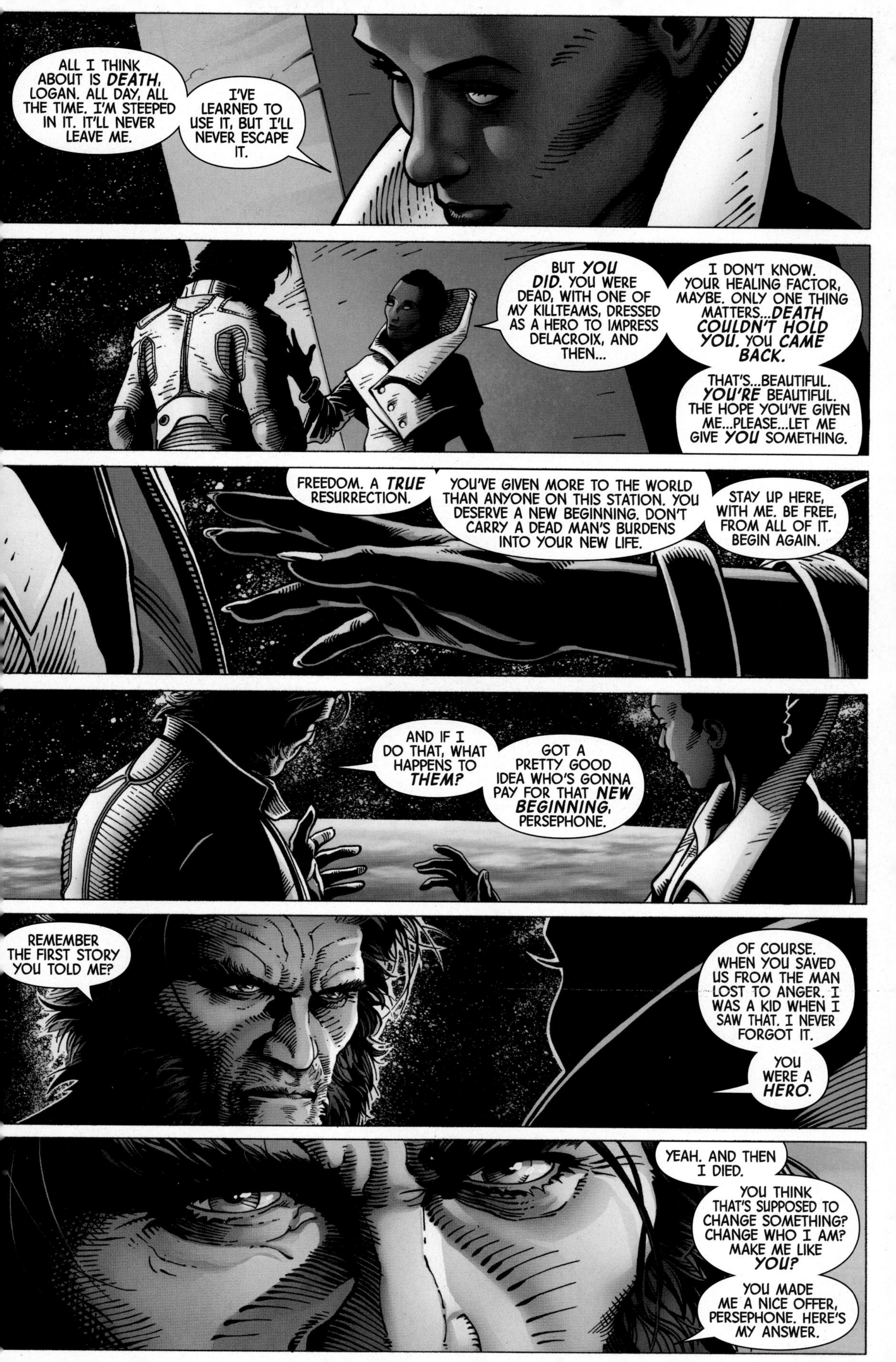
ALL I THINK ABOUT IS *DEATH*, LOGAN. ALL DAY, ALL THE TIME. I'M STEEPED IN IT. IT'LL NEVER LEAVE ME.
I'VE LEARNED TO USE IT, BUT I'LL NEVER ESCAPE IT.
BUT *YOU DID*. YOU WERE DEAD, WITH ONE OF MY KILLTEAMS, DRESSED AS A HERO TO IMPRESS DELACROIX, AND THEN...
I DON'T KNOW. YOUR HEALING FACTOR, MAYBE. ONLY ONE THING MATTERS...*DEATH COULDN'T HOLD YOU*. YOU *CAME BACK*.
THAT'S...BEAUTIFUL. *YOU'RE* BEAUTIFUL. THE HOPE YOU'VE GIVEN ME...PLEASE...LET ME GIVE *YOU* SOMETHING.
FREEDOM. A *TRUE* RESURRECTION.
YOU'VE GIVEN MORE TO THE WORLD THAN ANYONE ON THIS STATION. YOU DESERVE A NEW BEGINNING. DON'T CARRY A DEAD MAN'S BURDENS INTO YOUR NEW LIFE.
STAY UP HERE, WITH ME. BE FREE, FROM ALL OF IT. BEGIN AGAIN.
AND IF I DO THAT, WHAT HAPPENS TO *THEM?*
GOT A PRETTY GOOD IDEA WHO'S GONNA PAY FOR THAT *NEW BEGINNING*, PERSEPHONE.
REMEMBER THE FIRST STORY YOU TOLD ME?
OF COURSE. WHEN YOU SAVED US FROM THE MAN LOST TO ANGER. I WAS A KID WHEN I SAW THAT. I NEVER FORGOT IT.
YOU WERE A *HERO*.
YEAH. AND THEN I DIED.
YOU THINK THAT'S SUPPOSED TO CHANGE SOMETHING? CHANGE WHO I AM? MAKE ME LIKE *YOU?*
YOU MADE ME A NICE OFFER, PERSEPHONE. HERE'S MY ANSWER.

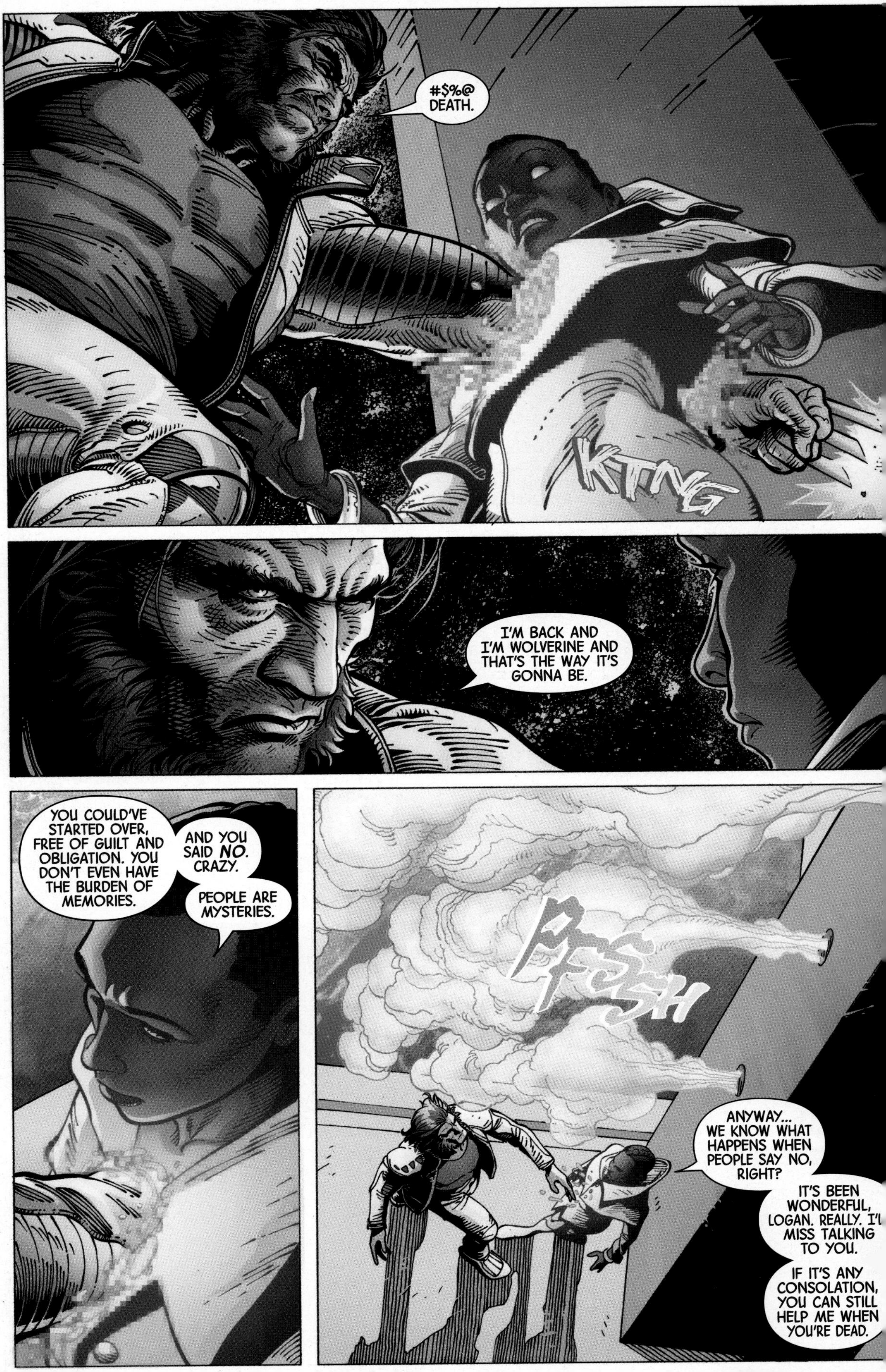

#$%@ DEATH.
KTING
I'M BACK AND I'M WOLVERINE AND THAT'S THE WAY IT'S GONNA BE.
YOU COULD'VE STARTED OVER, FREE OF GUILT AND OBLIGATION. YOU DON'T EVEN HAVE THE BURDEN OF MEMORIES.
AND YOU SAID NO. CRAZY.
PEOPLE ARE MYSTERIES.
PFSH
ANYWAY... WE KNOW WHAT HAPPENS WHEN PEOPLE SAY NO, RIGHT?
IT'S BEEN WONDERFUL, LOGAN. REALLY. I'L MISS TALKING TO YOU.
IF IT'S ANY CONSOLATION, YOU CAN STILL HELP ME WHEN YOU'RE DEAD.

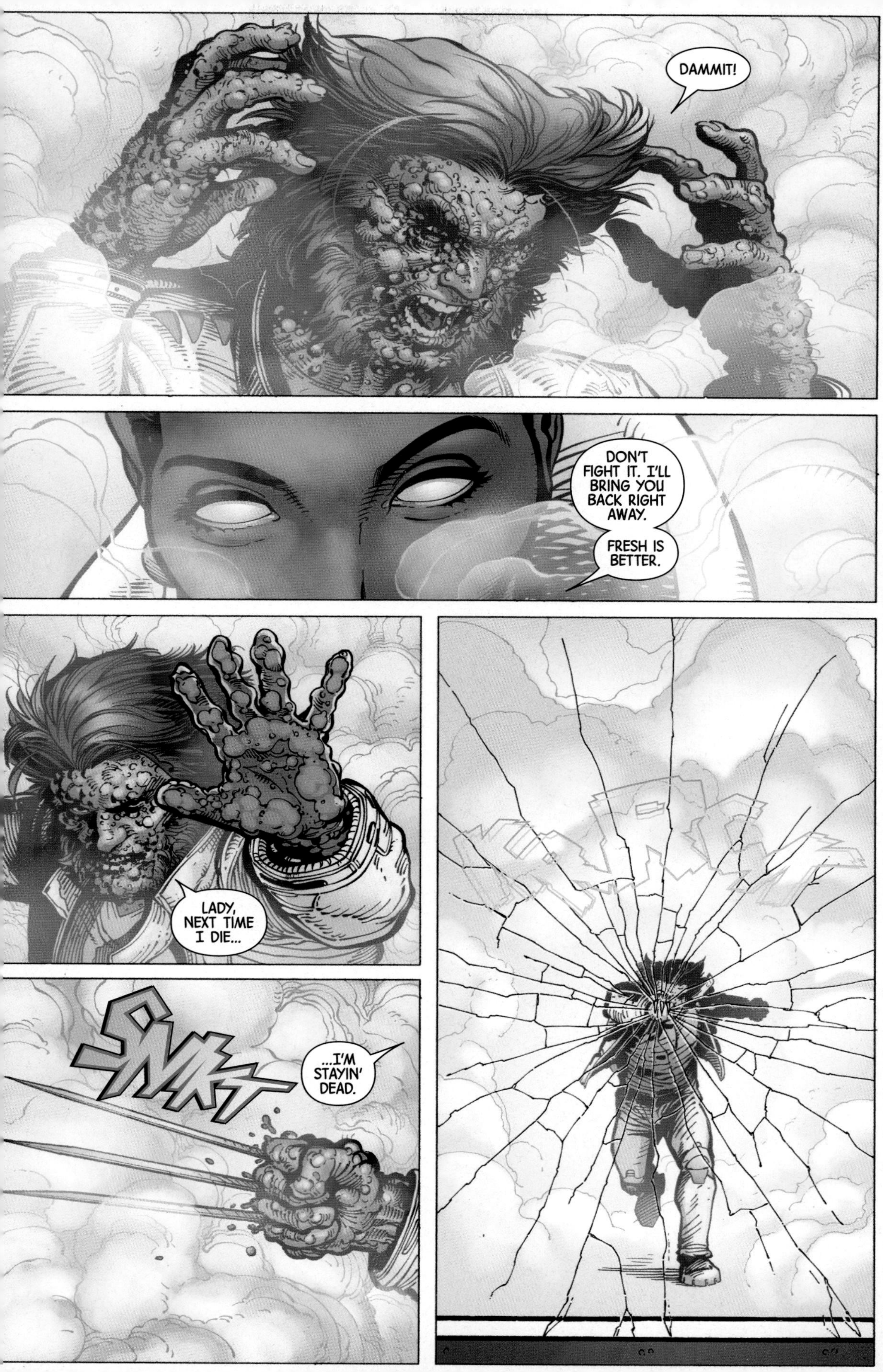
DAMMIT!
DON'T FIGHT IT. I'LL BRING YOU BACK RIGHT AWAY.
FRESH IS BETTER.
LADY, NEXT TIME I DIE...
SNIKT
...I'M STAYIN' DEAD.

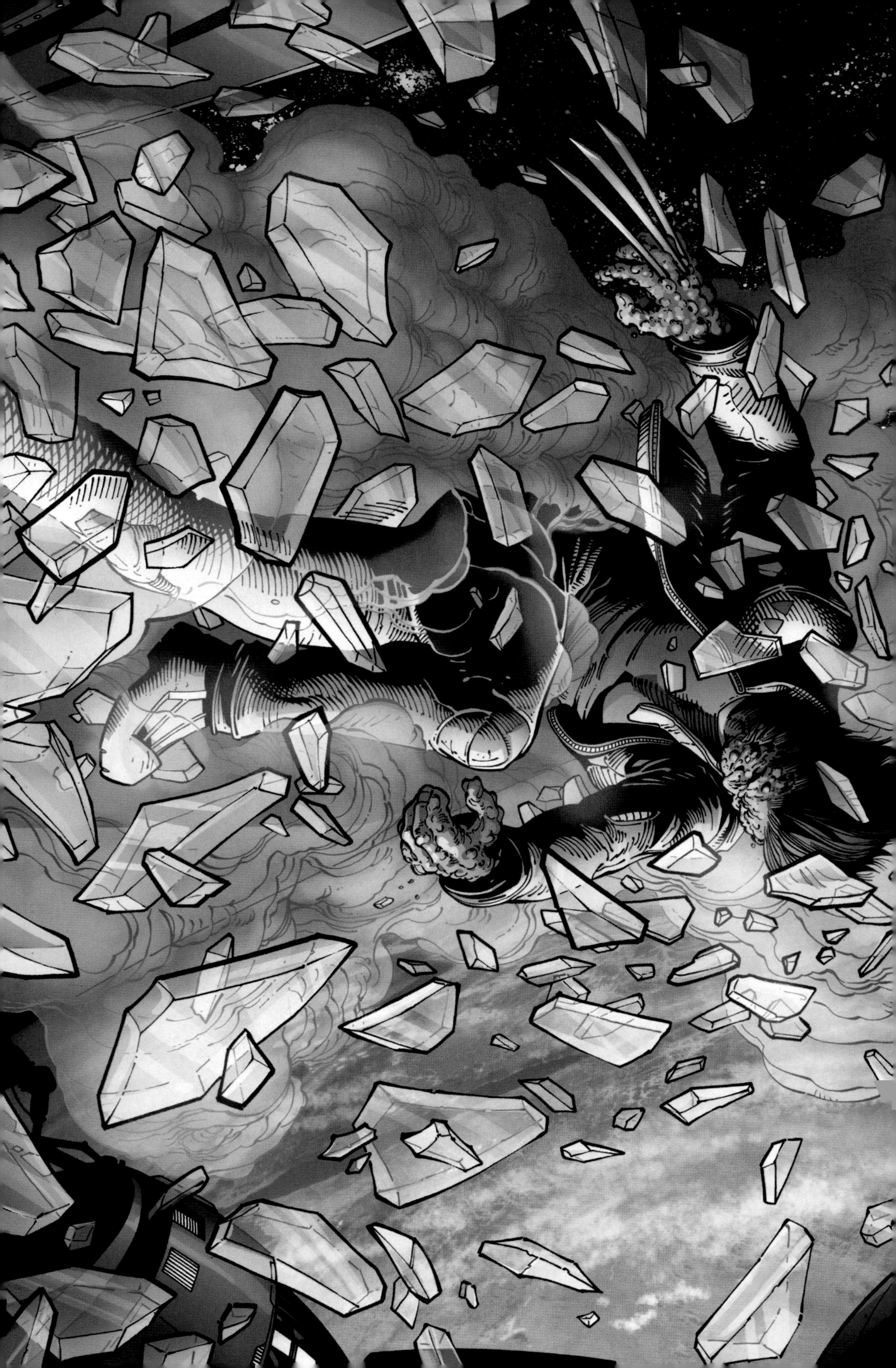

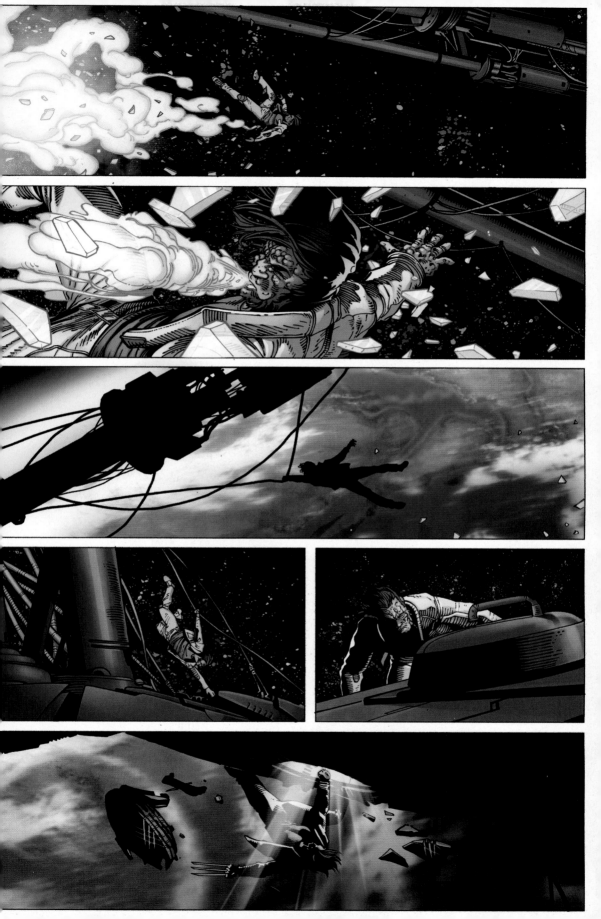

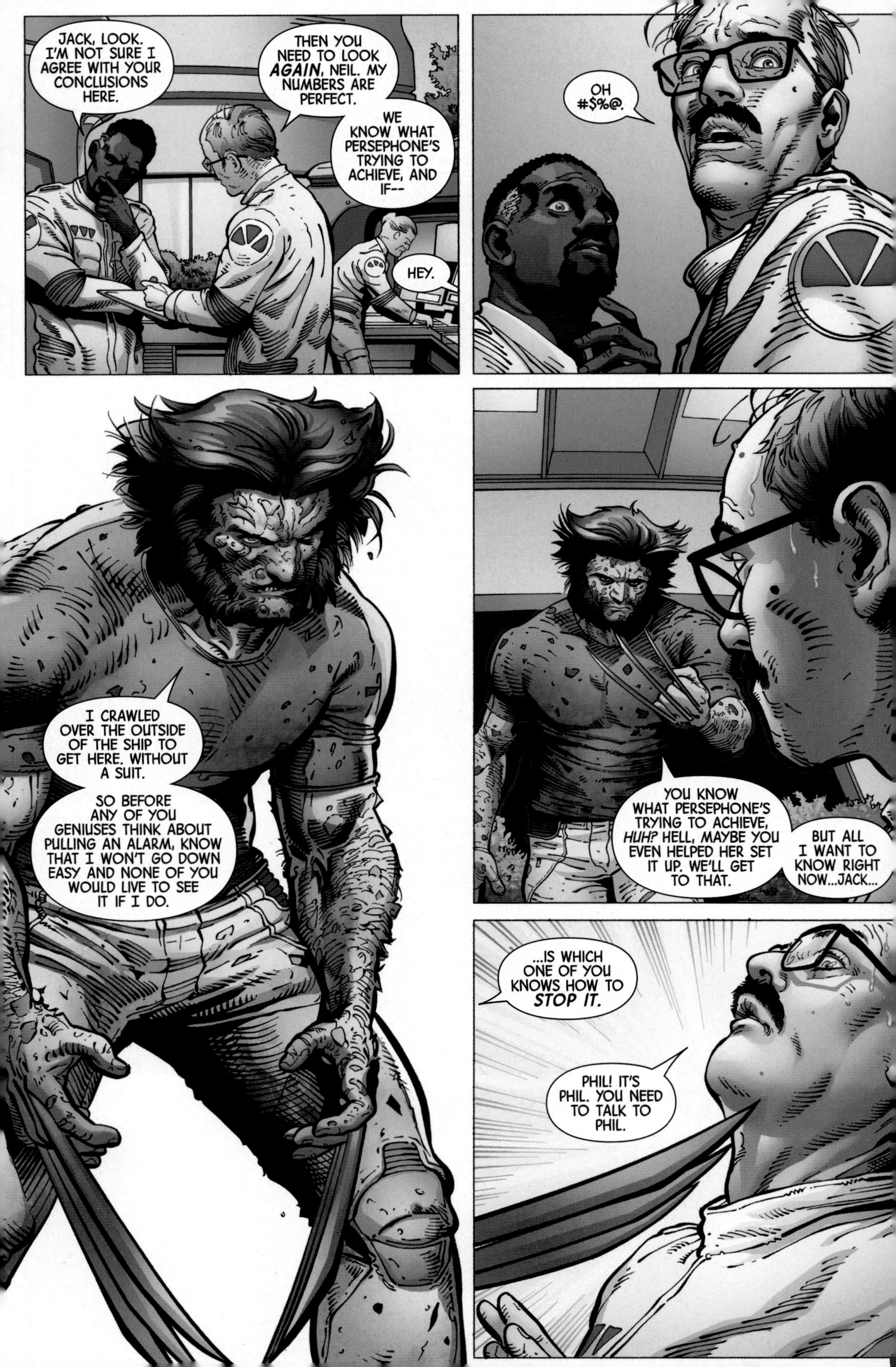
JACK, LOOK. I'M NOT SURE I AGREE WITH YOUR CONCLUSIONS HERE.
THEN YOU NEED TO LOOK *AGAIN*, NEIL. MY NUMBERS ARE PERFECT.
WE KNOW WHAT PERSEPHONE'S TRYING TO ACHIEVE, AND IF--
HEY.
OH #$%@.
I CRAWLED OVER THE OUTSIDE OF THE SHIP TO GET HERE. WITHOUT A SUIT.
SO BEFORE ANY OF YOU GENIUSES THINK ABOUT PULLING AN ALARM, KNOW THAT I WON'T GO DOWN EASY AND NONE OF YOU WOULD LIVE TO SEE IT IF I DO.
YOU KNOW WHAT PERSEPHONE'S TRYING TO ACHIEVE, *HUH?* HELL, MAYBE YOU EVEN HELPED HER SET IT UP. WE'LL GET TO THAT.
BUT ALL I WANT TO KNOW RIGHT NOW...JACK...
...IS WHICH ONE OF YOU KNOWS HOW TO *STOP IT.*
PHIL! IT'S PHIL. YOU NEED TO TALK TO PHIL.

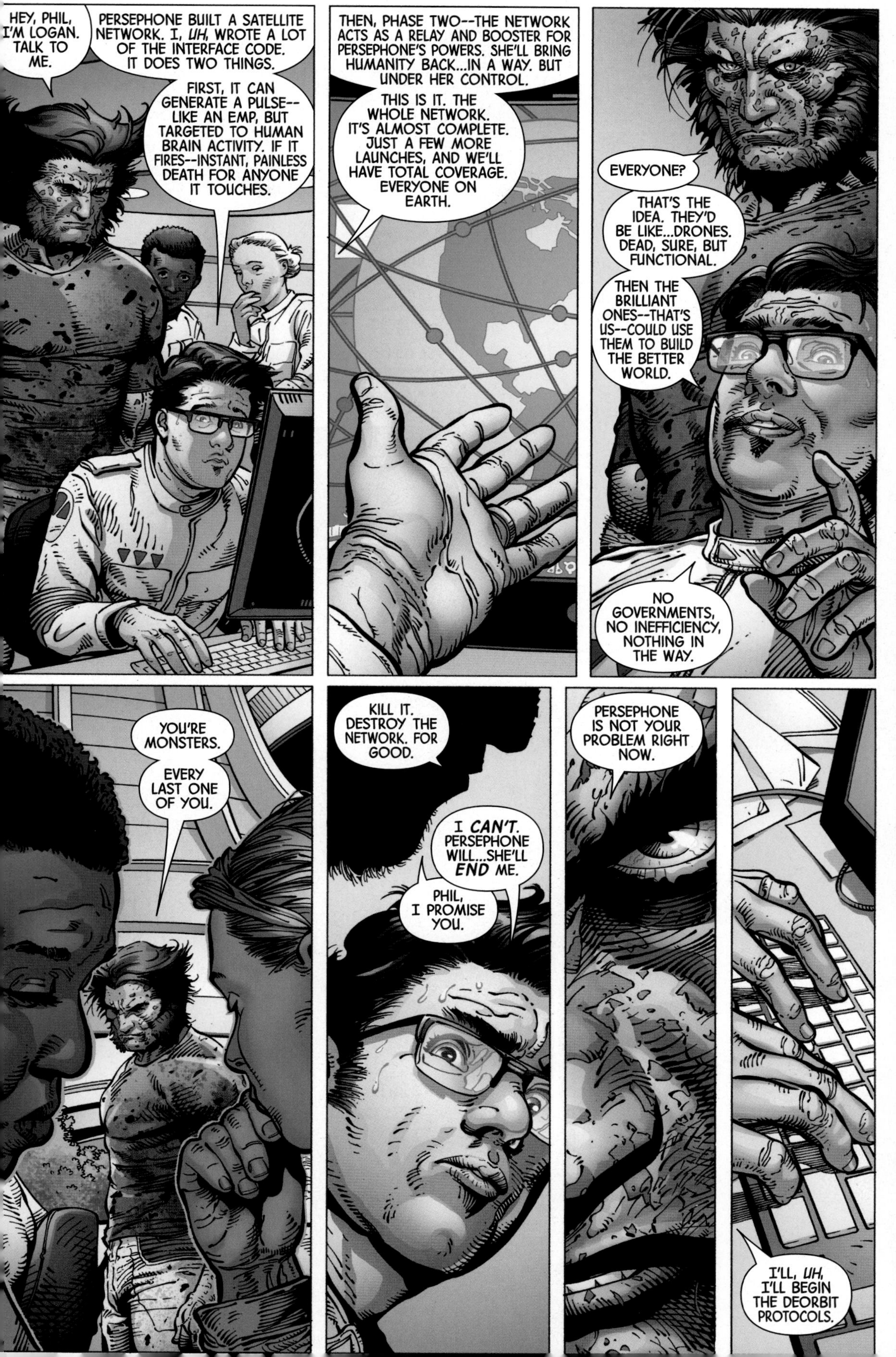
HEY, PHIL, I'M LOGAN. TALK TO ME.
PERSEPHONE BUILT A SATELLITE NETWORK. I, UH, WROTE A LOT OF THE INTERFACE CODE. IT DOES TWO THINGS.
FIRST, IT CAN GENERATE A PULSE-- LIKE AN EMP, BUT TARGETED TO HUMAN BRAIN ACTIVITY. IF IT FIRES--INSTANT, PAINLESS DEATH FOR ANYONE IT TOUCHES.
THEN, PHASE TWO--THE NETWORK ACTS AS A RELAY AND BOOSTER FOR PERSEPHONE'S POWERS. SHE'LL BRING HUMANITY BACK...IN A WAY. BUT UNDER HER CONTROL.
THIS IS IT. THE WHOLE NETWORK. IT'S ALMOST COMPLETE. JUST A FEW MORE LAUNCHES, AND WE'LL HAVE TOTAL COVERAGE. EVERYONE ON EARTH.
EVERYONE?
THAT'S THE IDEA. THEY'D BE LIKE...DRONES. DEAD, SURE, BUT FUNCTIONAL.
THEN THE BRILLIANT ONES--THAT'S US--COULD USE THEM TO BUILD THE BETTER WORLD.
NO GOVERNMENTS, NO INEFFICIENCY, NOTHING IN THE WAY.
YOU'RE MONSTERS.
EVERY LAST ONE OF YOU.
KILL IT. DESTROY THE NETWORK. FOR GOOD.
I CAN'T. PERSEPHONE WILL...SHE'LL END ME.
PHIL, I PROMISE YOU.
PERSEPHONE IS NOT YOUR PROBLEM RIGHT NOW.
I'LL, UH, I'LL BEGIN THE DEORBIT PROTOCOLS.

"THERE. IT'S DONE.

"THE SATS WILL ALL BURN UP IN THE ATMOSPHERE.

"BET IT LOOKS PRETTY NICE FROM DOWN THERE.

"IF THEY ONLY KNEW, *EH?*"

HONESTLY, THIS IS SORT OF A RELIEF. I WAS NEVER REALLY ON BOARD WITH ALL THIS. YOU'LL KEEP ME SAFE FROM PERSEPHONE, RIGHT?

IT WON'T BE LONG BEFORE SHE--

SHUT UP.

IF ALL THE SATELLITES ARE GONE...

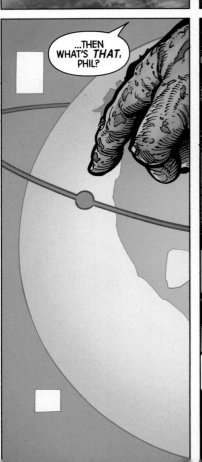

...THEN WHAT'S *THAT*, PHIL?

WELL... THAT'S *US*. THIS STATION.

CAN IT DO WHAT THE OTHER SATELLITES CAN? THE KILLING PULSE AND THEN THE REANIMATION?

YES, BUT ONLY ON WHATEVER AREA WE'RE ABOVE WHEN IT FIRES. YOU'RE TALKING AT *MOST* A FEW MILLION PEOPLE, AND THAT'S IF IT'S AN URBAN AREA.

A FEW MILLION...

SHUT IT DOWN.

I CAN'T. PERSEPHONE HA[S] CONTROL OVE[R] THE STATION

AND HONESTLY, IT'S ONLY A MATTER OF TIME BEFORE SHE NOTICES WHAT I DID AND-

TERMINATION PULSE FIRING SEQUENCE INITIATED. POWER DOWN ALL NONESSENTIAL EQUIPMENT. ALL PERSONNEL TO CRASH COUCHES.

WHERE DO I GO TO STOP IT?

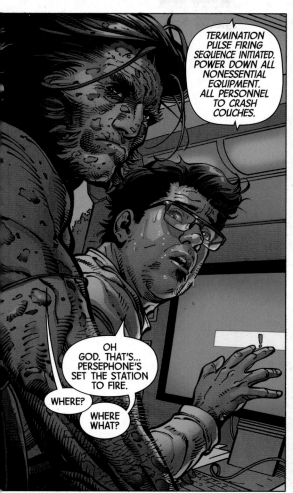

OH GOD. THAT'S... PERSEPHONE'S SET THE STATION TO FIRE.

WHERE?

WHERE WHAT?

ALL THE STATION'S OPERATIONAL STUFF IS THREE DECKS DOWN. THE PULSE DEVICE HAS TO BE SOMEWHERE DOWN THERE.

JUST...BE CAREFUL. IF YOU HIT THE WRONG PIECE OF EQUIPMENT, YOU COULD KNOCK THE WHOLE STATION OUT OF THE SKY.

YEAH, WELL, NO ONE ON EARTH'S GONNA SHED TOO MANY TEARS OVER ANY OF YOU.

BUT... YOU. YOU'D DIE TOO.

YEAH. AND ME.

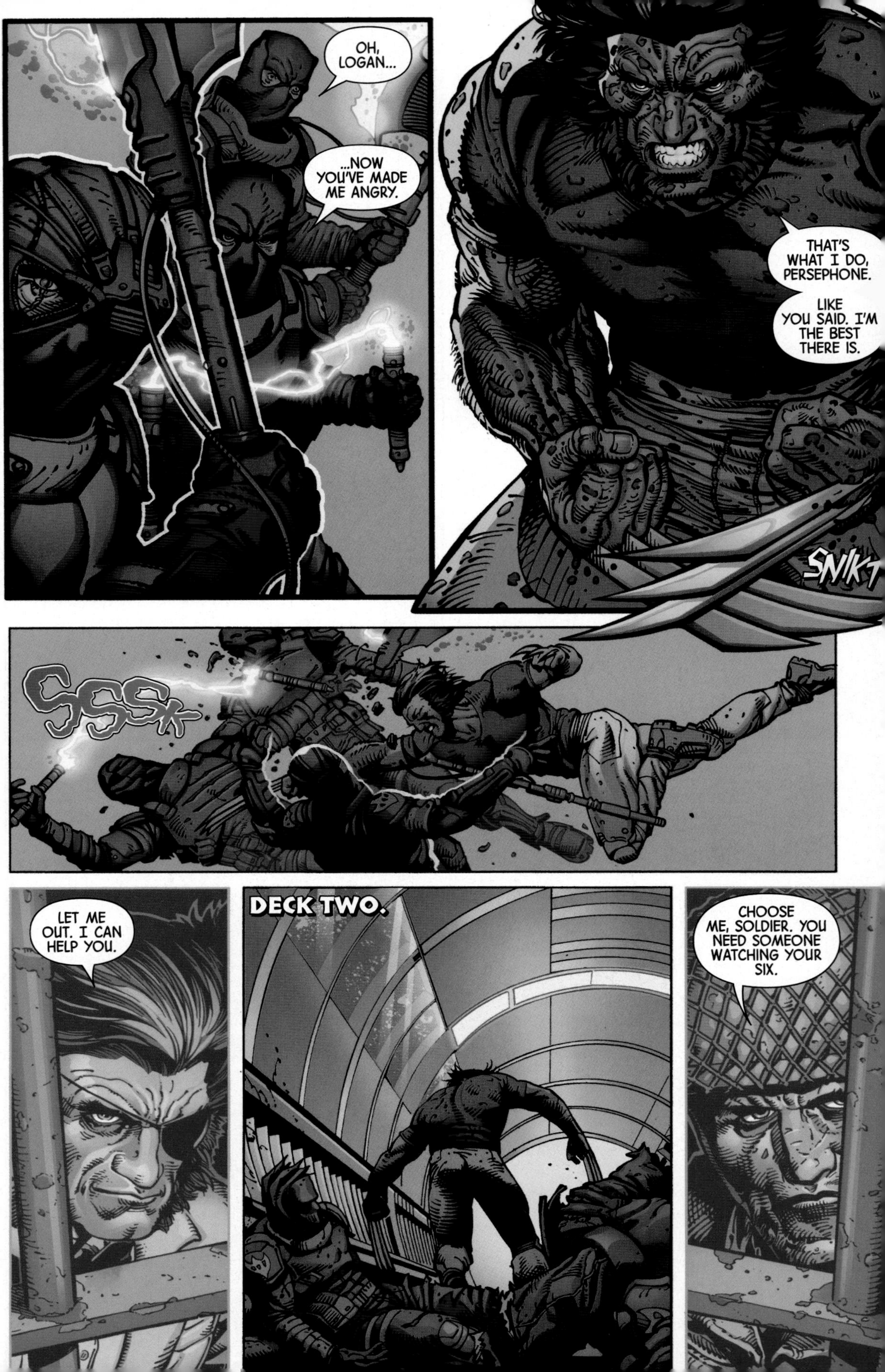
OH, LOGAN...
...NOW YOU'VE MADE ME ANGRY.
THAT'S WHAT I DO, PERSEPHONE.
LIKE YOU SAID. I'M THE BEST THERE IS.
SNIKT
SSSK
LET ME OUT. I CAN HELP YOU.
DECK TWO.
CHOOSE ME, SOLDIER. YOU NEED SOMEONE WATCHING YOUR SIX.

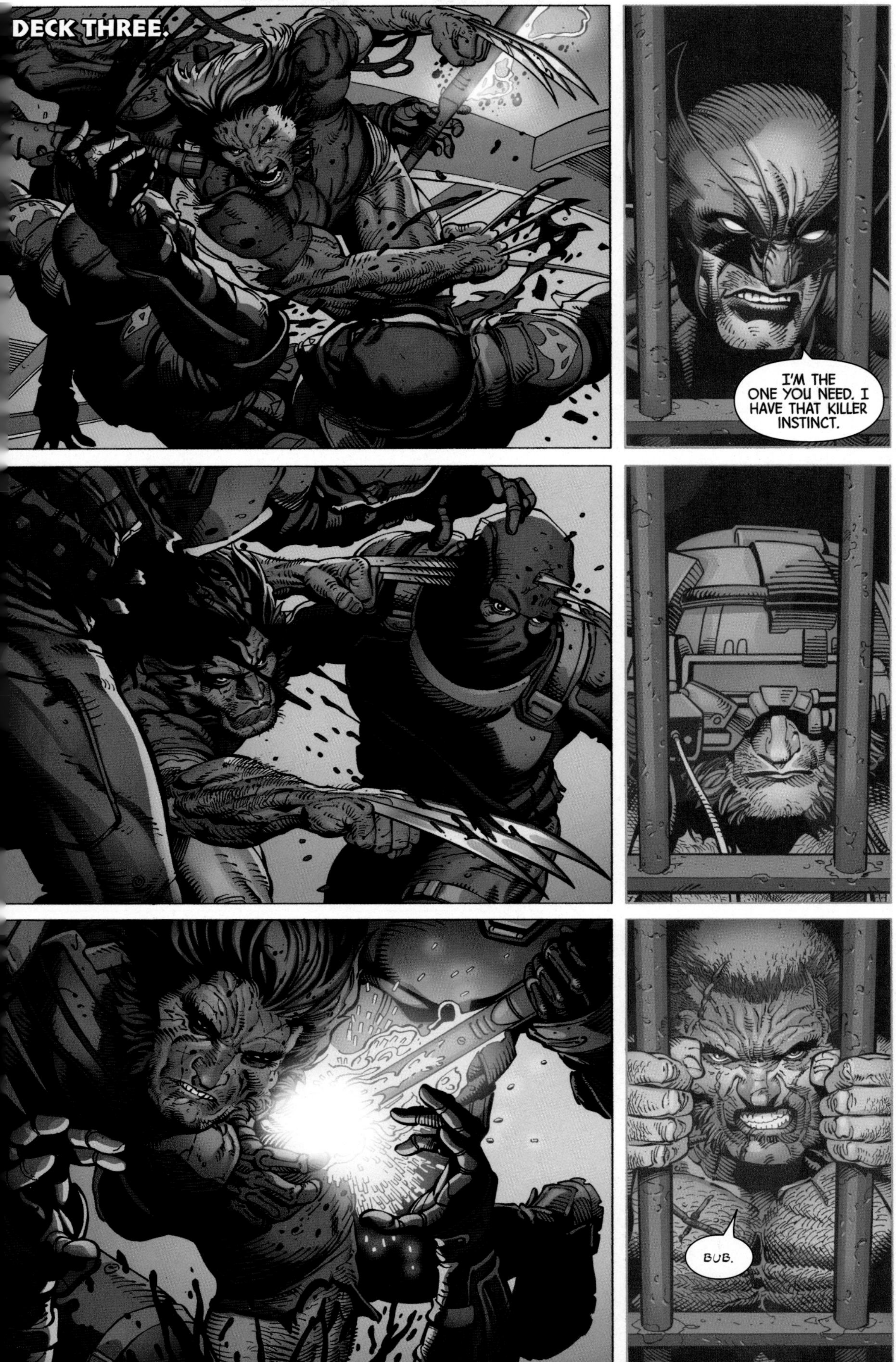
DECK THREE.
I'M THE ONE YOU NEED. I HAVE THAT KILLER INSTINCT.
BUB.

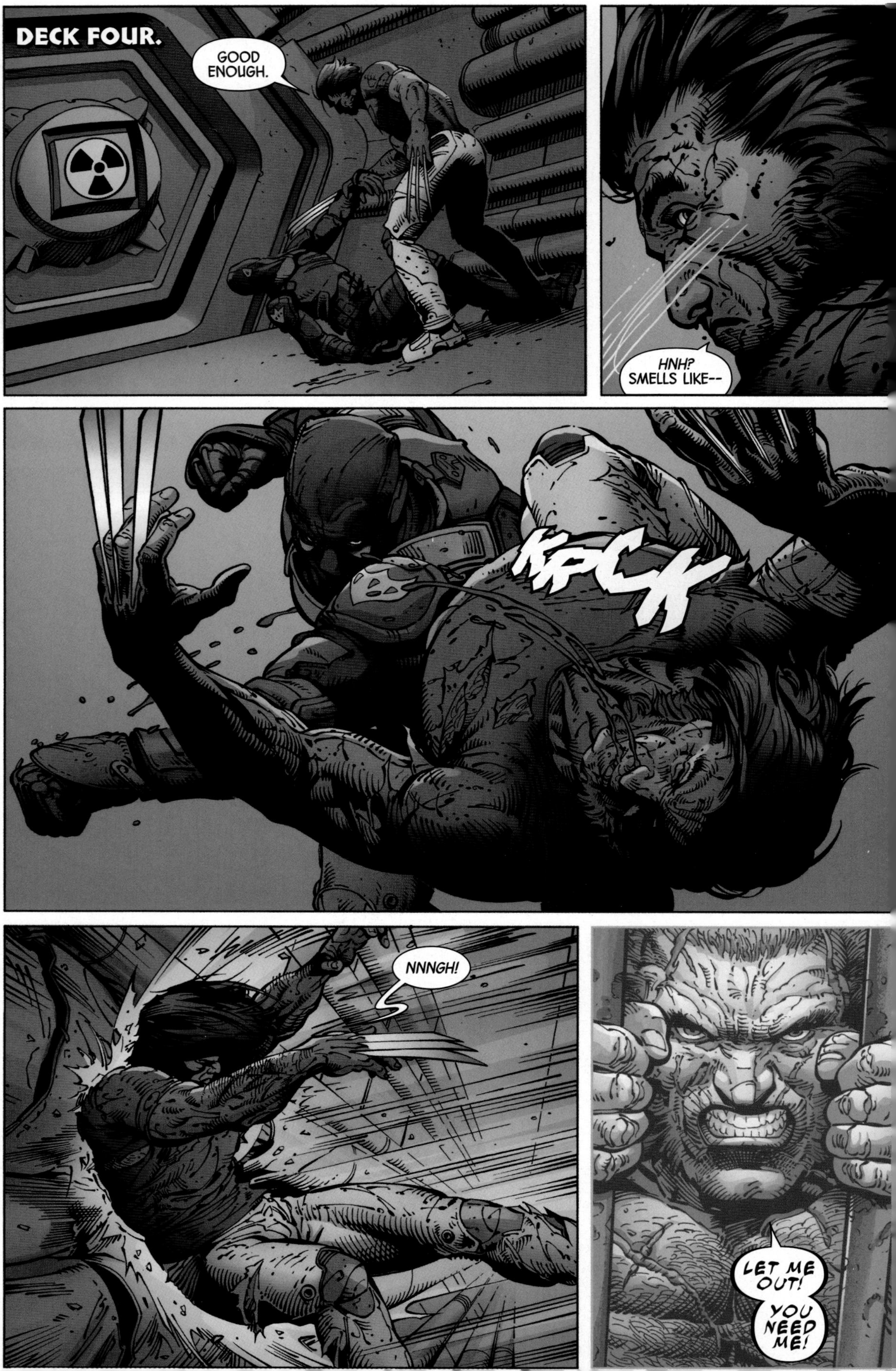
DECK FOUR.
GOOD ENOUGH.
HNH? SMELLS LIKE--
KRCK
NNNGH!
LET ME OUT!
YOU NEED ME!

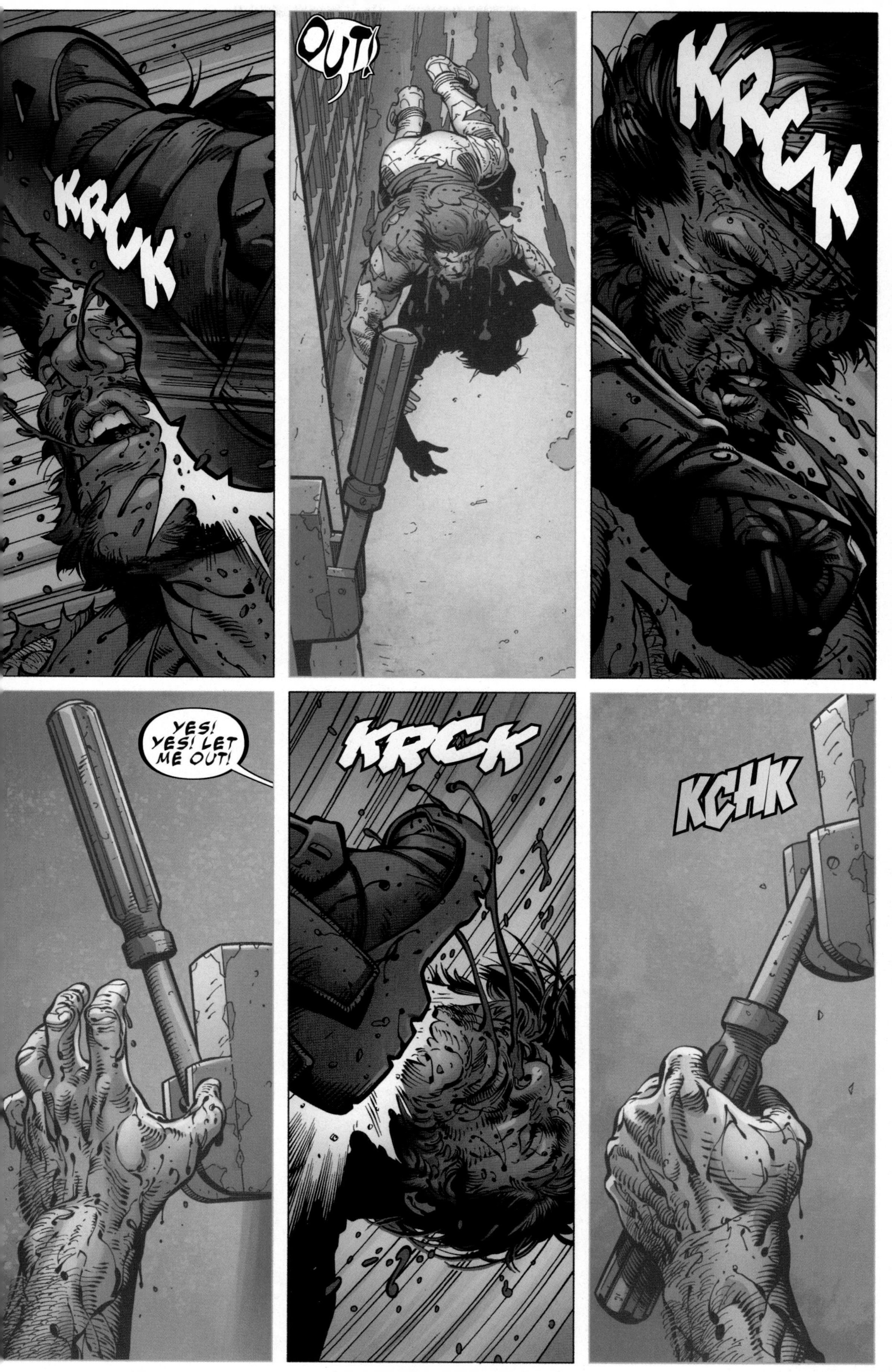
KRCK
OUT!
KRCK
YES! YES! LET ME OUT!
KRCK
KCHK

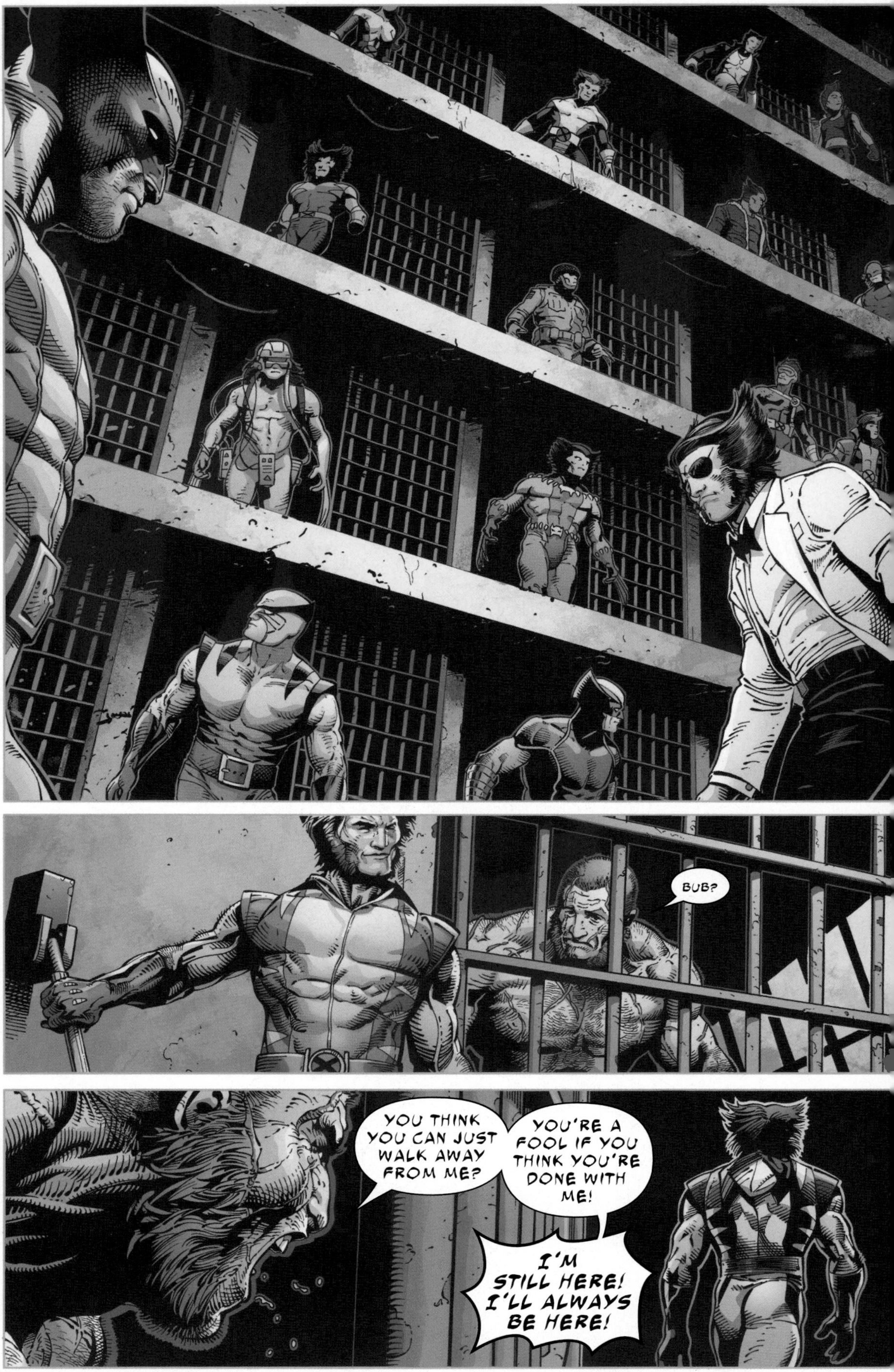
BUB?
YOU THINK YOU CAN JUST WALK AWAY FROM ME?
YOU'RE A FOOL IF YOU THINK YOU'RE DONE WITH ME!
I'M STILL HERE! I'LL ALWAYS BE HERE!

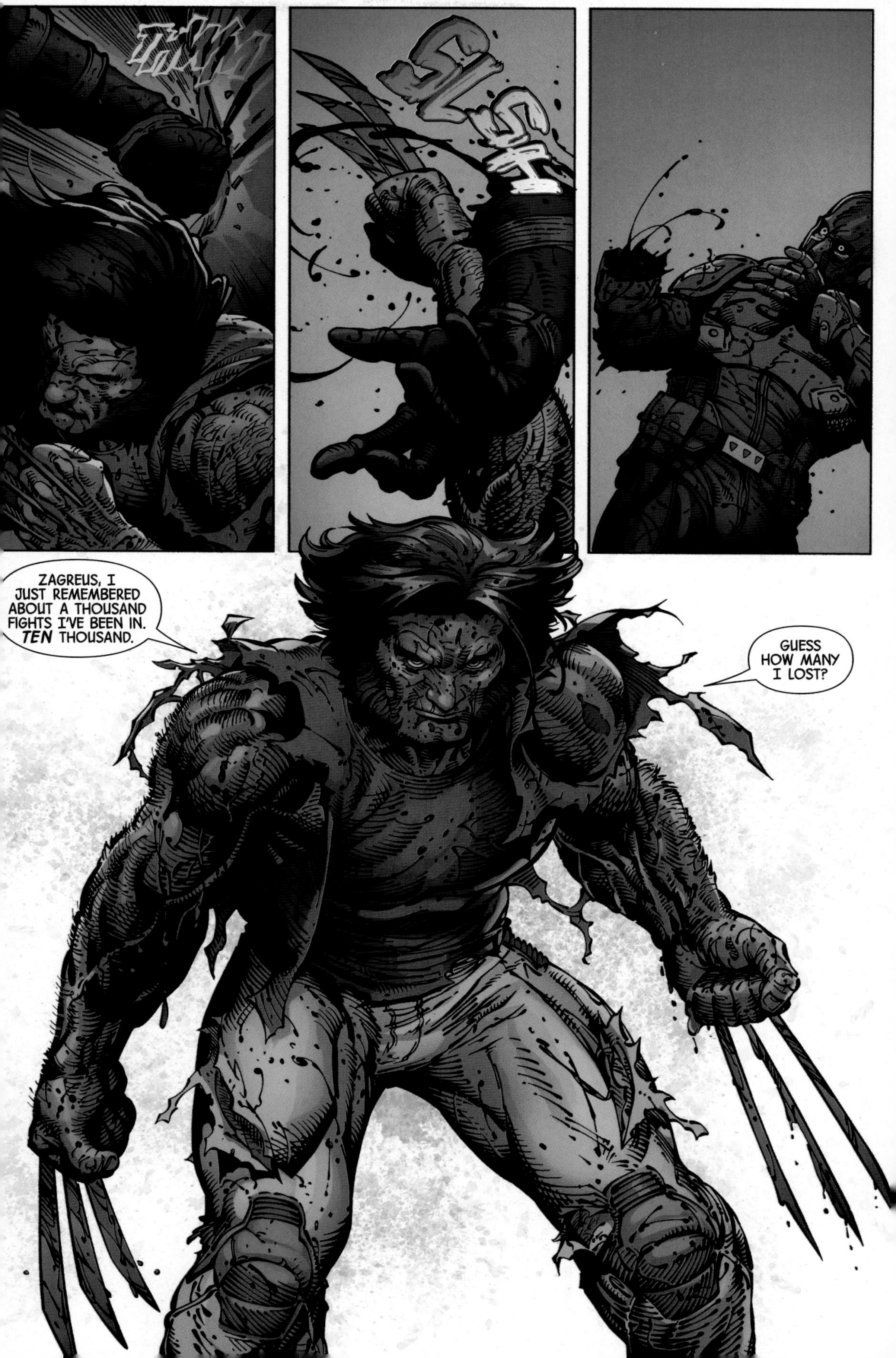
SLSH
ZAGREUS, I JUST REMEMBERED ABOUT A THOUSAND FIGHTS I'VE BEEN IN. ***TEN*** THOUSAND.
GUESS HOW MANY I LOST?

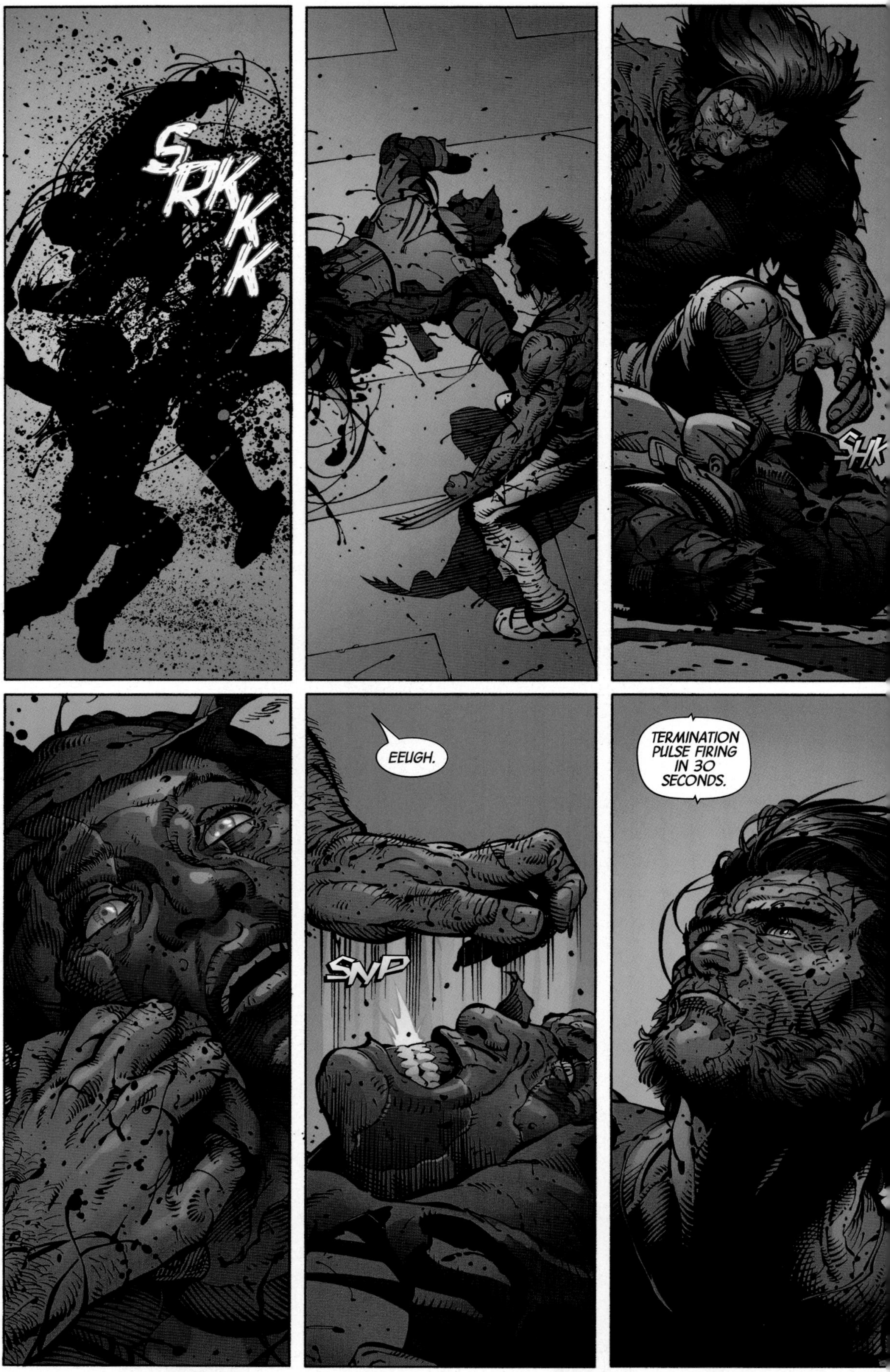
SRKKK
SHK
EEUGH.
SNP
TERMINATION PULSE FIRING IN 30 SECONDS.

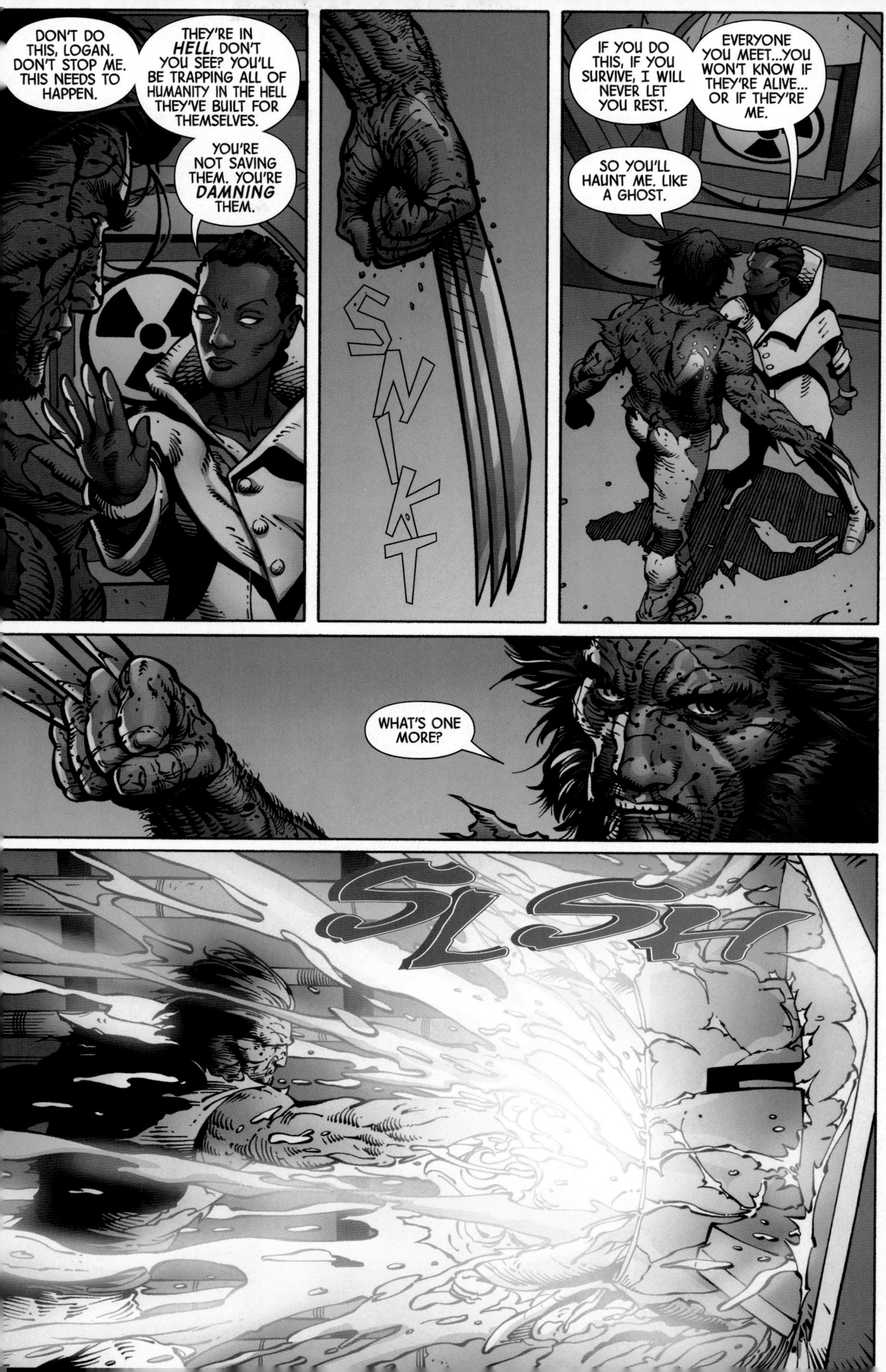
DON'T DO THIS, LOGAN. DON'T STOP ME. THIS NEEDS TO HAPPEN.
THEY'RE IN *HELL*, DON'T YOU SEE? YOU'LL BE TRAPPING ALL OF HUMANITY IN THE HELL THEY'VE BUILT FOR THEMSELVES.
YOU'RE NOT SAVING THEM. YOU'RE *DAMNING* THEM.
SNIKT
IF YOU DO THIS, IF YOU SURVIVE, I WILL NEVER LET YOU REST.
EVERYONE YOU MEET...YOU WON'T KNOW IF THEY'RE ALIVE... OR IF THEY'RE ME.
SO YOU'LL HAUNT ME. LIKE A GHOST.
WHAT'S ONE MORE?
SLSH

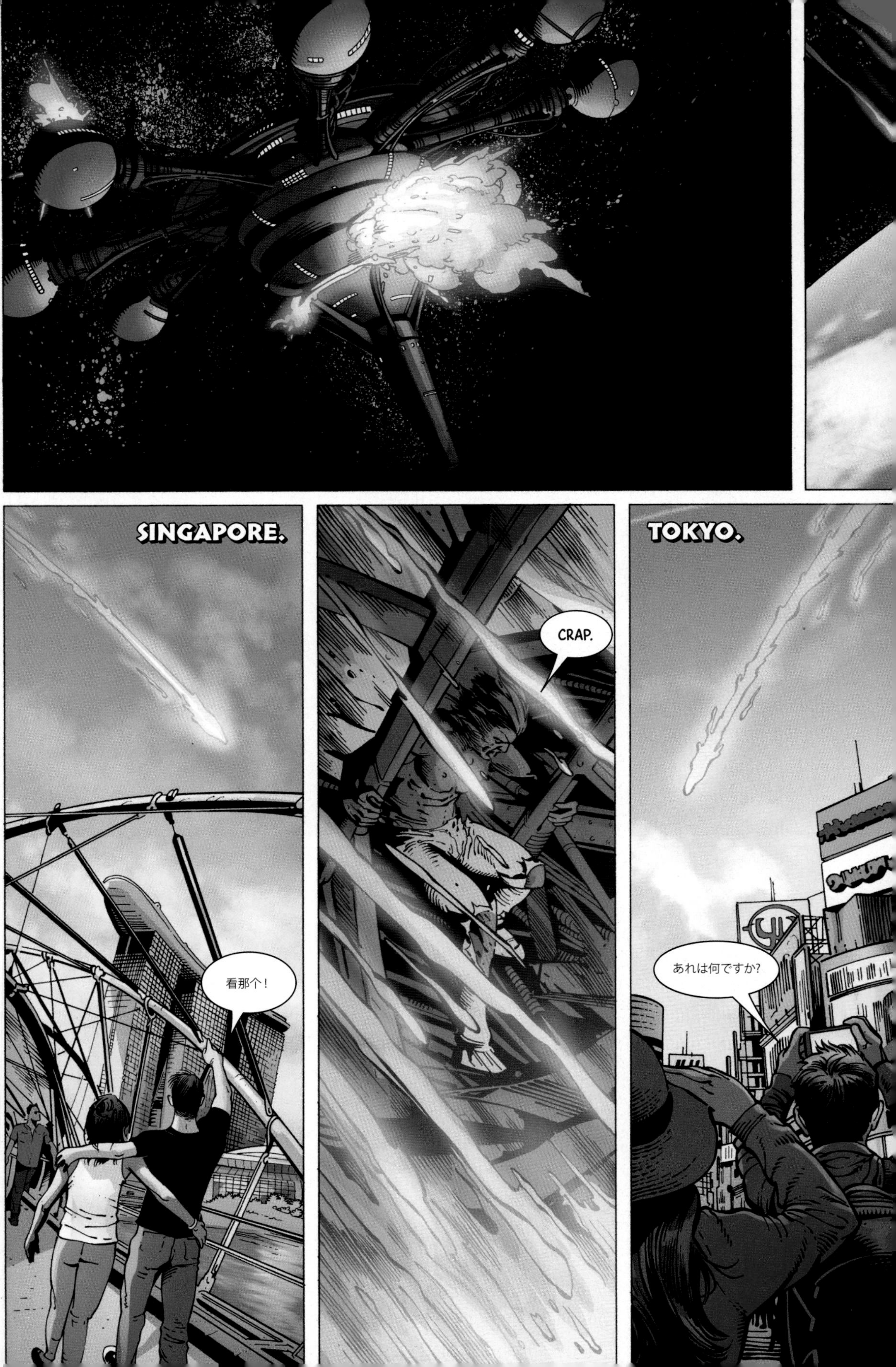
SINGAPORE.
看那个！
CRAP.
TOKYO.
あれは何ですか?

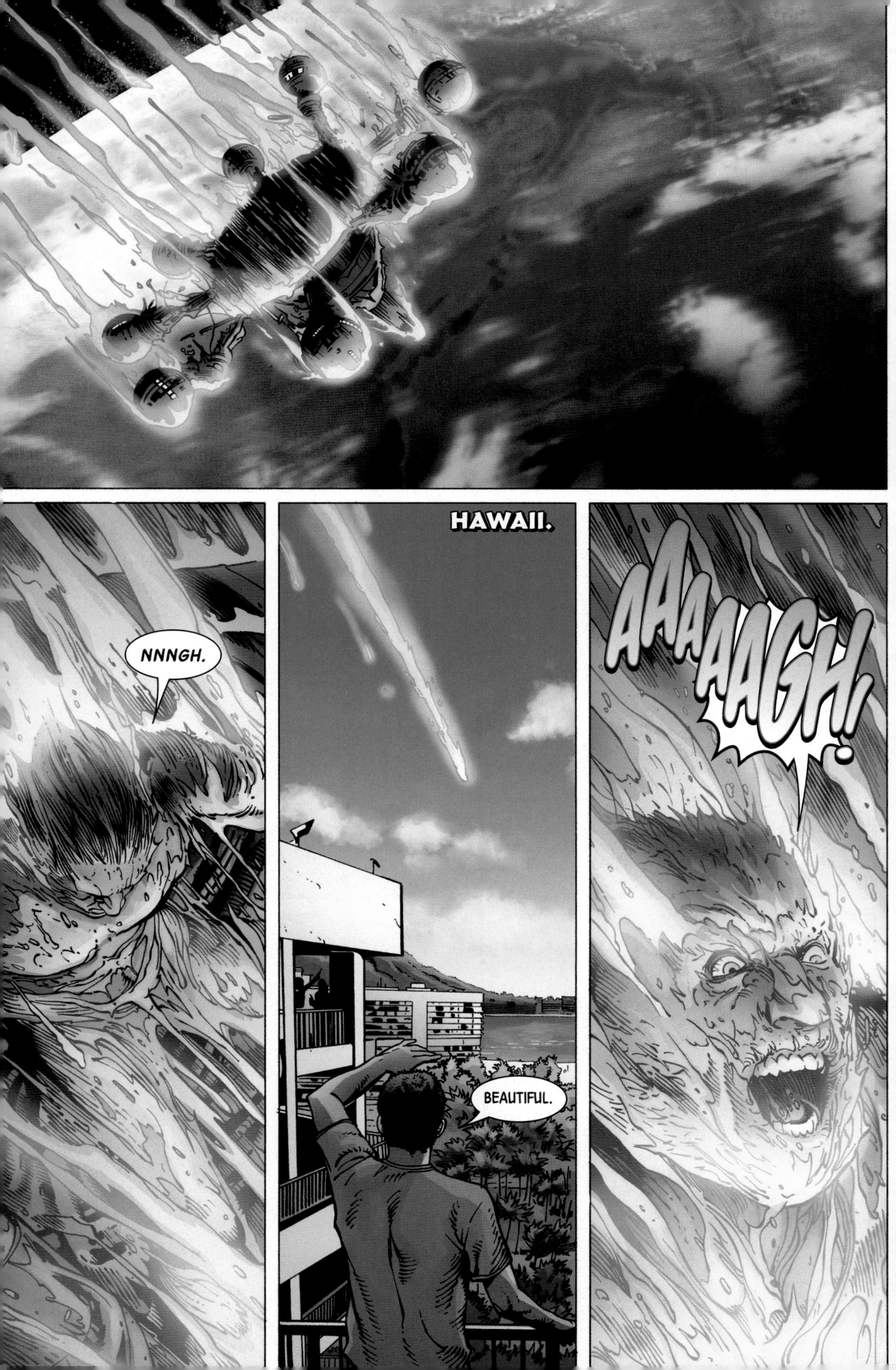
NNNGH.
HAWAII.
BEAUTIFUL.
AAAAAGH!!

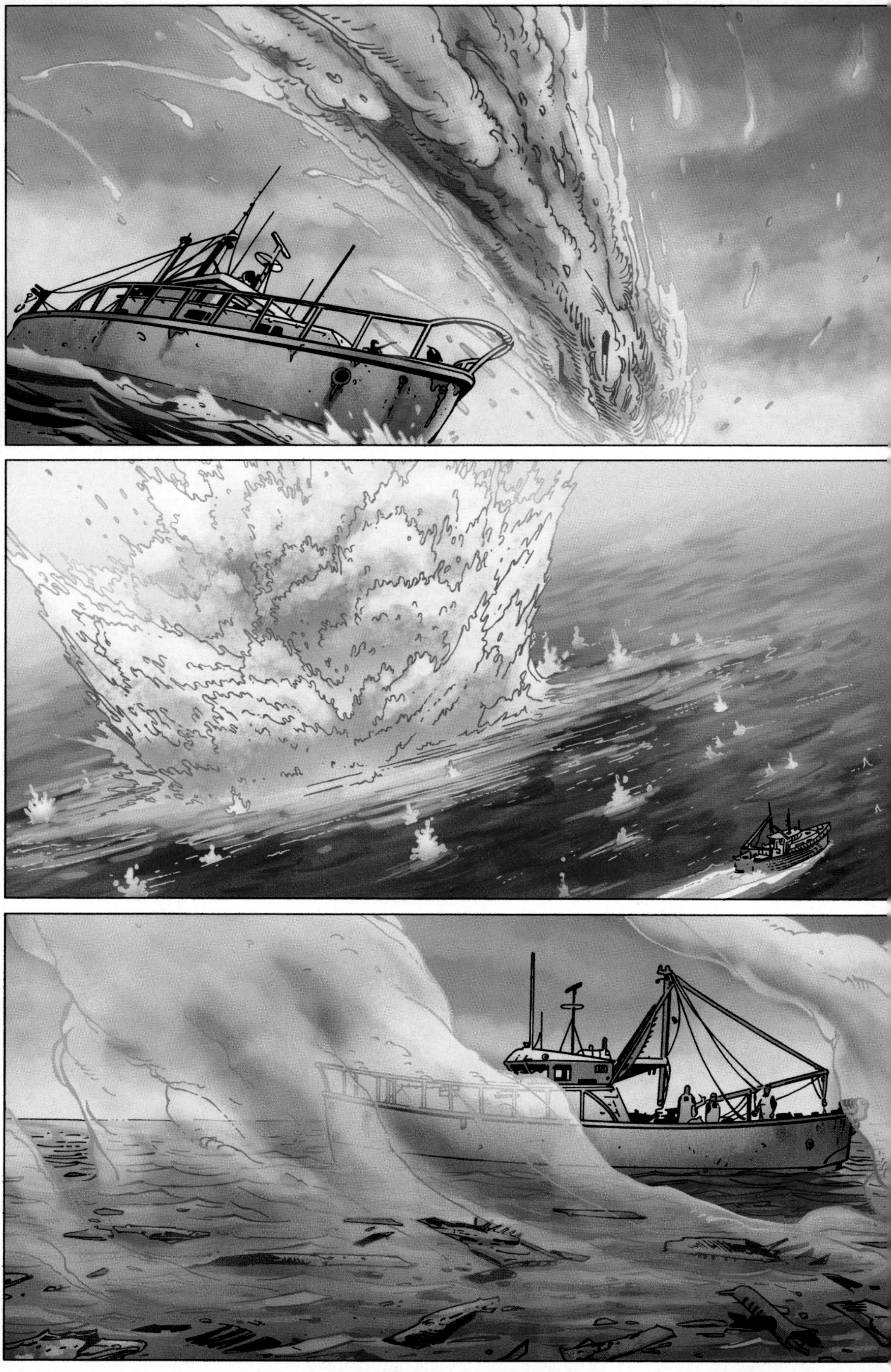

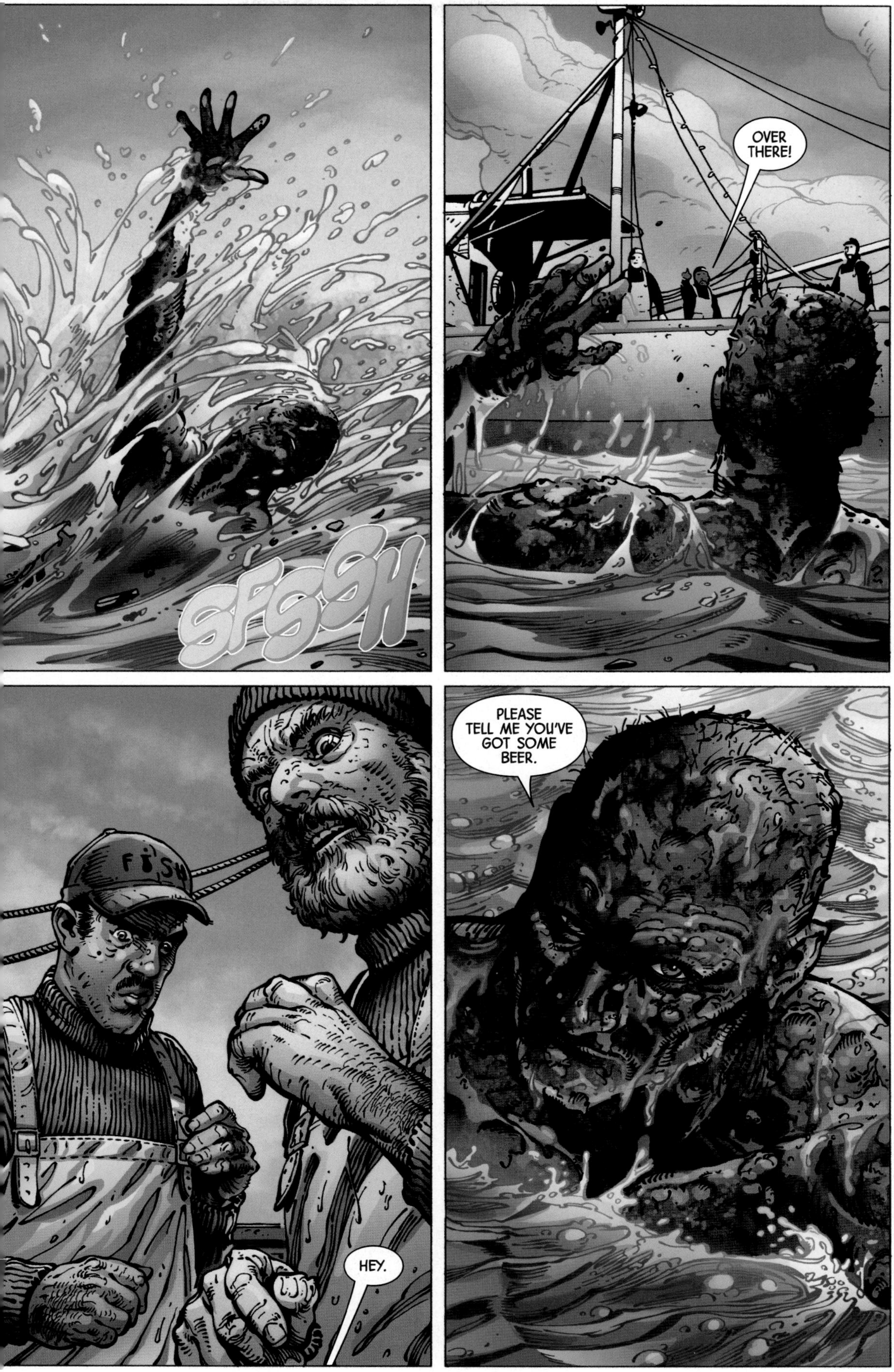
SFSSH
OVER THERE!
HEY.
PLEASE TELL ME YOU'VE GOT SOME BEER.

HNH.

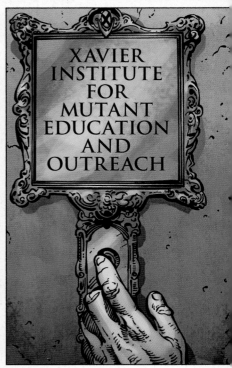

XAVIER
INSTITUTE
FOR
MUTANT
EDUCATION
AND
OUTREACH

#1 VARIANT BY **JOHN CASSADAY** & **LAURA MARTIN**

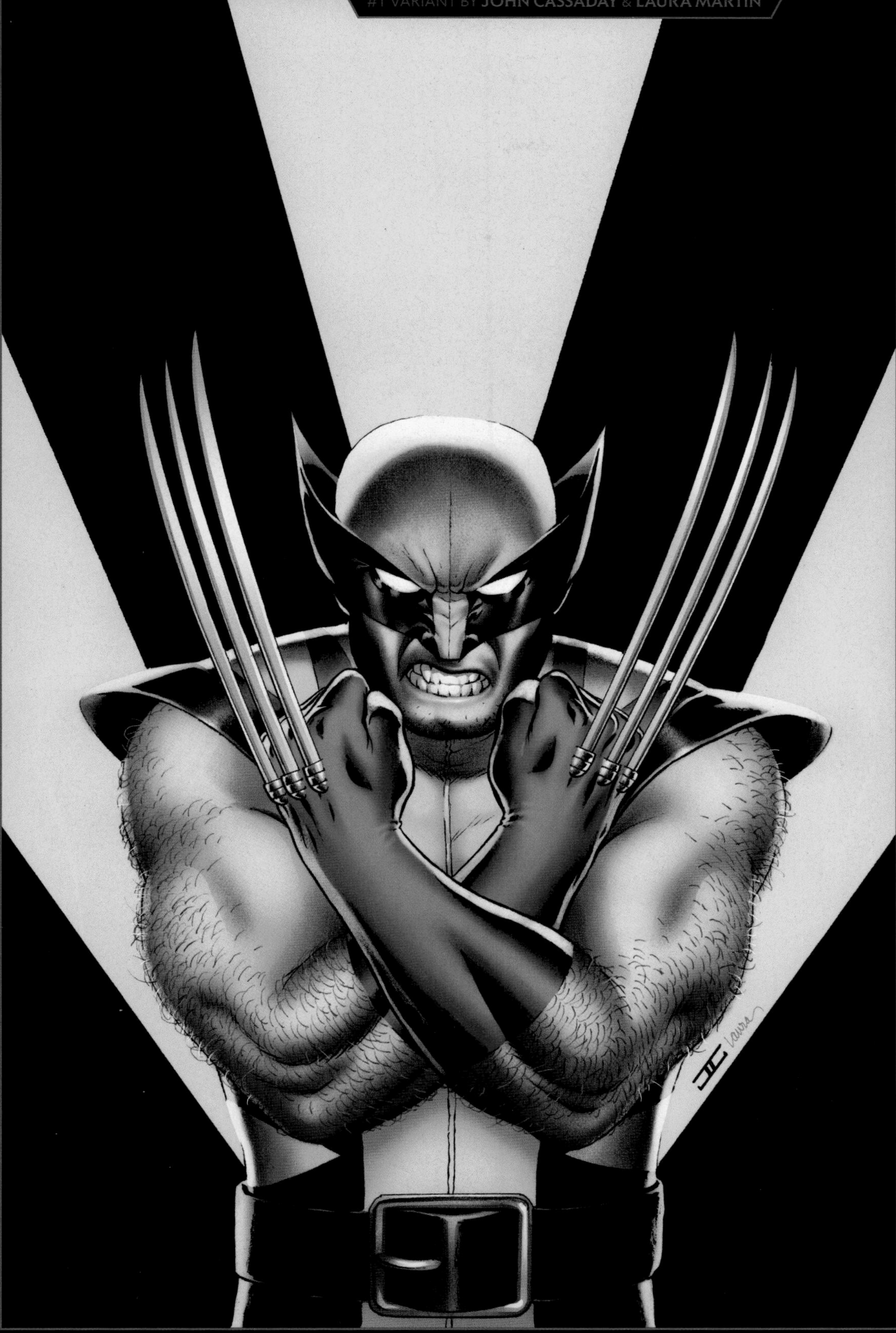

#1 VARIANT BY JOHN TYLER CHRISTOPHER

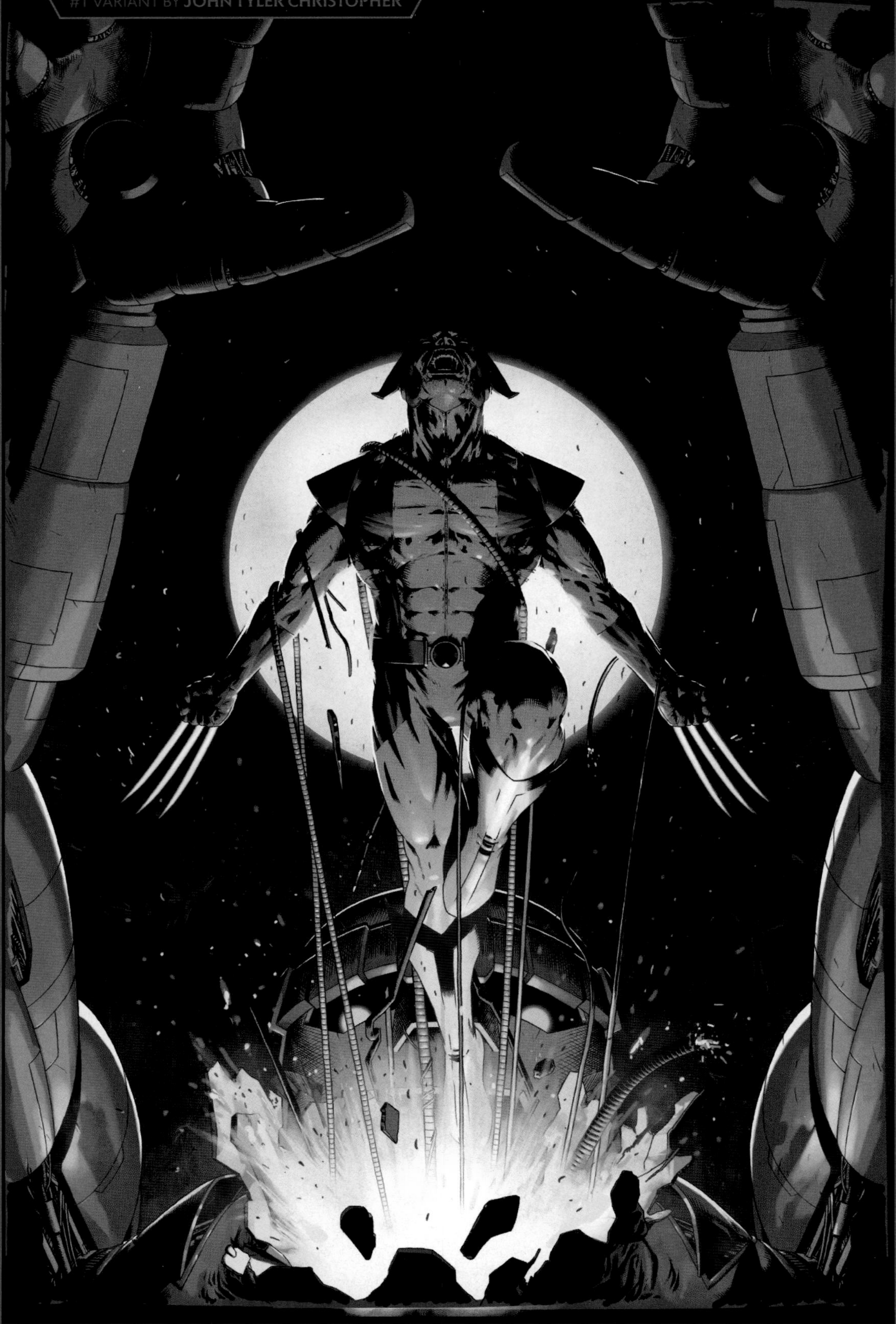

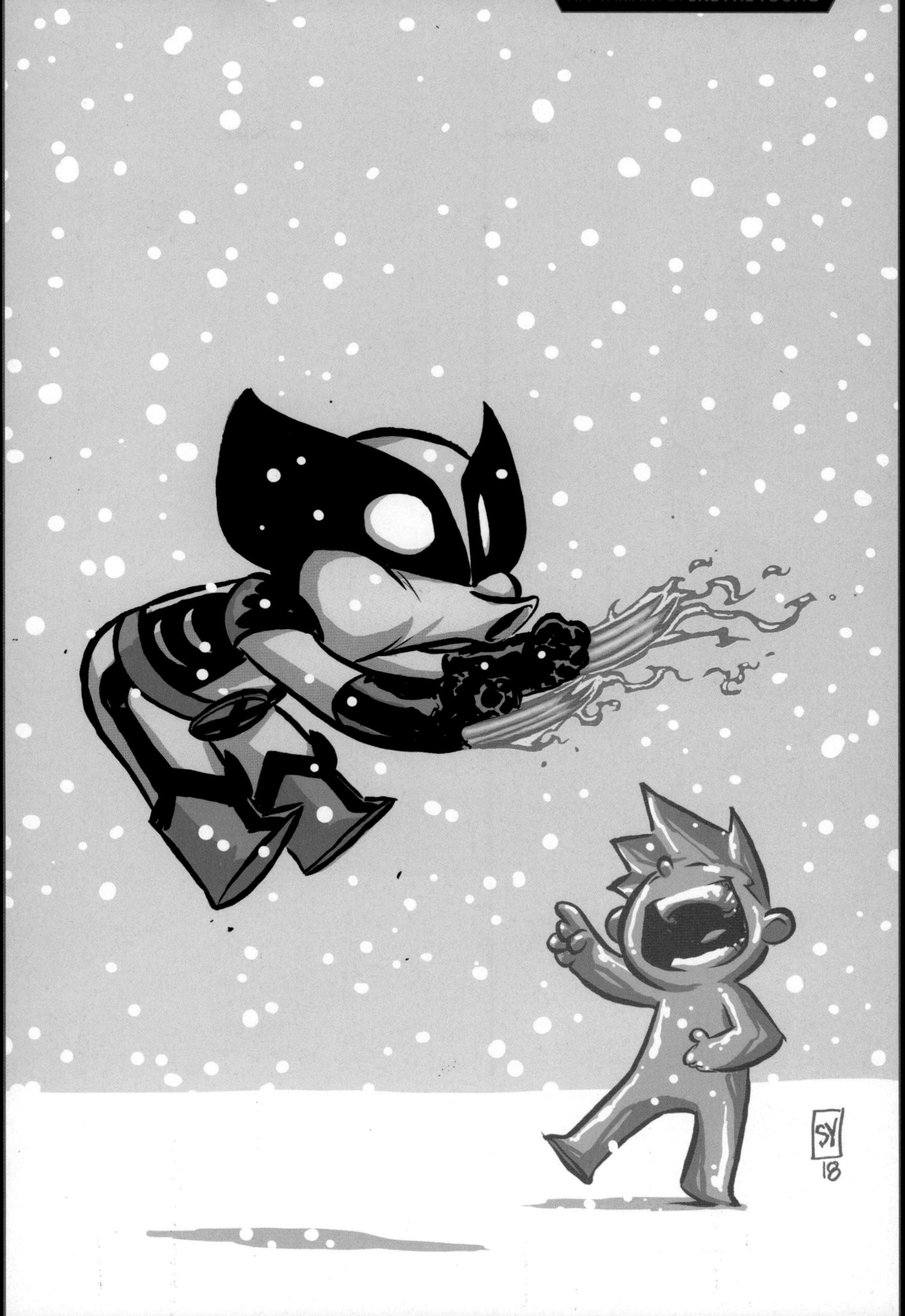
SY
'18

#1 VARIANT BY **LEINIL FRANCIS YU** & **SUNNY GHO**

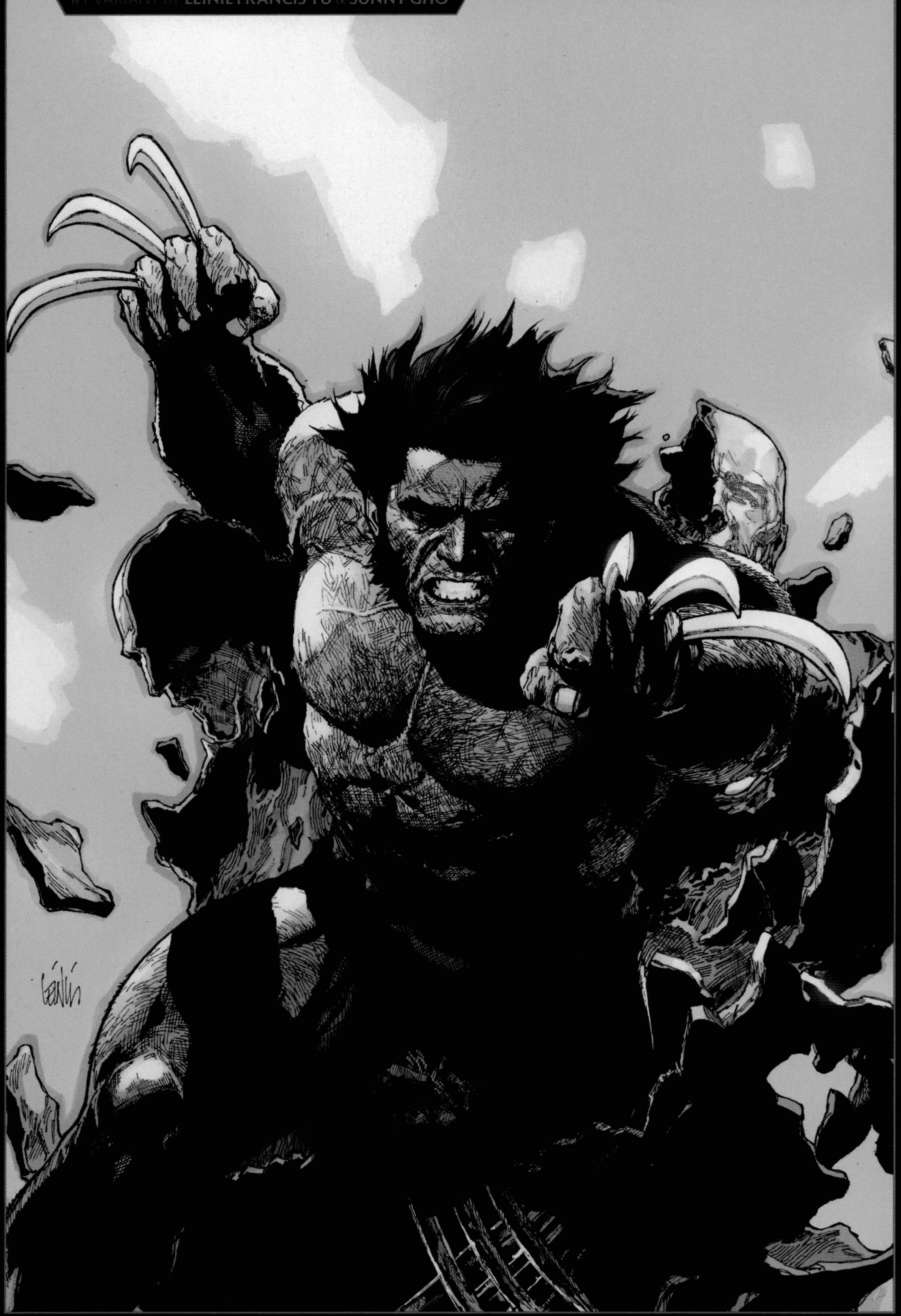

Leinil

#1 VARIANT BY **STEVE McNIVEN, JAY LEISTEN** & **LAURA MARTIN**

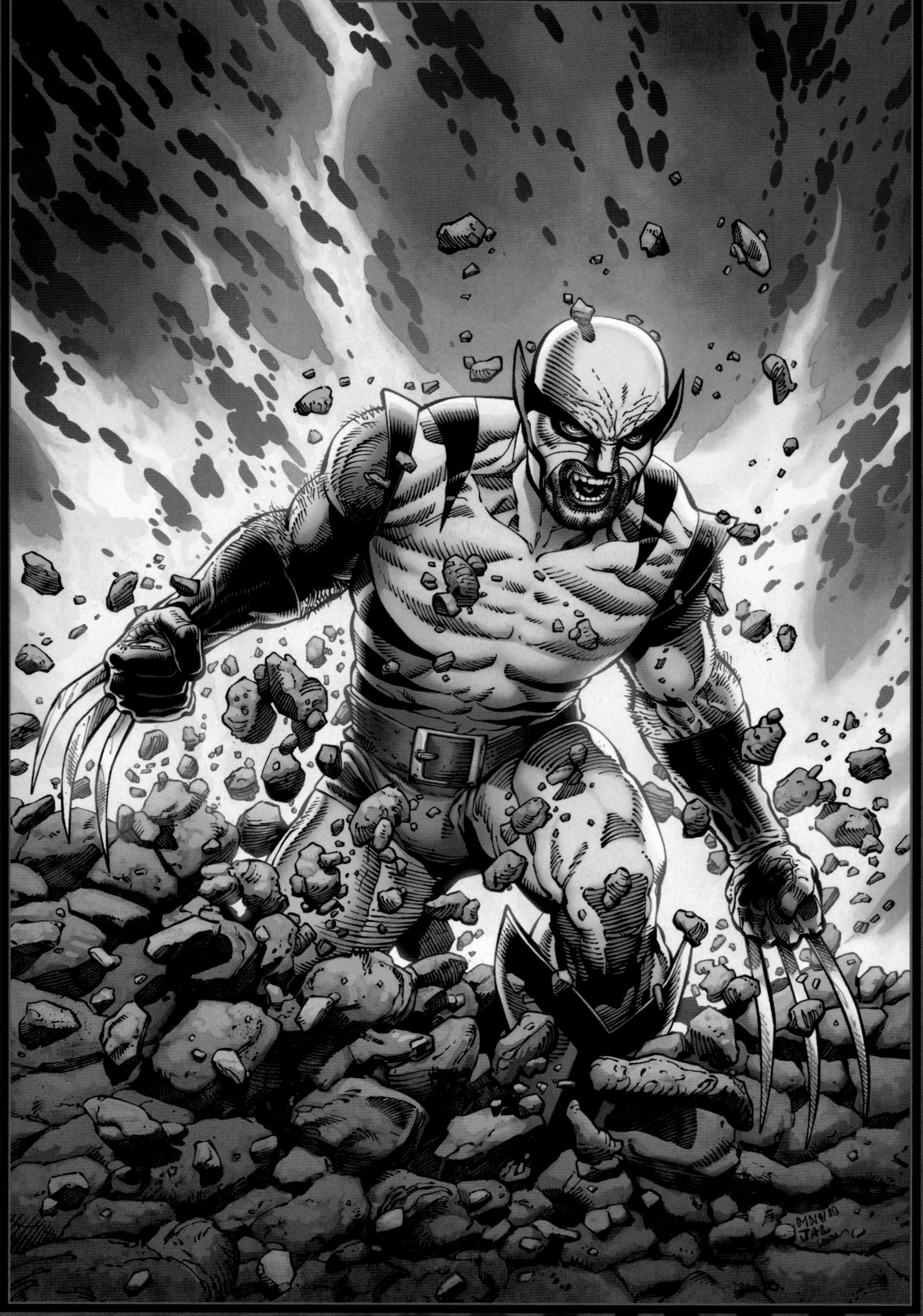

#1 VARIANT BY **STEVE McNIVEN, JAY LEISTEN & LAURA MARTIN**

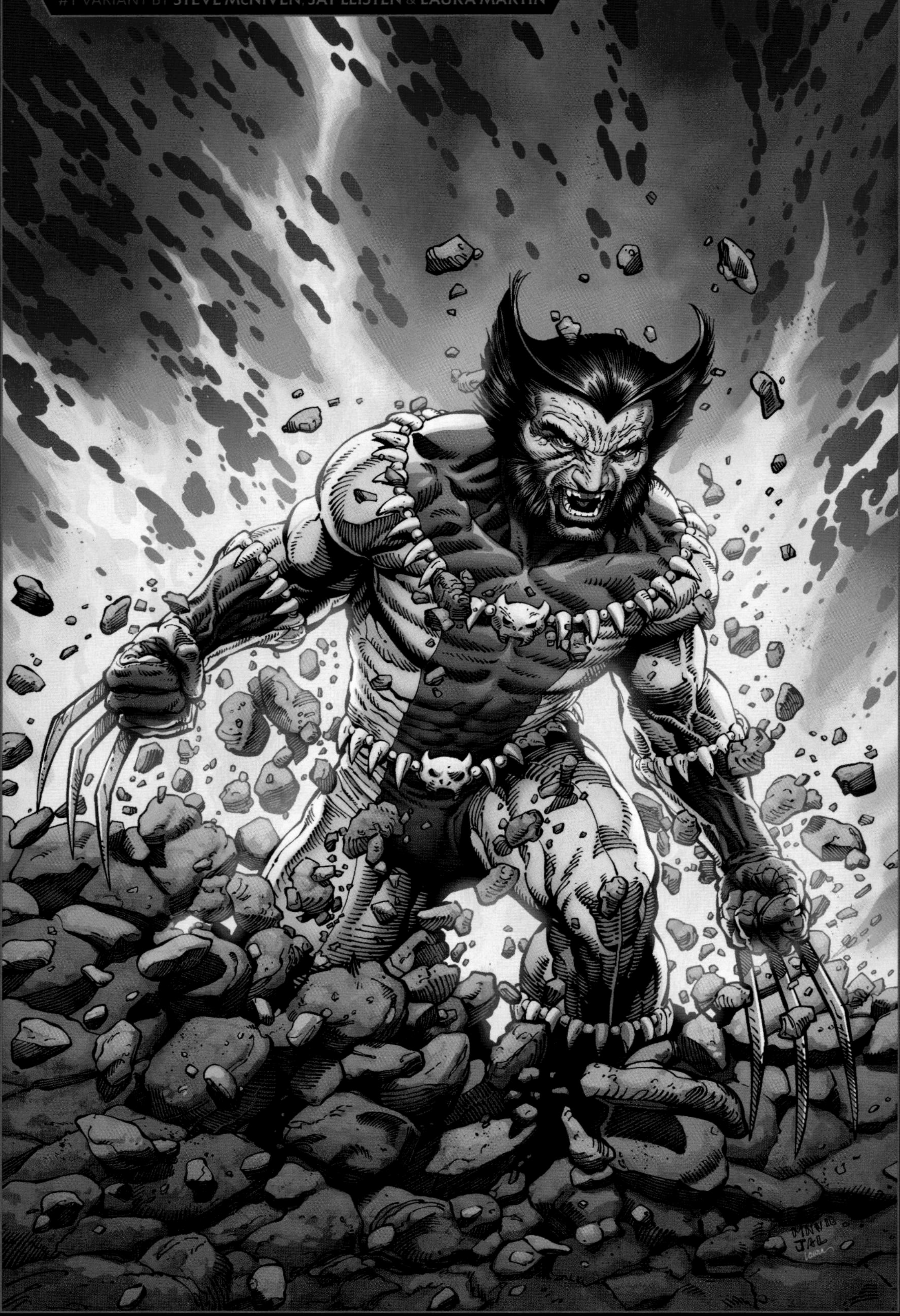

#1 VARIANT BY **STEVE McNIVEN, JAY LEISTEN** & **LAURA MARTIN**

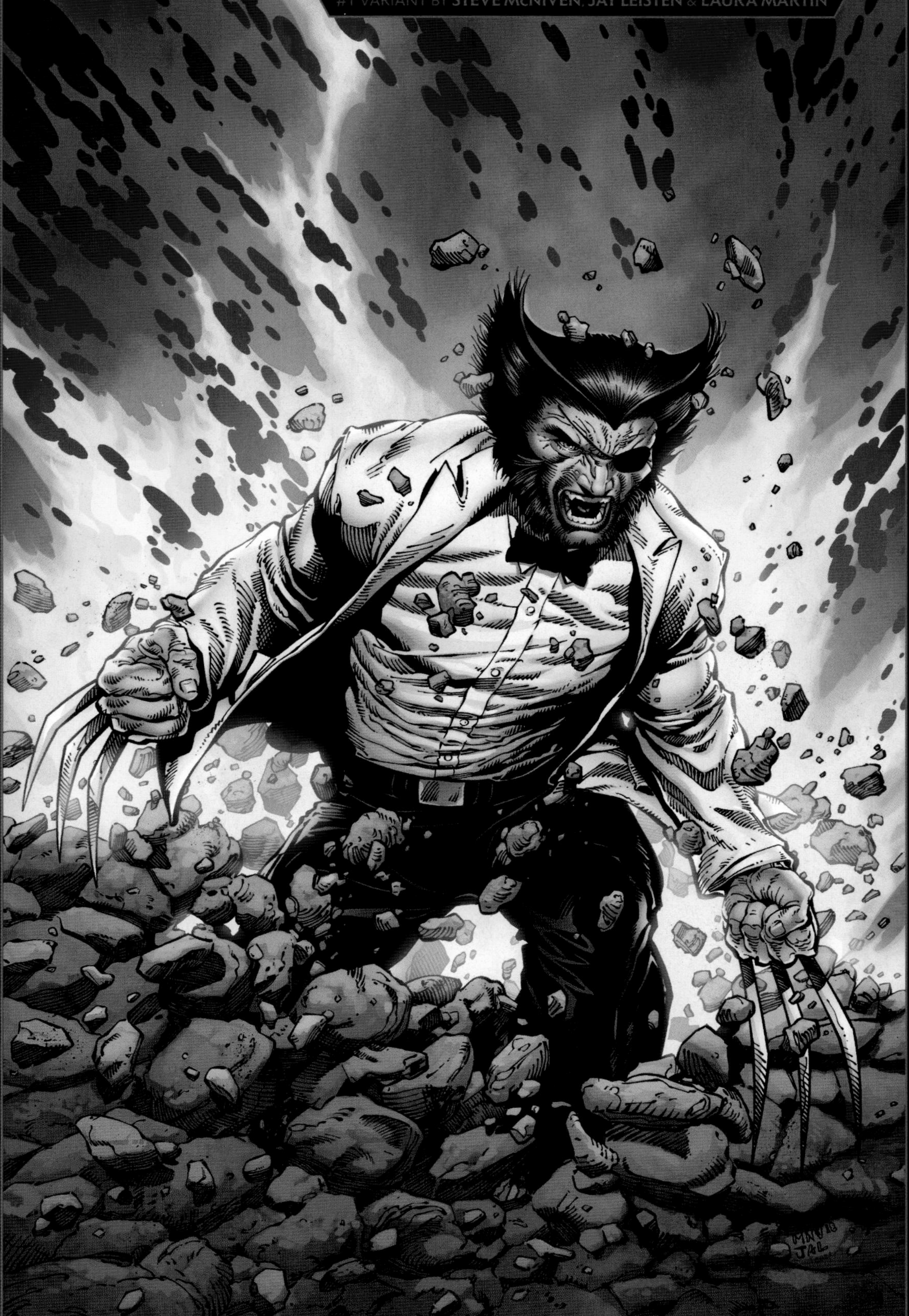

#1 VARIANT BY STEVE McNIVEN, JAY LEISTEN & LAURA MARTIN

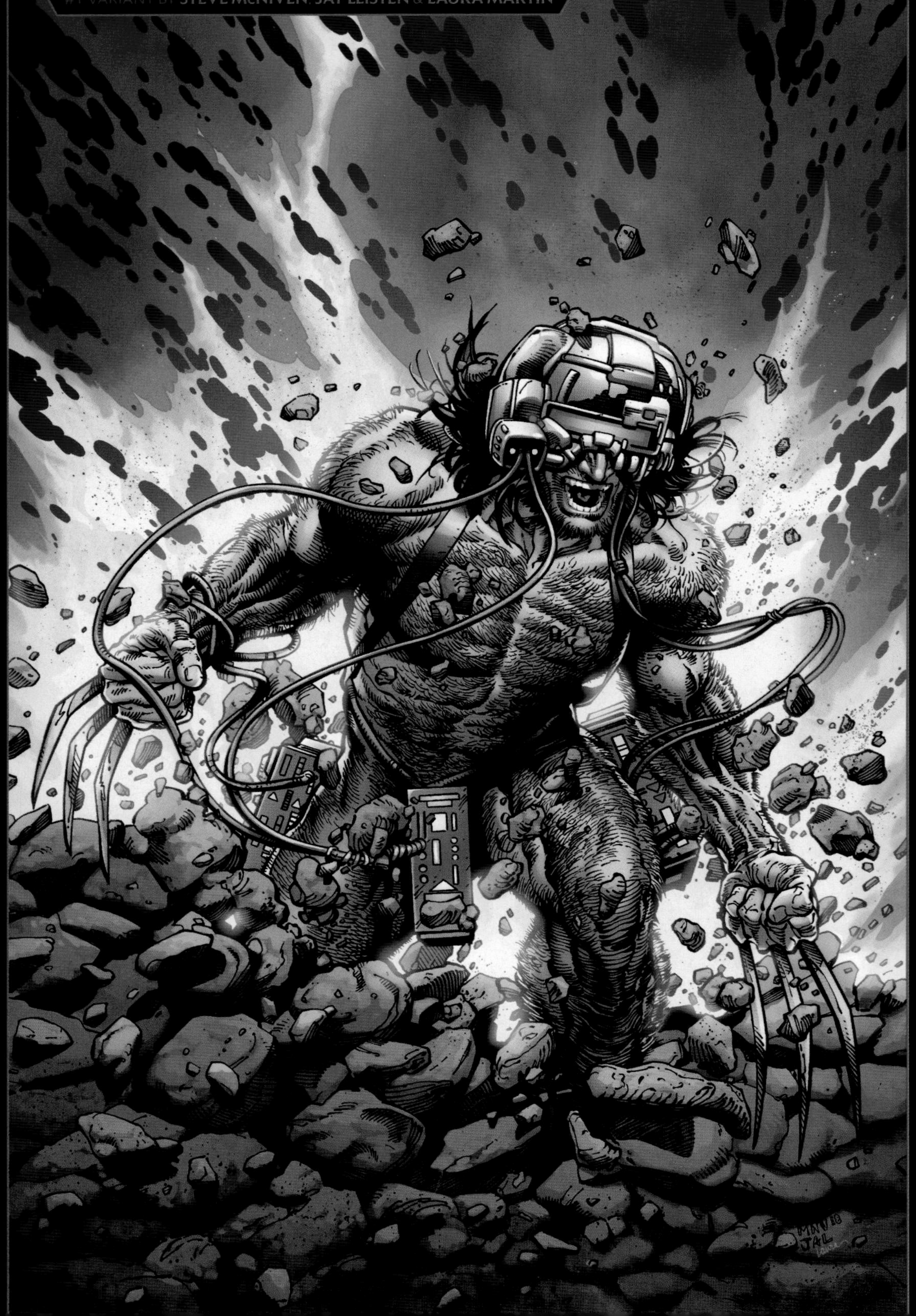

#2 VARIANT BY **DAVID MARQUEZ** & **RACHELLE ROSENBERG**

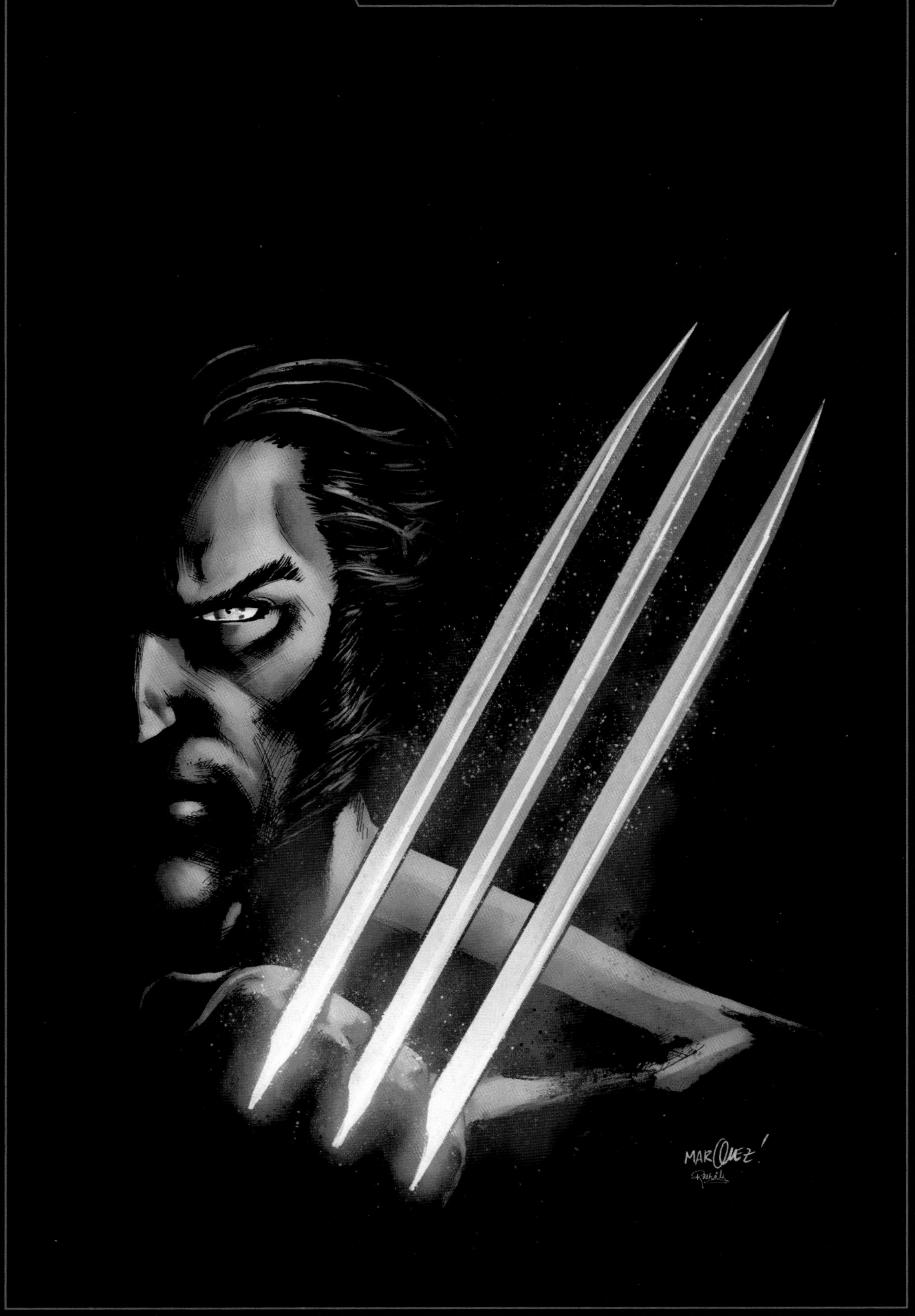
MARQUEZ!

#2 VARIANT BY **DECLAN SHALVEY** & **MATTHEW WILSON**

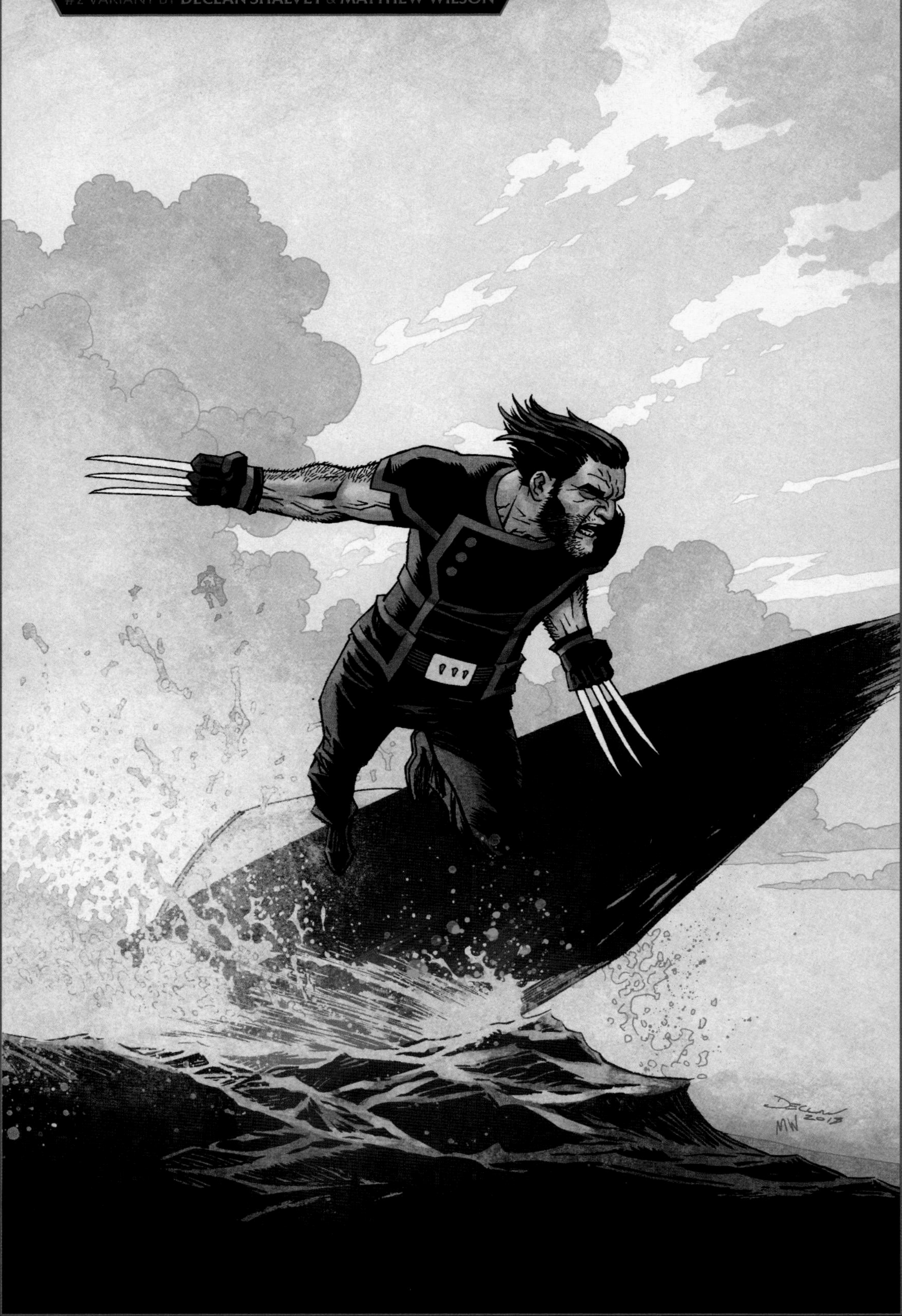

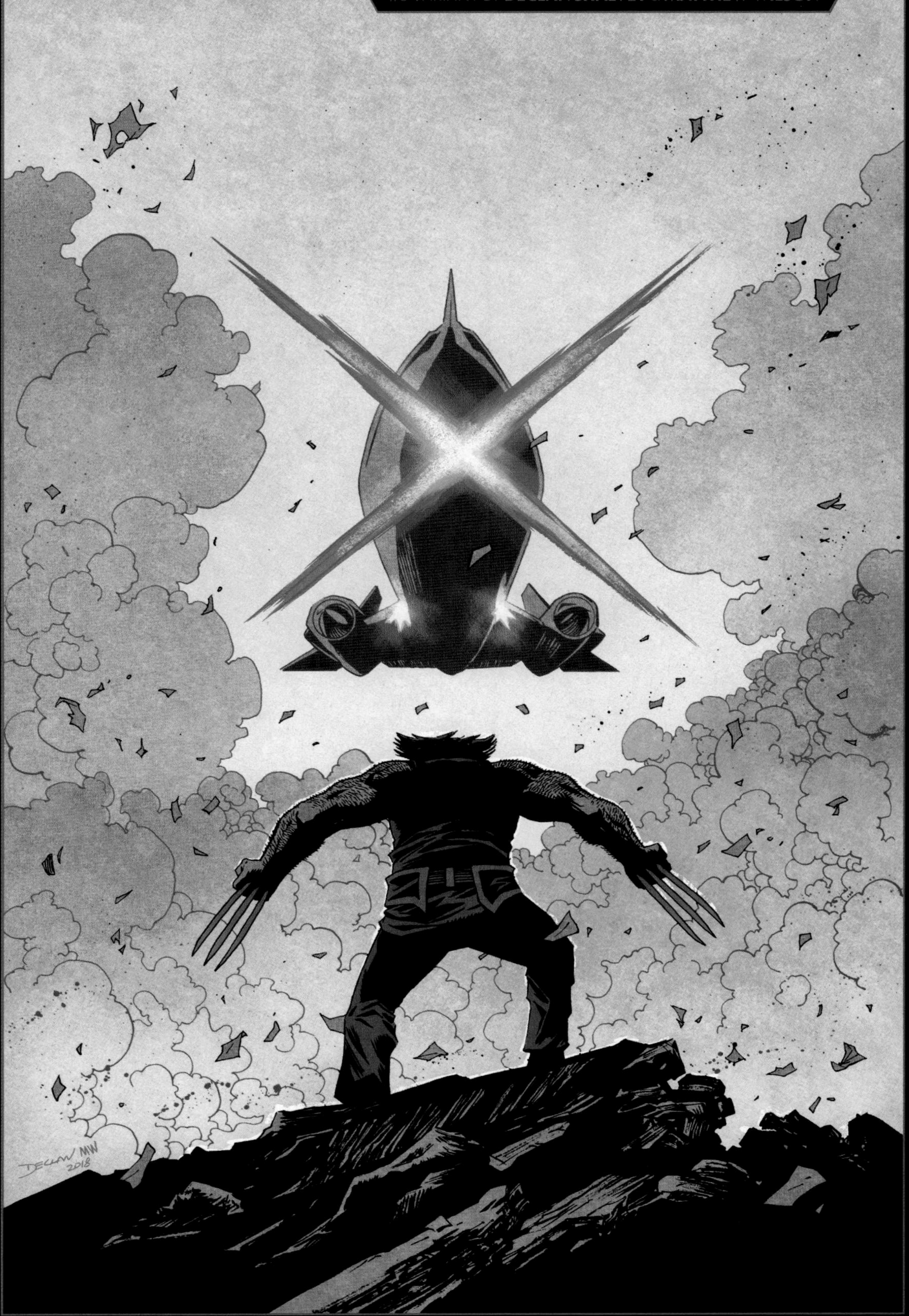
DECLAN MW
2018

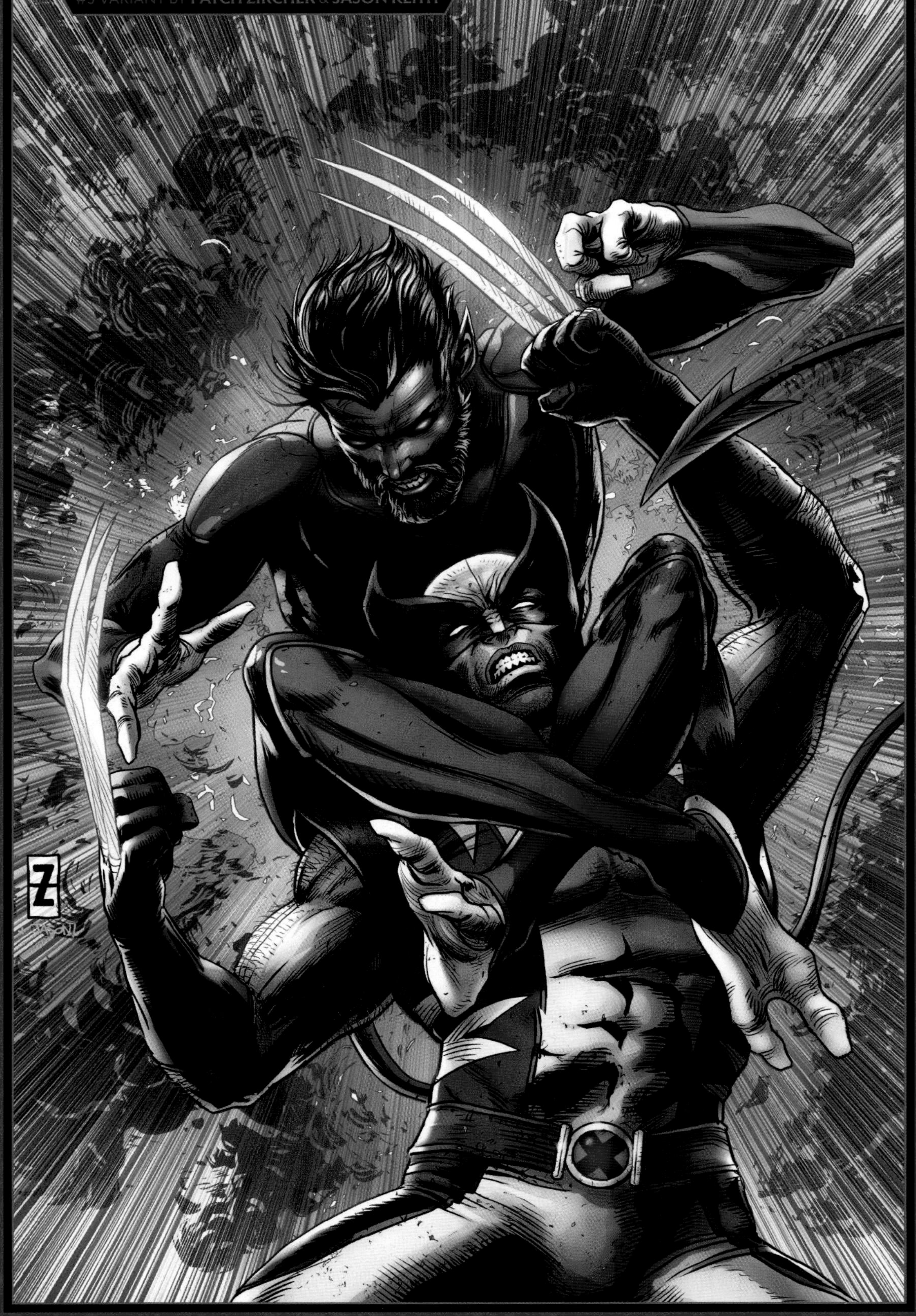

#4 VARIANT BY CHRIS STEVENS & JASON KEITH

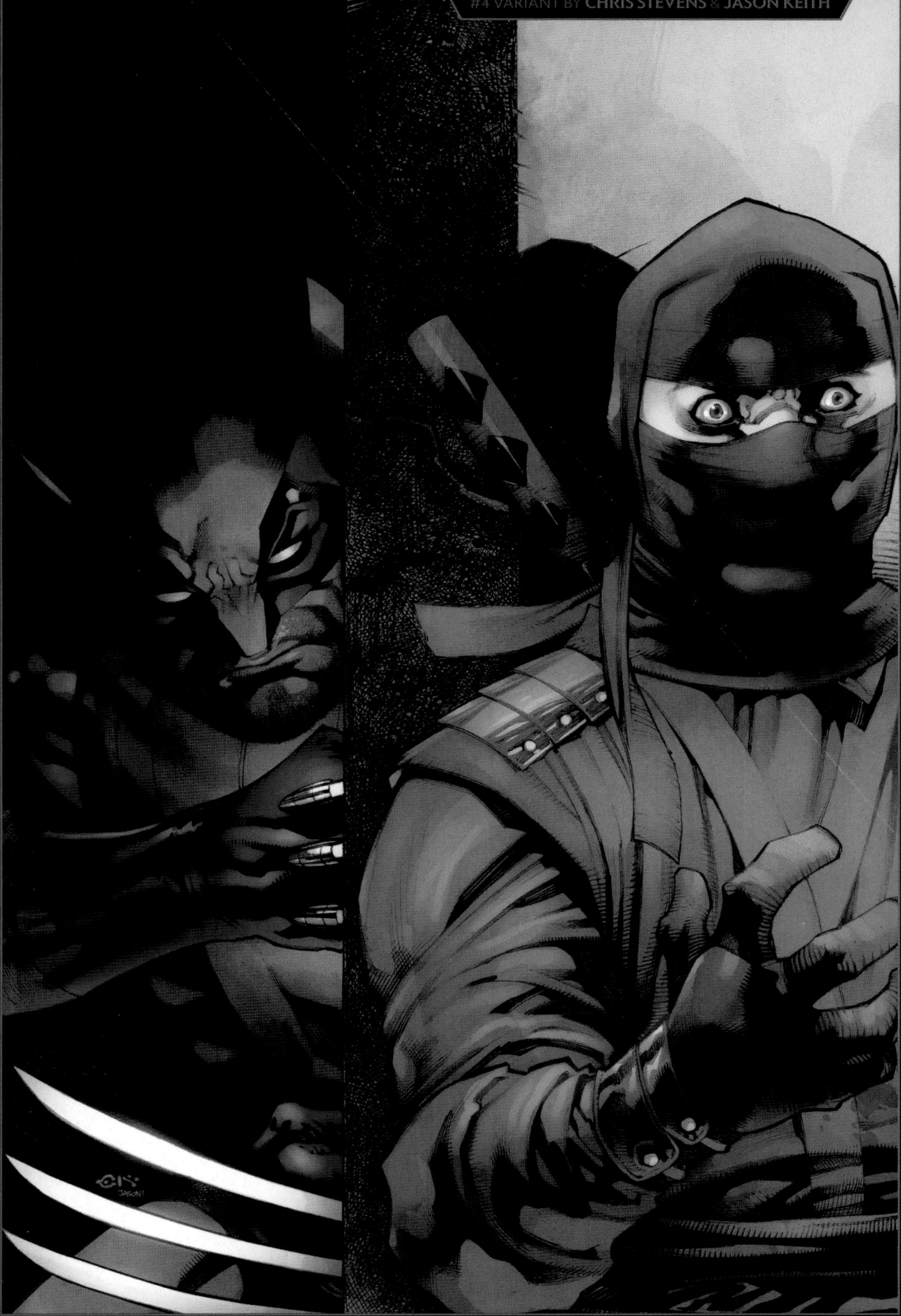

#5 VARIANT BY **ADI GRANOV**

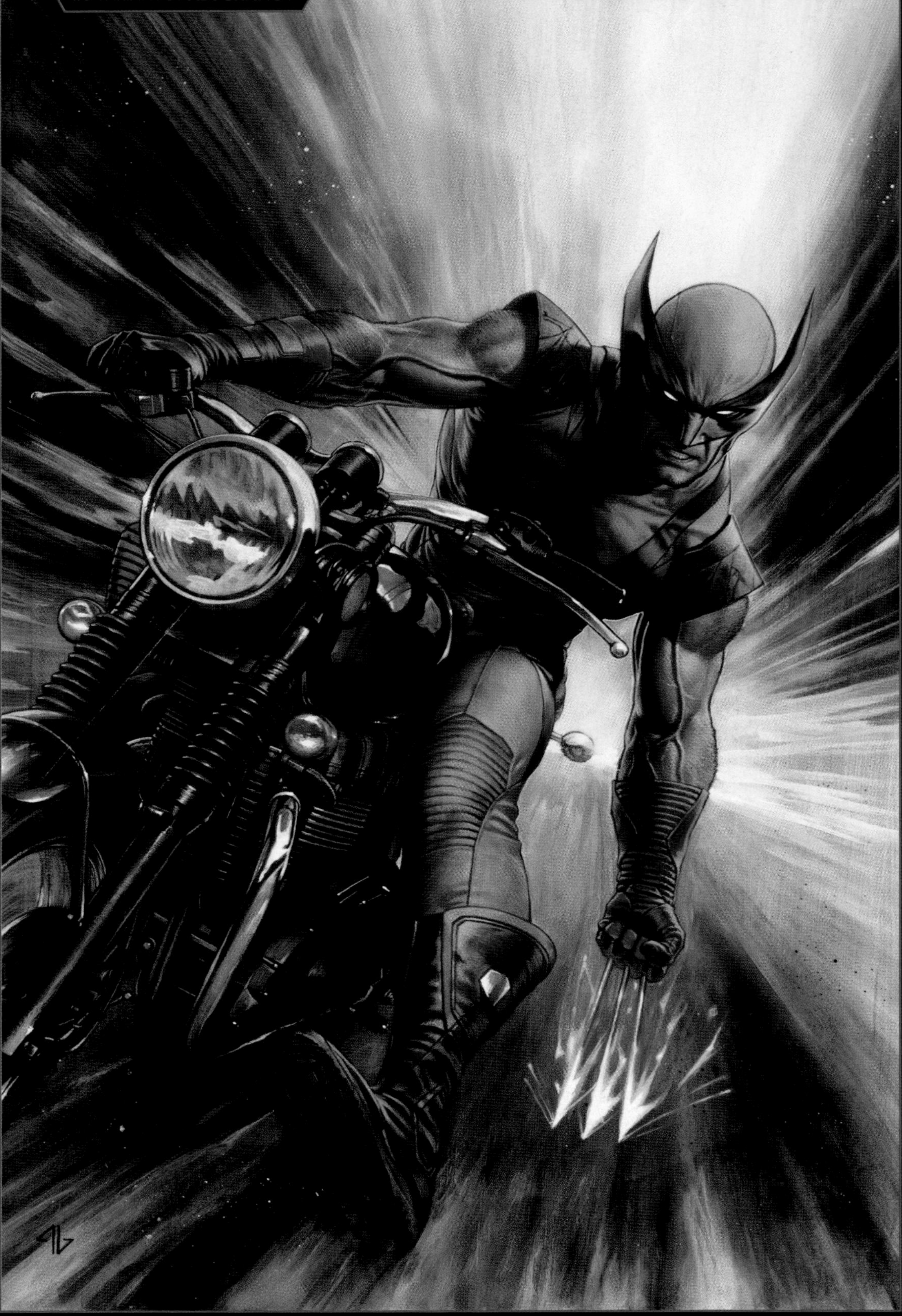

#5 VARIANT BY **ADAM KUBERT** & **JASON KEITH**

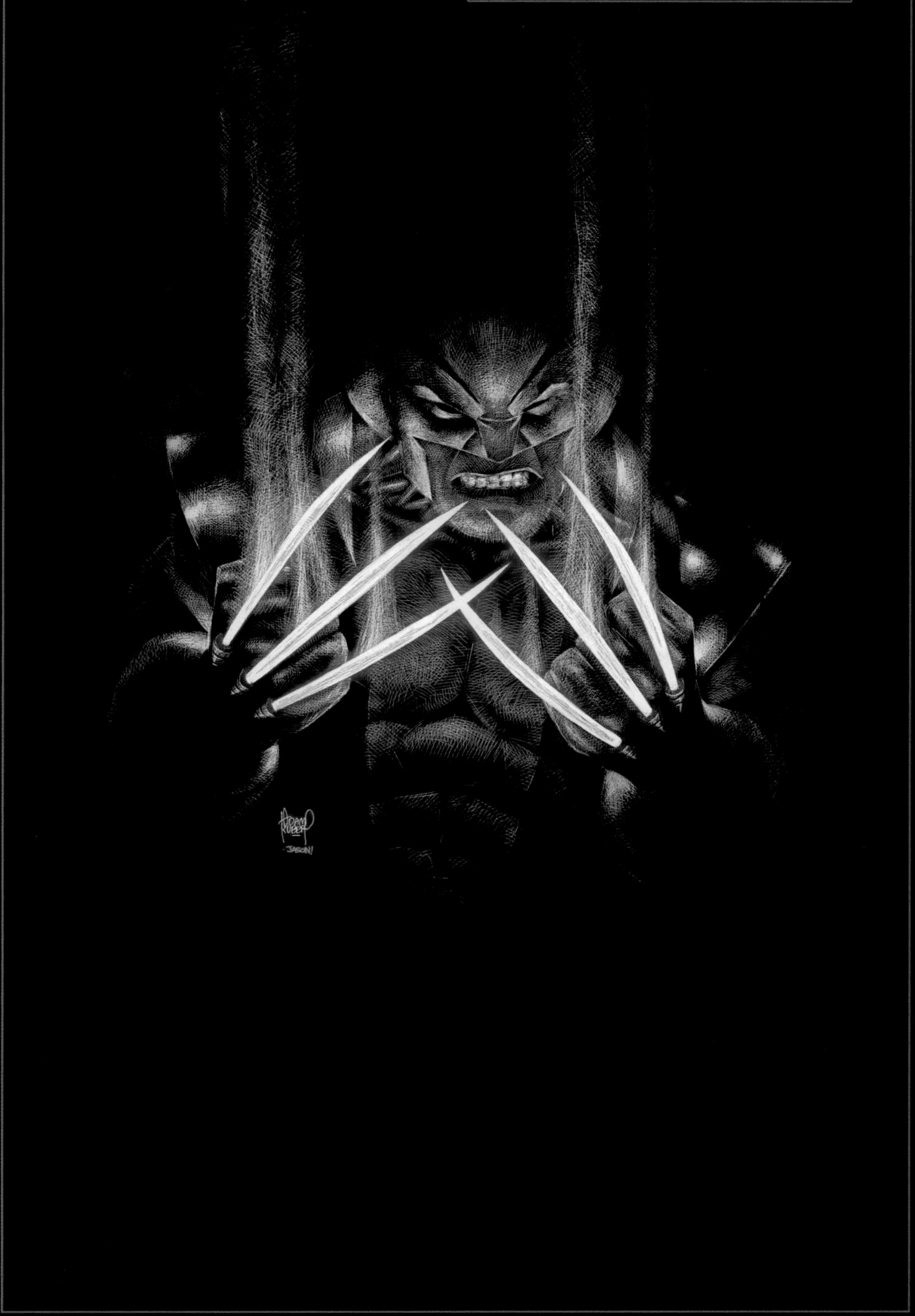

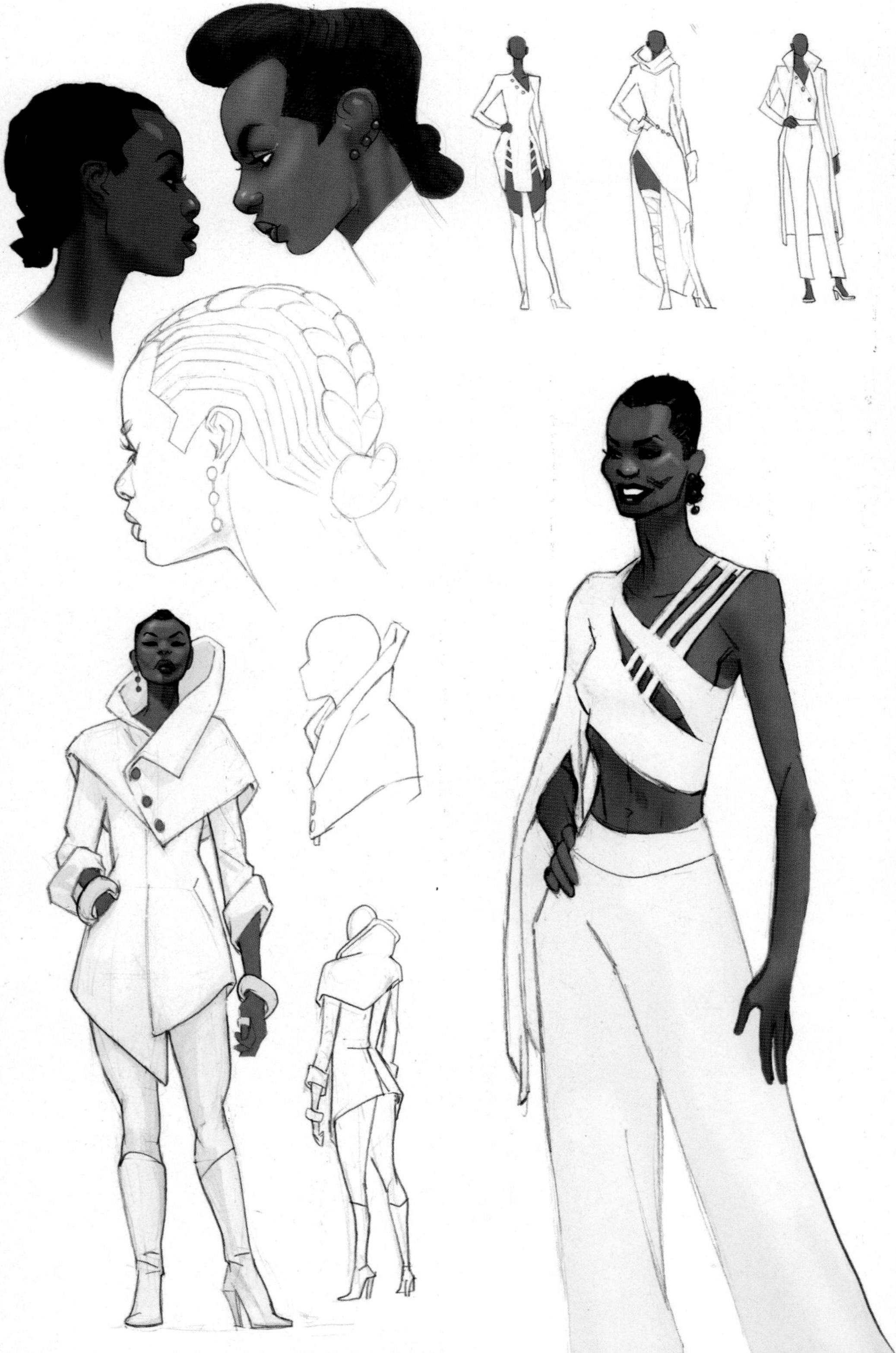

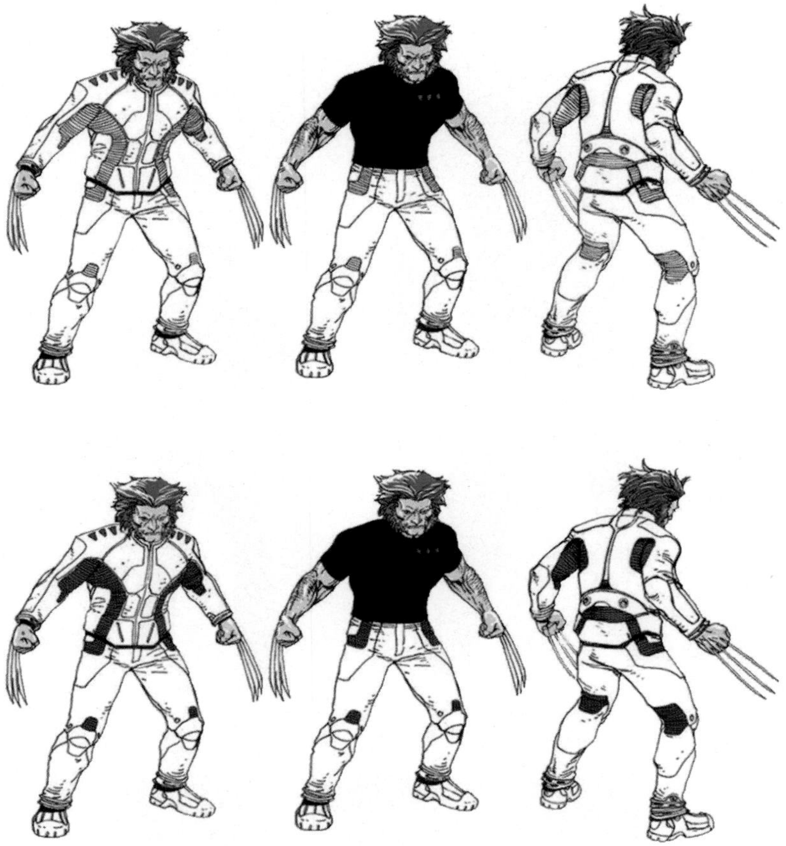

SPACESUIT

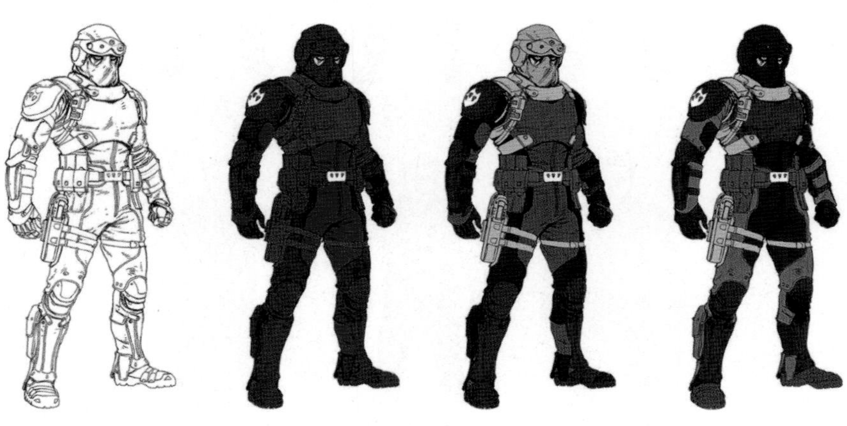

DEATH SQUAD

WOLVERINE "BLACK" COSTUME DESIGNS BY **DECLAN SHALVEY**

FINAL
A
B
C
D
E
F

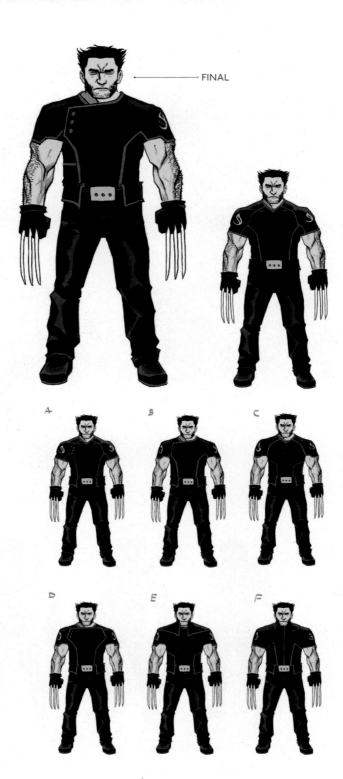